T
W

Gender Studies in Wales
Astudiaethau Rhywedd yng Nghymru

The aim of this series is to fill a current gap in knowledge. As a number of historians, sociologists and literary critics have for some time been pointing out, there is a dearth of published research on the characteristics and effects of gender difference in Wales, both as it affected lives in the past and as it continues to shape present-day experience. Socially constructed concepts of masculine and feminine difference influence every aspect of individuals' lives; experiences in employment, in education, in culture and politics, as well as in personal relationships, are all shaped by them. Ethnic identities are also gendered; a country's history affects its concepts of gender difference so that what is seen as appropriately 'masculine' or 'feminine' varies within different cultures. What is needed in the Welsh context is more detailed research on the ways in which gender difference has operated and continues to operate within Welsh societies. Accordingly, this interdisciplinary series of volumes on Gender Studies in Wales, authored by academics who are currently leaders in their particular fields of study, is designed to explore the diverse aspects of male and female identities in Wales, past and present. The series is bilingual, in the sense that some of its intended volumes will be in Welsh and some in English.

The first titles in this series include: Katie Gramich, *Twentieth-Century Women's Writing in Wales: Land, Gender, Belonging*; Jane Aaron, *Nineteenth-Century Women's Writing in Wales: Nation, Gender and Identity*; Paul Chaney, *Equality and Public Policy: Wales in Comparative Focus*; Ursula Masson, *'For Women, for Wales and for Liberalism'?: Women and Liberal Politics in Wales c.1880–1914*; Nickie Charles and Charlotte Aull Davies (eds), *Gender and Social Justice in Wales*; and Henrice Altink, Chris Weedon and Jane Aaron (eds), *Gendering Borders*. Further volumes currently in the planning stage include an essay collection on the suffrage movement in Wales edited by Sian Rhiannon Williams and Ursula Masson; a monograph by Sarah Prescott on pre-nineteenth century anglophone writing by women in Wales; another edited essay collection by Moira Vincentelli on Welsh women artists; and a Welsh-language volume by Cathryn Charnell-White on gender in eighteenth-century Welsh literature by men and women.

Twentieth-Century Women's Writing in Wales

Land, Gender, Belonging

Katie Gramich

UNIVERSITY OF WALES PRESS
CARDIFF
2007

British Library Cataloguing-in-Publication Data
A catalogue record for this book is available from the British Library.

ISBN 978-0-7083-2086-0

Typeset by Columns Design Ltd, Reading
Printed in Great Britain by CPI Antony Rowe, Wiltshire

Contents

Acknowledgements

My main debts are to my students over the past twenty years, who have impressed me with their enthusiasm for and critical acumen in exploring the field of Welsh women's writing. Delegates at the annual Association for Welsh Writing in English conference at Gregynog Hall over the same period have also provided me with invaluable ideas and an opportunity to discuss and debate the field with like-minded people. For even longer than that, my family has encouraged and borne with me. Latterly, Cardiff University has afforded me the opportunity to teach my specialisms once more and to return to finish the research begun many years ago. I am grateful to Dawn Harrington at Cardiff for her help with preparing the manuscript. My particular thanks are due to M. Wynn Thomas and Tony Brown, and, above all, to Jane Aaron and Stephen Knight, who have been invariably supportive and inspirational.

Acknowledgments

Introduction

It is a truism that women's writing has often been marginalized. Until the last few decades of the twentieth century, the accepted literary canons of virtually all European countries were overwhelmingly male. Moreover, as Susanne Hagemann has pointed out with reference to Scottish literature,[1] women writers from small nations frequently suffer a double marginalization and consequent neglect. If that is true of Scotland, how much more is it so of Wales, the smallest of the four nations within the British Isles and prey to being overlooked as insignificant or simply amalgamated into that curious hybrid called 'England-and-Wales'. Finally, Welsh women writers who have written in Welsh suffer a further burden of marginalization, by virtue of the general ignorance of and lack of interest in minority languages. It is no wonder then that, suffering triple or quadruple marginalization, Welsh women writers have been until very recently virtually invisible.

Most academic works which purport to cover 'British' literature of the twentieth century tend to neglect Welsh women writers almost entirely, as well as Scottish and, to a lesser degree, Irish ones. Elaine Showalter's *A Literature of their Own: British Women Writers from Brontë to Lessing* (1977), is a case in point, discussing only English novelists of the period. As R. S. Thomas said, 'Britishness is a mask. Under it there is only one nation, and that is England.'[2] Nevertheless, a British identity has been, and continues to be, available to all Welsh women, and it is an identity which has sometimes been of great political and emotional importance to them. Is the neglect of Welsh women writers justifiable, then, if we can assume that Welsh identity and experience can safely be subsumed into, and represented by, other 'British' women writers? The question to be asked of Welsh women's writing is similar to that

1

posed by the historian Deirdre Beddoe: 'is there a distinctive Welsh women's history, as opposed to a general British women's history?'[3] Beddoe concluded that there certainly was a separate Welsh women's history, 'shaped by a distinctive Welsh culture . . . itself largely defined by Nonconformity', and she traced differences in spheres such as education, employment, migration, industrialization, health, and gender roles and expectations, to name but a few. As Beddoe drily remarks, 'the English experience is "after all" not a universal one'.[4]

Given the volume and diversity of the literary works produced by Welsh women during the last century, it is inevitable that a literary history such as this must be selective. Since Welsh women writers have been largely excluded from traditional histories of British women's writing, implicitly because it is assumed that they are somehow included in, or indistinguishable from, 'British' literature, one of the principal foci of this study will be to examine the ways in which Welsh women writers present Wales and Welsh identity as distinct from other nations and identities. In stating this aim, I am well aware that some women writers, including Welsh ones, have viewed the whole concept of national identity as anathema, a view taken to its extreme in Virginia Woolf's declaration: ' as a woman I have no country. As a woman I want no country. As a woman my country is the whole world.'[5] Nevertheless, even such a combative rejection of national identity betrays a passionate relation to it. Moreover, feminist repudiation of nationhood such as Woolf's is often historically specific; Woolf's is couched in an anti-war polemic of extreme urgency, written in the late 1930s. When the nation is seen in spatial, geographical or topographical terms, that repudiation is seldom made. Indeed, Woolf's own *Orlando*[6] is an example of a text by a woman writer which expresses a passionate and nostalgic attachment to the land of England, and to a particular country estate – Knole – regarded as distilling the quintessence of Englishness, while at the same time subjecting expansionist British imperialism to mockery.

We are familiar with the idea that nations and nationalism are human constructs, but it may be more difficult in day-to-day lived experience to regard the land itself as a construct, however much it has been shaped and changed by human habitation. This may be especially true of Wales, a small country where transport and communication links have been – and to an extent still are – difficult. In such a setting, allegiance and a sense of belonging to one's 'square mile' can be very strong and, as I hope to demonstrate, the 'square mile' itself can be manipulated by writers into a microcosm of the larger whole which is Wales. Anthony D. Smith has argued persuasively that nations and nationalism cannot be explained or understood solely as modern 'inventions', *pace* Anderson, Gellner, Hobsbawm and Ranger;[7] rather, modern conceptions of belonging and nationality are reconstructions, based on shared myths and traditions. Smith's notion of the 'ethnoscape' – 'the identification of a land with "its" people and a people with "its" land, and the emotions to which this attachment gives rise'[8] is particularly helpful in understanding the relationship between Welsh people and Wales. Time and time again in examining the constructions of Wales presented in the work of twentieth-century Welsh women writers, we observe the construction of a particular 'ethnoscape', in which notions of Welshness and belonging are embodied in the female character inscribed within an ancestral landscape.

In what follows I aim to address a number of questions relating to Welsh women writers and their literary representations of Welshness. These include the following: how have women conceptualized Wales spatially in literary terms? Is Wales seen as a land which belongs to them, despite being a 'land of the fathers'? Is Wales seen as a conquered land or a colony? Are the places of Wales regarded as appropriated or dominated?[9] Is Wales personified and, if so, how? Is it seen largely in terms of a wild landscape of mountains and valleys or is it domesticated and tamed? How are its towns and cities represented? Is it figured in metaphorical or religious terms, such as a blessed, cursed or promised land? How does industry interact with the land and affect its inhabitants? How do gender categories intersect with spaces in the land? Do women writers see their land as a provider, sustainer, something to be exploited or dominated, a source of wealth or status, or perhaps beyond human control?

In *Nineteenth-Century Women's Writing in Wales: Nation, Gender and Identity*, Jane Aaron traces the development of a gendered Welsh nation in the work of its women writers. The present volume extends a narrative history of Welsh women's writing in both languages into the twentieth century, exploring the differing ways in which modern female writers have built on that nineteenth-century construct of 'the nation'. Its approach is based on feminist cultural geography, as detailed below, examining how Wales itself is conceived in these literary works as a place in which

Welshness and womanhood can be lived and performed. The work is a recuperative literary history, along similar lines to Elaine Showalter's seminal text, *A Literature of their Own: British Women Novelists from Brontë to Lessing*. Showalter's text, however, as I have observed, failed to mention any Welsh authors. Her title is taken from John Stuart Mill's *The Subjection of Women* (1869), a revolutionary text which, as we shall see, is read avidly by a character in a 1911 novella by a Welsh woman writer[10] and which proposed that 'if women lived in a different country from men . . . they would have had a literature of their own'.[11] *Twentieth-Century Women's Writing in Wales: Land, Gender and Belonging*, then, is an assertion and a demonstration of a distinctive Welsh female literary tradition and a declaration that Wales is 'a different country', represented as such by its modern women writers.

The volume is arranged chronologically and divided into five main chapters. It discusses both Welsh-language and English-language writers and covers several genres, including the short story, the novel and poetry, and, to a lesser extent, drama, travel writing and creative journalism. It is intended to provide a complement and, to some extent, a corrective to extant works of Welsh literary history, which tend to focus primarily on male authors, sometimes exclusively so. The volume builds on recent scholarship in Welsh women's history and gender studies (for example, the work of Deirdre Beddoe, Siân Rhiannon Williams, Ursula Masson), in nineteenth-century Welsh women's writing (Jane Aaron), and on post-colonial readings of Welsh writing in English (Stephen Knight, Kirsti Bohata, Jane Aaron, M. Wynn Thomas), as well as on the important republication of women's literary work in the Honno Classics/Clasuron Honno series.

Welsh women's writing in the twentieth century is concerned not only with history (the temporal), but also with geography (the spatial). Accounts of Welsh literary production have hitherto, and understandably, been historicist in nature. Indeed, it would be difficult to make sense of later nineteenth-century women's writing without, for example, tracing the influence of the 1847 'Blue Books' Report on the state of education in Wales upon it. The Report is a historical document and the 'research' which produced it was a historical event. But the outcome of those historical facts was a discourse which had far-reaching consequences on the ways in which Welsh women conceived of their place in the world and of

Wales itself as a place.[12] This study will therefore shift the balance from the historical to the spatial, which will allow for a truly *literary* study, examining the imaginative ways in which Welsh women have created the space called Wales in their fictions and verses. The chapters will offer literary analyses of the texts, followed by a theoretical conclusion, which will seek to provide a synthesis of and framework for the literary analyses. The approach here will be derived from cultural geography, which concerns itself with examining the structural forces that shape human experience. In the twentieth century in Wales, this will mean tracing the way in which modernization, industrialization and urbanization have transformed traditional, rural modes of life. A glance at the streets of settlements in the Rhondda Valley is sufficient to persuade us that spatial organization is ideological – it maps out the environment in such a way as to enforce and naturalize social inequality and the inequitable distribution of wealth. It is also gendered, creating spaces of and for the performance of femininity and masculinity, respectively. This study sets out to explore the ways in which Wales's literary women have responded to that ideologically charged and gendered space known as Wales – how they have imagined and represented it, transformed, contested or embraced it.

Just as power and identity need to be understood as fluid, so space can no longer be understood as 'absolute'. Not only does the meaning of places change over time (the Big Pit mining museum 'means' something very different today from when, in the early twentieth century, it was a thriving working mine), but also spaces can mean conflicting things for people at the same time. This is particularly true in literary representations of Wales: for example, the chapel containing the Revivalist prayer-meeting is a sinister place for Allen Raine, but a place of revelation and redemption for her contemporary, Sara Maria Saunders.

In chapter 1, 'Sacred Place: 1900–1920' the literary production of the Welsh women writers of the beginning of the twentieth century is examined; these were the direct inheritors of the nation-building efforts of their nineteenth-century predecessors. At the same time, they were also affected ideologically by the aftermath of the Blue Books Report of 1847 and the subsequent campaign to redeem Wales, and the Welshwoman particularly, from the calumnies of that Report. The women writers of the 1900s were, however, on the whole more overtly politically aware than the earlier writers. They were deeply affected by the Home Rule movement, as well as by campaigns for temperance and suffrage, both of which can be seen as feminist movements in the Welsh context. One writer, Eluned Morgan, focuses on her homeland, the Welsh colony in Patagonia, and this is analysed as a construction of an alternative, 'new world' Wales. Welsh women writers dedicated to these causes contributed copiously to the Welsh periodicals of the time, many of which were masterminded by O. M. Edwards, who acted as mentor to several Welsh women writers of this generation. The chapter will analyse the constructions of Wales as a cultural, religious and political space in the writing of individuals including 'Allen Raine' (Ada Puddicombe), Eluned Morgan, Gwyneth Vaughan, Sara Maria Saunders, 'Moelona' (Elizabeth Mary Jones) and Edith Nepean.

Particular attention is given to the influence of the 1904–5 Revival on a range of these writers, examining how this new wave of religious fervour seemed to re-energize constructions of Wales as the land of redemption, a sacred space in which women had a particularly important and transformative role to play. Dorian Llywelyn calls this the 'soteriological landscape', that is, the land-scape of salvation. As Llywelyn points out, 'for many peoples throughout history the nation has been understood essentially as a religious reality'.[13] Nevertheless, that sacred place was in the proc-ess of being desecrated, not only by industrialization and urbaniza-tion, but by the depredations of the First World War, all of which are reflected in the transformed landscape of Wales represented in the work of the next generation of Welsh women writers.

In chapter 2, 'Fallen Place: 1921–1945', I trace the way in which a number of Welsh women writers of this generation, understand-ably, lose faith in Wales as a soteriological landscape or 'land of the white gloves', and their writings represent a Wales of political activism, labour unrest, unemployment, rural depopulation and poverty. Some writers (such as Eiluned Lewis, in her 1934 bestseller *Dew on the Grass*) nostalgically evoke a Welsh rural idyll, while acknowledging the encroaching proximity of the industrialized South. Kate Roberts's rural north-west Wales, meanwhile, is itself industrialized, and Roberts writes movingly of a changing cultural and political landscape, in which women's lives and labour are foregrounded. The effects of the First World War on Welsh women at home are recorded in these writings, most movingly in the scene near the end of Roberts's 1936 novel *Traed mewn Cyffion* where a mother receives news of her son's death in a language, English, which she does not understand. The Second World War is also addressed by writers such as Lynette Roberts (in *Poems*, 1944, *Gods with Stainless Ears*, 1951) and Kate Bosse-Griffiths (in *Fy Chwaer Efa*, 1944), who see the mechanized talons of war tearing through Wales. Hilda Vaughan dramatises the un-idyllic aspects of life in rural mid Wales, focusing particularly on issues of women's inheritance and land-ownership, for instance in *The Soldier and the Gentlewoman* (1932). Indeed, one of the recurring tropes of the Welsh women's writing of this era is that of dispossession and eviction; arguably, the women of Wales have been cheated of the 'sacred place' promised by the 1904–5 Revival and have been left instead with a fallen land, literally scarred and bereft of many of its young people.

In the third chapter, 'Awakening Place: 1946–1977', the period which saw a transformation of women's lives in Wales is considered. There was a transformation in the sense that many participated in the resurgence of nationalist feeling, as evidenced by their prominence in the political campaigns of Plaid Cymru and Cymdeithas yr Iaith. Many, too, gained a new sense of international identity through identification with the burgeoning women's movement from the late 1960s onwards.

There is also a strongly elegiac sense of loss, particularly with regard to the Welsh language and its culture. With a palpable dualism between ideologies of conservatism and radical protest, it is not surprising to find that these women writers' representations of Wales differ fundamentally, from the lyrically evoked Bardsey Island of Brenda Chamberlain's *Tide-Race* (1962) to the lively but impoverished industrial south Wales towns of Menna Gallie's novels. Nevertheless, there is a strong sense of vibrancy in these disparate spaces, a sense of Wales awakening into a modern world of divided allegiances and political actions, in which women's traditional roles are beginning to dissolve and metamorphose into different forms.

Chapter 4, 'Feminist Place: 1978–1997', focuses on the outpouring of literary work in both languages in this period, which can be seen as, in some senses, the fruit of the women's movement, which had its origins in the previous decade. The politicization of women's conceptions of Wales and Welshness is continued and intensified in some writers' works, though that political landscape is also tempered by a new lyricism in the diverse works of poets such as Menna Elfyn and Hilary Llewellyn-Williams, novelists such as Angharad

Tomos and Siân James, and playwrights such as Lucinda Coxon and Sharon Morgan. The 1979 Referendum, in which devolution was rejected, did not appear to attenuate Welsh women's sense of Wales as a separate and special entity; on the contrary, Welsh women tended to speak up for Wales against Thatcherism, the Falklands War, the closure of the mines, and the proliferation of nuclear weapons.

The title of chapter 5, 'Hybrid Place: 1997–2005', reflects the growing tendency to regard modern Welsh writing as a post-colonial literature. According to Bill Ashcroft *et al.*, 'The gap which opens between the experience of place and the language available to describe it forms a classic and all-pervasive feature of post-colonial texts.'[14] Recent criticism has fruitfully explored the theory that modern Welsh writing is post-colonial, though this approach has also incurred voluble opposition, mainly from historians. However, the 'yes' vote in the Devolution Referendum of 1997 and the subsequent creation of the Welsh Assembly have undoubtedly changed both the concept and the reality of 'Wales' as a political and, possibly, a cultural and social place. If Wales was colonized by England and seduced into the fiction of 'Britishness', contemporary Wales could be seen as finally emerging from that colonial dream. The work of the writers just after the turn of the twentieth century seem to portray the uneasiness described by Ashcroft *et al.* in their description of the gap between language and reality. Allen Raine, for example, clearly had ambitions to create an independent fictive Wales, yet the language and genre at her disposal are frequently inadequate for the task. It may be that Welsh women writers in the twenty-first century now have the freedom to forge a truly post-colonial vision of Wales in their work, in whichever language they choose. Certainly, the Wales of contemporary women writers' work is diverse – from the suffocating intensity of Trezza Azzopardi's Cardiff streets in *The Hiding Place* (2000) to the hybrid and polyvocal cultural space of a north Wales kitchen in Charlotte Williams's *Sugar and Slate* (2002).

A drive along the A470 from north to south Wales will convince us that Wales is a heterogeneous entity, and it is not surprising to find this heterogeneity represented in the literary works of Welsh women in the twentieth century. Moreover, Welsh women writers have not infrequently drawn attention to internal differences in their writing on Wales – between Caernarfonshire and 'the South' in

Kate Roberts's prose, for instance, or between the western Cardiganshire coast and the Valleys of the south-east in the novels of Allen Raine. This study does not attempt to present Wales as a homogeneous whole, except when writers themselves are performing this ideologically charged feat of spatial reinvention. Rather, it will draw attention to the different versions of Wales found in the work of writers from differing parts of the country, the different 'shapes she makes', as Menna Elfyn puts it in one of her best-known poems.[15] At the same time, it will argue that the writings of these modern Welsh women authors form a recognizable and distinct body of work, which manifests particular characteristics at particular points in twentieth-century history, revealing that there are unexpected correspondences and interrelationships between Welsh women's literary works in both languages throughout the century.

1 Sacred Place: 1900–1920

Although literary histories have occasionally ignored the turns of centuries as boundaries for the construction of periods and movements in literature,[1] it is still common to speak in terms of neatly parcelled centuries as meaningful units of literary history. This book considers twentieth-century Welsh women's writing within just such a framework, and it is certainly true that some characteristics of twentieth-century writing are markedly distinct from those of previous centuries. At the same time, it is important to note that the turns of centuries are porous boundaries, at best. Many of the characteristics distinguishable in late nineteenth-century Welsh women's writing continue relatively unchanged into the first decades of the new century. Several important women writers' work straddles the two centuries. Moreover, certain historical events and pervasive ideologies from much earlier in the nineteenth century continue to exert an influence on women's writing. One significant example is the effect of the 1847 *Report of the Commission of Inquiry into the State of Education in Wales*, the so-called *Blue Books*, which continued to be powerfully felt in women's periodical publications well after the turn of the century.[2] Women writers still felt the pressure to refute the allegations of the Blue Books about the impropriety and sexual licence of Welsh women and, at the same time, to emphasize the cultural value of the Welsh language, which had been so comprehensively calumnied in 'Brad y Llyfrau Gleision'.[3] It might be argued, indeed, that the continuing backlash against the Blue Books was partly responsible for the essentially conservative nature of Welsh women's writing in the early decades of the twentieth century, though other social and economic reasons must also be acknowledged.

Elsewhere in the literary world, the first decades of the twentieth century witnessed the cataclysmic shift which is nowadays labelled as 'modernism'. Virginia Woolf, one of its most influential exponents, indeed announced that 'on or about December 1910 human character changed'.[4] We understand Woolf to be talking about a distinct shift in human social relations on the one hand, and on the other the burgeoning of a new aesthetic movement. In December 1910, Woolf's friend Roger Fry had organized the famous first exhibition of post-Impressionist painting in London, followed up by another two years later. Writers such as Katherine Mansfield cited that exhibition as a turning point in their own artistic development, inspiring them to attempt something bold and new. This exhibition did not reach Wales – was it therefore a case of Wales remaining isolated from the new European movements in art, music and literature, a quiet colonial backwater which complacently got on with its own affairs, largely in its own language?

Certainly, Wales at the turn of the century was by no means a backwater politically. The Labour party had its origins in the industrial and social ferment of the south Wales valleys in the later decades of the nineteenth century. Neither was it a backwater economically or industrially, for in 1900, Wales was producing and exporting a large percentage of the world's coal, steel and other goods, such as slate, copper and textiles. Its towns were expanding prodigiously, immigrants were pouring in, and port cities like Cardiff were becoming a vibrant melting-pot of different cultures. At the same time, though, Wales's traditional cultural difference was being eroded in the gradual decline of the Welsh language and the growing Anglicization of society.

What were Welsh people concerned about in January 1900? A glance at the newspapers and periodicals tells us that they were concerned with, among other things, socialism, temperance, suffrage, home rule and the disestablishment of the Church. So the decline of the Welsh language evidently did not mean that Wales had been seamlessly sewn into the fabric of the British Empire. It was still asserting its otherness, primarily from England, in many different ways. It elected the first socialist MP, Keir Hardy, at the very start of the century. It also had a different approach to gender roles and responsibilities. Despite the continuing conservative backlash against the allegations of the Blue Books, Wales retained an ambivalent attitude to the hegemonic English ideology of separate spheres, as exemplified in the very public careers of prominent women such

as 'Cranogwen' (Sarah Jane Rees), who was very far from conform-
ing to the ideal of 'the angel in the house'.[5]

At the turn of the century 'Cranogwen' was still a dominant force
in Welsh women's writing, despite being in her sixties by this time.
That she was regarded as an exemplar by a number of younger
women writers is suggested, for example, by the poem 'Cranogwen',
by 'Buddug', which expresses an admiration not far short of
adulation:

> Rwyf bron a'th addoli, anfarwol Granogwen,
> 'Rwyt wedi fy synnu, a'm swyno yn lân,
> Y mae dy athrylith a'th awen ddisgleirwen,
> Yn twymo fy enaid – yn ennyn fy nghân.
> Dy ryfedd hyawdledd a'th ddwys dduwiolfrydedd,
> A'th ddoniau gwahanol enillodd fy serch:
> Pwy bellach faidd wadu nas gall arucheledd
> A mawredd meddyliol babellu mewn merch?[6]

> [I almost worship you, deathless Cranogwen,
> You've amazed me and charmed me for so long,
> Your genius and your dazzling skill with the pen,
> Quicken my soul – and inspire my own song.
> Your rare eloquence and intense piety,
> Your many different gifts have won my admiration:
> For who today can claim that superiority
> And intellectual greatness can't exist in woman?]

'Cranogwen' was indeed a formidable woman: poet, teacher,
preacher, editor, temperance campaigner, sailor, she won the Crown
in the National Eisteddfod and was a renowned public speaker. In *Y
Gymraes* (The Welshwoman) of January 1900 Cranogwen herself
wrote a tribute to another, younger, Welsh woman poet, Ellen
Hughes, who published two collections of verse, under the titles
Sibrwd yr Awel (1887) and *Murmur y Gragen* (1907). Another
member of this nest of female poets of the time was 'Ceridwen Peris'
(Alice Gray Jones), who was also a regular contributor to the
journals of the day, such as *Y Gymraes* and *Y Frythones* (The
Female Brython), and, like her fellow poets, was also an enthusiastic temperance campaigner. Although these poets are not afraid to
address political and social issues in their verse, it is undeniable
that, technically and formally, they are conservative writers, whose
poetic diction is virtually indistinguishable from verse written at
least half a century previously. There is no significant shift in terms
of form or diction between Cranogwen's *Caniadau* (1870) and

Ceridwen Peris's volume of the same title, published late in her life in 1934. Elsewhere, of course, James Joyce was gleefully declaring the demise of 'poetry for ladies',[7] but in Wales such pleasant verse appeared to be flourishing, though Ceridwen Peris at least tried, ineptly, to express the viewpoint of the working-class woman in poems such as 'Cân Gwraig y Gweithiwr'[8] (Song of the Worker's Wife).

All these Welsh-language poets and the occasional English-language Welsh poet of the period present strongly patriotic views of Wales in their verse. To an extent this emphasis may be seen as a direct reflection of the contemporary Home Rule campaign, as well as a continuing refutation of the accusations made in the Blue Books. Cranogwen's personal influence cannot be underestimated, either; when she declares in her poem 'Fy Ngwlad' (My Country) that she intends to spend her life in the service of her country ('wele fi, / Fy ngwlad, am dreulio mywyd i'th wasnaethu di'[9]), and condemns those few traitors who repudiate their homeland, it is not surprising to see many other female writers of the time virtually queuing up to say much the same thing.

This consonance of theme and style may be attributed partly to the existence of a strong literary culture in the field of periodicals, which flourished in the late nineteenth century and the first decade of the twentieth in Wales. O. M. Edwards was a key figure in this movement, as was Cranogwen herself. The titles of the publications themselves speak eloquently of the patriotic impulse underpinning them: it is hard to miss the patriotic allusion in titles such as *Cymru* (Wales), *Cymru'r Plant* (Children's Wales), *Y Genhinen* (The Leek), *Y Gymraes* (The Welshwoman) and *Y Frythones* (The Female Brython, that is, descendant of ancient Brythonic-speaking Welsh people).

Among prose-writers, one of the earliest in the century was another protégée of O. M. Edwards, Winnie Parry, who wrote for *Cymru* and *Cymru'r Plant* between 1893 and 1907 and went on to edit *Cymru'r Plant* from 1908. She published a novel, *Sioned*, in 1906 and a collection of stories and poems, *Cerrig y Rhyd*, in 1907. As Jane Aaron points out, Parry's work heralds a new outlook in twentieth-century Welsh women's writing, turning away from the unbending image of the Welshwoman as 'pur fel y dur' (pure as steel). Parry herself was different from the nest of contemporary poets discussed above in that she was generally less didactic, particularly in the novel *Sioned*, which is notable for the 'modern' raciness of the first-person narrative and in the humorous and satirical tone. But what kind of conception of Wales does this novel and her other works present?

Sioned is a sixteen-year old girl who is sharp-witted, clever, and funny; she adores her older brother, Bob, and enjoys taking the wind out of the sails of anyone who is too serious or pretentious. The chief appeal of the novel is in the language, which sounds authentic and natural, bubbling over with the energy of Sioned herself. She puts pepper on the pillow of Jacob Jones, the super-cilious, pious theological student who comes to stay, and takes her revenge for his snubbing of her by enjoying his discomfiture in sneezing his way through his first chapel service. When she goes to buy her mother a pair of spectacles, the shopkeeper, in an attempt to discover what strength the glasses required should be, asks her what age her mother is, to which she replies:

> 'Twn i ddim, a 'taswn i yn gwybod faswn i ddim yn deyd wrthach chi, achos tydi o ddim o'ch busnas chi, mwy nag ydi o'm busnas i faint ydi'ch oed chi,' meddwn i reit siarp, achos 'roeddwn i'n weled o'n hy dros ben yn f'holi i am beth 'toedd 'nelo fo ddim â fo. A 'blaw hynny, fedra i ddim diodda i bobl ddeyd 'y ngeneth i' wrtha i.[10]

> ['I dunno, and even if I did I wouldn't tell you 'cos it's none of your business, any more that it's any of my business how old you are', said I pretty sharply, because I thought it was a bit of a cheek for him to be cross-examining me about something that had nothing to do with him. And besides, I can't bear anyone calling me "my girl" like that.']

Sioned's world is the world of her 'square mile', a traditional, Welsh-speaking, north Wales village with a strong sense of commu-nity and propriety. It is only when she is sent off to live with her aunt and uncle in London in order to attend an 'Establishment for young ladies' that she begins to realize her distinct Welsh identity and her love for the 'sacred place' of home. Trapped in her uncle's dark, gloomy house, Sioned longs for:

> fy llofft bach yn yr hen Dŷ Gwyn, lle medrwn weld i waelod y Cae Hir dim ond codi ar f'ista yn 'y ngwely . . . a chysgod yr hen dŷ yn gorfadd arno fo, a'r haul yn scleinio ar 'i gwr pella fo, ac fel roedd yr hen goeden onnen yn crafu'i dail yn erbyn un ochr o'r ffenast; ac mi oedd gâs gin i yr hen dai llwydion hyll, bob un 'r un fath a'u gilydd, oedd i gwelad o ffenast y llofft lle roedd modryb wedi fy rhoi i i gysgu.[11]

[my little bedroom in old TŷGwyn (White House), where I could see to
the bottom of the Long Field just by sitting up in bed ... and the
shadow of the old house lying across it, and the sun shining on its
furthest corner, and how the old ash tree scraped its leaves against one
edge of the window; and I really hated the old ugly, grey houses, all
exactly alike, that could be seen from the window of the bedroom
where Auntie had put me to sleep.]

At the same time, she becomes aware of her Welshness when she is
surrounded by English speakers; she longs to hear her own language
and, when she hears an old drunken tramp mumbling away in
Welsh on a doorstep, she recklessly gives him a half-sovereign. The
girls at the 'Establishment' mock Sioned and regard her as 'some
wild creature from the woods' ('ryw greadur gwyllt o'r coed').[12]
When it becomes clear that Sioned will never be tamed or
Anglicized, her brother Bob comes to fetch her home, much to her
jubilation.

Despite the gleeful irreverence of *Sioned*, however, the stories
and poems of Parry's *Cerrig y Rhyd* (1907), aimed at a juvenile
audience, tend to be cloyingly pious, sentimental and didactic. The
same writer who could, in *Sioned*, challenge some of the comfortable familial and social assumptions underpinning Welsh society,
was also capable of writing stuffily unrealistic fables reinforcing
restrictive gender ideologies. In 'Y Plas Gwydr' (The Glass Palace),
for example, the little girl Maggie learns the lesson of submission
and self-abnegation in a dream experience, in which any symptom
of a bad mood cracks the walls of a beautiful glass palace. When she
emerges from her dream she is ready to buckle under and be
eternally amiable to her annoying younger siblings. The stories use
fairy-tale formulae and end happily ever after, once the protagonists
have learned their moral lesson.

However, there are some authentic-sounding children's voices in
Winnie Parry's poems, particularly in 'Fy Ffrog Newydd' (My New
Frock), in which a little girl rails against the constrictions placed
upon her by her new frock. Implicit is an attack upon the gender
restrictions symbolized by the dress; the little girl would much
rather be without it, a state which she associates with freedom,
freedom to accompany her brother, Bob, to see the wren's nest in the
hedge.[13] 'Hen Ferch' (Old Maid) is a story about Barbara, who
sacrifices her own happiness for the sake of her disabled sister.
Though this is a story drenched in sentimentality, it does champion
the 'old maid', who is the object of people's scorn, and shows her

self-abnegating heroism. The collection as a whole seems obsessed with the death of parents and/or children, represented with pious sentimentality, for example 'Breuddwyd Nadolig' (Christmas Dream) concerns the freezing to death of the little match-seller, Bobbie; Margiad, the little orphan in 'Dros Foel y Don' (Over the Mountainous Wave), drowns on her odyssey to her grandparents' cottage, since she is so afraid of being sent to the workhouse. All these deaths end with a comforting picture of the dead child's happy reward in heaven. Even the translation into Welsh of a poem by Longfellow ('The Castle by the Sea') has as its theme the death of a child.

Saunders Lewis's verdict on Winnie Parry is cutting: 'her stories are neither children's stories nor adults' stories but rather . . . stories for adults who have retained the intellectual level of children' ('nid yw ei straeon hi nac yn straeon plant nac yn straeon pobl mewn oed, ond straeon ydynt . . . i bobl mewn oed a gadwodd safonau deall plant').[14] Though Kate Roberts gave some praise to her work in published reviews in *Y Faner*, in private correspondence with Lewis she tended to agree; referring to works by Winnie Parry and Moelona in a letter of 1928, she complains: 'They're as insipid as apple jam. I think people who write like this should be put in jail to prevent them from writing any more' ('Maent mor ddiflas â jam afalau. Credaf y dylid rhoi pawb sy'n sgrifennu fel hyn yn jêl rhag iddynt ysgrifennu rhagor')[15].

The ambiguity over the target audience of some texts, as alluded to by Saunders Lewis's comment on the work of Winnie Parry, might also be applied to a short novel entitled *Cit*, by Fanny Edwards (1908). This text comes from *Cymru'r Plant* and constitutes a first-person autobiographical narrative by Cit Stevens, an orphan. Cit's story often adopts the child's point of view, but equally sometimes adopts the retrospective narrative perspective of an adult; in this and other respects, it bears similarities with nineteenth-century female *Bildungsromane*, such as Charlotte Brontë's *Jane Eyre*. However, Cit's story is distinctively Welsh. For example, when she becomes a governess with the Pennant Jones family, she is forced by them to attend church, rather than chapel.

There is some social comment in the novel about the ill-treatment of maidservants both in Wales and England; we know that a large proportion of the huge number of female domestic staff employed at this time were Welsh women from rural areas with few other employment opportunities.[16] The novel also deals with migration:

the male protagonist goes to make his fortune in America (a very common trope in women's fiction of this period), while female servants are often forced to go and work in English cities. Cit's friend Poli's view of her stay in Liverpool is bleak:

anghofia i byth trueni yr ystrydoedd culion hynny. Ro'n i yn diolch bob cam o'r ffordd mod i wedi ngeni a magu mewn pentref tawel yng Nghymru ... Ar bob llaw, budreddi a thlodi, a phob gwyneb bron a stamp hagr pechod wedi suddo yn ddwfn arno. Dynion a merched yn gorwedd ar y pavements ... a'u llygaid wedi pylu gan effeithiau y ddiod feddwol ... Yr oedd y rhegfeydd a'r sgrechiadau, a rhyw chwerthin dieflig lanwai'r ystrydoedd, yn ddigon i godi arswyd ar y cryfaf.[17]

[I'll never forget the wretchedness of those narrow streets. I gave thanks every step of the way home that I was born and raised in a quiet village in Wales ... I saw on every side of me, filth and poverty, and every face bore the ugly stamp of sin carved deeply upon it. Men and women lying on the pavements ... their eyes glazed by the effects of alcoholic drink ... The curses and screams and some devilish laughter which filled the streets were enough to horrify even the strongest.]

Clearly, the novel is at least partly a temperance tract, which presents Wales as 'gwlad y menig gwynion'[18] (the land of the white gloves), where Cit naturally assumes that while travelling she will go to the temperance mission for her meal,[19] rather than risk the dangers of a tavern. There is also an implicit cultural nationalism underlying the text, which pours scorn on those Welsh families who affect Anglicized habits and forget their Welsh. The prodigal son returns from America in time to claim his inheritance and is finally reunited with the faithful Cit. The narrative is at the same time a *Bildungsroman*, with a suitably romantic happy ending, and a national narrative of return to the native land in order to uphold and perpetuate the Welsh language and culture, together with Welsh values of piety and sobriety.

As mentioned previously with regard to poetry, there is much tonal and thematic similarity between prose fiction by women writers in English and Welsh at the turn of the century. One example of an Anglo-Welsh novel which appeared soon after the turn of the century is *A Maid of Cymru* (1901) by the sisters Mallt and Gwenffreda Williams, writing under the pseudonym 'The Dau Wynne'.[20] This work first appeared in 1900–1 as a serial in the English-language patriotic journal *Young Wales*. The novel, as the title suggests, is highly nationalistic. Stephen Knight sees it as a 'powerfully ideological, anti-imperial anti-romance', perceiving in it a 'real sense of anti-colonial resistance',[21] though Jane Aaron's view of the novel in her *Pur fel y Dur* is much more negative, emphasizing its class-based conservatism.

What sort of conception of Wales does this 'patriotic romance' put forward? Initially, the heroine, Tangwystl Hywel, is seen beyond the borders of her country, in England, where she is viewed as exotic and seductive (though pure, of course) by the English protagonist, Garry Thoyts. She is placed in a 'Celtic' milieu, staying with a Breton woman and associated with music. Garry, meanwhile, is a colonial farmer in 'the wilds of Breda's Land',[22] though he secretly hankers after being a soldier like his elder brother, who is stationed in Aden. The initial English setting (under western hills, with idyllic old courts, chestnut trees, a college and a promenade), then, is hemmed around with territories of spatial and cultural otherness. Tangwystl's body is from the first associated with the landscape of her homeland: 'he caught the glance of eyes, showing under their dark lashes, mistily blue, as distant mountain peaks veiled in summer haze'.[23] Parallels are made between 'Breda's Land', a faraway island, and Wales, suggesting a colonial connection: Lord Entwhistle sends his cousin Garry to look after his quarries in Wales: 'The quarries are situated in the wilds of Wales, but after Breda's Land, you won't object to that I know.'[24] Entwhistle, however, opines that 'the natives require a firm hand'.[25] There is an affectionate description of the Welsh landscape, in which the Welsh-speaking Tangwystl and Lleuci Hywel are lying on a hilltop, and Tangwystl's view of the panorama before them is fervently patriotic:

> gloomy and sombre and bare as the dyffryn [valley] was, it possessed a grandeur, a wild and striking beauty of its own, and to the eyes now resting on it – the blue eyes of a dreamer, a mystic, and an enthusiast – it was the most beloved spot on earth.'[26]

The young women themselves are strongly associated with the land: 'swift and nimble of foot as their own native ponies',[27] though in view of the fact that Tangwystl meets her end being trampled underfoot by wild mountain ponies, this simile is somewhat macabre. Gweni (the maid) is described as 'a typical Cymraes ... she wore innumerable garments, not unworthy of an Esquimeaux'.[28] Again, the connection is made with the exotic 'Other'. Elor Meirch, the Hywels' house, is described as an old manor-house, bare, unadorned and dignified, filled with solid oak furniture. Neverthe-less, there is a sense of the end of a particular class: 'it's just the one old family that's left hereabouts now',[29] says Nani Pritchard. Tangwystl parodies English arrogance and disdain of Wales:

> She drew up her slender form, stuck an imaginary eyeglass in one eye, and trailed up and down the dim-lit hall, looking over her shoulder to drawl, 'Horrid place, Wales! Horrid weather. Always raining. Here, quarryman John Jones, if I catch you talking that gibberish Welsh, YOU call a language, with quarryman Evans again, I'll dock you of a day's pay.' There! That's how English officials act in Cymru . . .[30]

Though the novel is limited by the formulaic aspects of the romance genre and by its upper-class perspective, it does not shy away from acknowledging poverty, and the picture given of the peasantry is a positive one. The description of the circumstances of Gwilym Parri, protégé of the bard Ab Crawnant, is very stark and may be seen as foreshadowing R. S. Thomas's Iago Prydderch:

> He lived on a poor little farm away on the Mynydd Cynidr, reclaimed in bygone days from the mountain wastes. He had lived there all his life, and his father and grandfather before him. Up in the cloud country he toiled all day, every day through the seasons, rising at dawn to labour in the stony fields that could so ill repay him, for a bed-ridden grandame and half-witted sister were dependent on him. All day he was working, and when night came he felt fit only to lie down and sleep the heavy brutish sleep of the toiler. But poor and obscure and hard-worked as he was, he had been dowered with the bard's beautiful soul . . .[31]

The novel's ideology appears rather confused: Tangwystl rides through the village like Lady Bountiful and, as Jane Aaron points out, even 'Deio Goch, the blacksmith, so called from his republican principles . . . touch[es] his forelock' to her.[32] Yet Tangwystl herself is teased for her imperious airs, and says, 'God-mother Lloyd avers that I am a sad republican.'[33] Despite this confusion, the text is clear in its lament for the depopulation of the Welsh hill-country: charac-ters always seem to be going to far-flung foreign parts, for instance, Gwilym wants to go to New Zealand, while Hoel (*sic*) heads off to the South Seas. Tangwystl reflects on

> the deserted homesteads – once happy centres of life and industry and a rude prosperity – now in ruins through lack of inmates on the Penrhiwceibr and in Glyncelyn – that there was hardly a farm in

the Three Valleys that had not given one stalwart son or blooming
daughter to lifelong exile, and now the young bard of whom Dyffryn
predicted great things was going the same road, leaving his native land
– the wild hills and valleys of Cymru – for ever . . .[34]

Notwithstanding this complaint about rural depopulation, the
Dau Wynne's representation of Wales is by no means exclusively
rural; they acknowledge the industrial and urban dimension of
Welsh people's experience, while emphasizing a common cultural
heritage. For example, 'the iron and steel workers of Dowlais and
Rhymney and Cyfarthfa, the miners and surface-men from many a
colliery' enthusiastically attend the eisteddfod.[35] The novel also
features a quarrymen's strike, but this episode is resolved in an
unintentionally farcical manner when the bard's speech about the
glories of Wales's past, combined with Tangwystl's irresistible singing, persuade the men to go back to work. Industrial relations in the
real Wales of the time were hardly that simple.

In the novel, the English are seen as 'materialistic' and 'utilitar-
ian', engaged in 'conquest of the world',[36] whereas the Welsh are
seen as poetic, dreamy, liable to 'abandon' themselves in impractical
pursuits.[37] A pan-Celtic sentiment is expressed, referring to 'our
sister nation, Alban'[38] and to 'my brother Celt of Brittany'.[39] The
Hywels are evicted from their ancestral home, Elor Meirch, through
the underhand tricks of an Englishman, Byng Orris, which brings
real sadness to Tangwystl. This appears to be a recurrent theme in
Welsh women's writing: women are time and again evicted or left
homeless, and are frequently powerless to remedy their loss. A
similar trope is found in the work of Hilda Vaughan (discussed
later), though she manipulates her plot in order to effect revenge on
the Anglicized patriarchy which has usurped the woman's place in
Wales. In *A Maid of Cymru*, however, eviction also afflicts Welsh
male characters, notably Gwilym Parri, who loses his cottage
through sheer poverty.

In terms of the expected romance plot, the Dau Wynne's novel is
surprisingly dissident. When her suitor, Cadwgan, addresses Tangwystl as his 'sweet maid of Cymru . . . or shall I call you my fair
white rose?' she tartly responds, 'You will not find a rose in me, sir,
you must look elsewhere.'[40] Presumably, here, Tangwystl is reject-
ing Englishness and femininity, both associated with the emblem of
the rose. The novel resists marriage as a happy-ever-after ending,
emphasizing Tangwystl's mysticism and asceticism – it is suggested
that, in an earlier age, she would have been a saint or a hermit. As it

turns out, Tangwystl is saved from marriage, on the eve of her wedding. Before she dies, however, she writes a message to her future husband in her own blood, urging him to devote himself to Wales!

Despite its melodrama, the novel's ending is metaphorically apt, uniting Tangwystl with the body of the hills she loves so uncompromisingly. She dies in a cave, trampled by the wild Welsh ponies to which she herself has earlier been compared. Outside, lightning strikes, echoing the fire (*tân*) of her own name and her nickname, Fflamgoch (Red Flame), as well as the fervency of her patriotism. The novel tends to celebrate female spaces – domestic interiors – but at the same time asserts women's right to dominate public spheres, such as in the public meeting of striking quarrymen, the outdoor eisteddfod and the pan-Celtic festival. Tangwystl is notably unconventional in her lone wandering over her beloved hills in all weathers and all times of the day and night (again, a characteristic which unites the heroines of early twentieth-century Welsh fiction in both languages). In gender terms, this novel figures the woman as redeeming the man (Cadwgan) from his foolhardy repudiation of his nationhood. She is also strong-minded in her rejection of the English suitor, Garry, who, contrary to the conventions of the romance, does not return to claim his prize at the end of the novel. There are strong female characters apart from Tangwystl herself, too, notably Mali the soothsayer and Blodwen Cadwaladr, the bard's granddaughter.

In another work by one of the 'Dau Wynne', Mallt Williams, the short story 'David', there is a similar moral dilemma, but seen from the man's point of view.[41] Just as Garry Thoyts is rejected by Tangwystl because he is English, in 'David', Gwen rejects her fiancé, David, because he has converted to Methodism. The depiction of Nonconformity here is very positive, and the story is a condemnation of the narrow-minded prejudice of Gwen and others in the community. Again, the issue of possession of the land itself arises, since David is denied the tenancy of the farm he has set his heart on when the Squire learns of his conversion. At the end of the story, David is poised to leave Wales to be a missionary in the South Seas; he is presented as a heroic martyr, in contrast to the worldly and narrow-minded Gwen.

Migration, then, can be seen as an important trope in these early twentieth-century works, and it is certainly reflective of the experience of thousands of Welsh people of the time, whether it be internal migration from rural west and north Wales to the industrial valleys of the south-east or migration to far-flung places, often still outposts of the British Empire. A key writer who gives vivid expression to the experience of migration is the Welsh-language writer, Eluned Morgan. When Morgan announces, referring to the ocean, 'this is my home' ('dyma fy nghartref')[42] in *Gwymon y Mor* (Sea-Wrack, 1909), her account of the sea journey across the Atlantic to Patagonia, she is literally as well as metaphorically correct, since she was actually born on board the ship *Myfanwy* as her parents emigrated to Patagonia in 1870. Morgan's travel writing is extraordinarily vivid and personal, invariably couched in the first-person voice and giving an impassioned account of the countries she visited in her unusual life. As the daughter of one of the founders of the Welsh colony in Patagonia, known as 'Y Wladfa' in Welsh, Eluned Morgan's passionate Welsh nationalism is unsurprising. Yet her attachment to Patagonia itself and, indeed, to the continent of South America, with which she identifies, is as striking. What is interesting is the way in which Morgan conjoins these two national allegiances, combining them with a strong religious faith bearing traces of pantheism.

Dringo'r Andes (Climbing the Andes, 1904) is, formally, a hybrid text including a first-person narrative frequently addressing the 'dear reader', extracts from diaries kept on the journey, a letter from an Indian chief, accounts of the history of the Welsh settlement in Patagonia, and snatches of poetry, hymns and songs. Its initial presentation of Y Wladfa is both of a colony imitating its origins in rural Wales ('Welsh farmers trying to make their homesteads like the white cottages of Wales' / 'ffermwyr Cymreig yn ceisio gwneud eu cartrefle fel bythynnod gwynion Cymru'[43]) and of a quasi-biblical Promised Land (in reference to the township of Rawson – 'here was the Canaan of the old colonists' / 'yma oedd Canaan yr hen wladfawyr').[44] She emphasizes the brotherly solidarity and friendship forged between the Welsh and the native Indian people, in contrast to the violent oppression of the Indians practised by the Spanish settlers. Like her contemporary Gwyneth Vaughan, (discussed later), Morgan laments the present state of Wales, with its urbanization and industrialization, suggesting that Y Wladfa is an attempt to recreate the old rural Wales of the past. Morgan is a

thoughtful narrator, constantly mediating between her Welsh readership and the South American landscapes and experiences she
narrates. On occasion, she uses similes calculated to strike a chord
of familiarity with her readers, such as the encounter with a black
farmer in the foothills of the Andes, who is described as being 'as
black as the coal of the Rhondda Valley' ('cyn ddued â glo Cwm
Rhondda').[45] However, she points out that racism was alien to her
experience before she crossed the Atlantic. She mounts a sustained
attack on the imperialism of the white man, who has decimated
indigenous tribes all over the world; it is notable, though, that she
excludes the Welsh from the category of 'white man', aligning them
instead with indigenous peoples. The Spanish, the Americans and
the English are all seen as guilty of persecuting 'small nations'
('cenhedloedd bychain')[46]. She refers to the Indians as 'plant Natur',
and it is clear that she herself is one of the same tribe, so to speak.

When the travellers reach the Andes, they are welcomed by a
Welsh community living in places such as 'Capel y Llwyn, Tŷ Coch,
Afon Llwchwr, Troed yr Orsedd' – 'magical and melodious Welsh
names' ('enwau Cymraeg swynol a phersain')[47]. As Morgan
remarks, they were nine thousand miles away from Snowdonia, and
yet the place-names, the language and culture of the people here
were completely Welsh. She presents Y Wladfa as threatened on all
sides by a hostile Roman Catholicism; the Welsh are a small band of
Protestants in 'the savage lion's den' ('ffau'r llewod rheibus').[48] The
landscape itself is described in emotional and awe-filled detail – the
condors circling the summits, the giant fuchsia trees bending low
over the waterfalls, the amazingly camouflaged insects attracted by
the campfire at night. There are persistent references to Y Wladfa as
an Edenic garden which needs to be carefully nourished and tended;
Morgan ends by urging Welsh readers to go there – ironically
enough – to study the purity and beauty of their own language. She
expresses a similar sentiment in *Gwymon y Mor*, where she states:

Oes heb wreiddiau yw ein hoes ni, ac yn byw ar sudd yr hen dderi fu,
ond fe dderfydd y nodd bywiol cyn hir ac yna bydd rhaid dychwel i'r
mynyddoedd, ac ail-blannu a magu gwreiddiau iach, gonest – dyna
pryd y daw'r glewion yn ôl ac y gwawria'r oes aur.[49]

[Ours is an age without roots, living on the sap of the old oaks of the
past, but the vital goodness will come to an end before long and then
there will be a return to the mountains, to plant again and foster some

healthy, honest roots – that's when the heroes will return and the golden age will dawn.]

Clearly, Morgan sees the future of Wales in South America; as she sails down the coast of Argentina in *Gwymon y Mor* she reflects that the El Dorado of the future will be here, in the South. The settlements in Y Wladfa are the beginnings of that future El Dorado; she describes them lovingly as 'little Welsh villages nesting on the banks of the river Camwy' ('pentrefi bychain Cymreig sy'n nythu ar lan afon Camwy').[50] The metaphor of the villages *nesting* beside the river brings to mind the idea of migratory birds, as well as conjuring up an atmosphere of contentment, cosiness, protection and belonging. Ernest Gellner has suggested that the Romantic notion of 'roots', which Eluned Morgan returns to repeatedly, perhaps paradoxically offers individuals a sense of personal liberty, since the nation-state 'did not insist that the identity of culture be there from the start: it was enough if there was a recollection of origins and a deep desire to return to the sources of one's vitality and true identity'.[51]

Romantic roots are also characteristic concerns of Gwyneth Vaughan, the pen-name of Annie Harriet Hughes, a largely self-educated woman from rural Merioneth who published extensively in the Welsh-language journals, such as *Y Cymro* and *Y Brython*, in the first decade of the century. She later republished three of her novels in separate volumes, leaving another novel unfinished in the pages of *Y Brython*. The tenor of her works is both patriotic and religious, though she makes use of both humour and romance in her adaptation of the novel genre to her own purposes. In the Preface to her novel *O Gorlannau y Defaid* (From the Sheepfolds, 1905), she states her purpose in writing the work as being to record and memorialize some of the 'vanishing landmarks' of Wales and Welsh life. It is interesting that she foregrounds the land itself, in her reference to the 'vanishing landmarks', for in the novel that follows the landscape of Wales plays a very prominent part. It acts as a 'lieu de memoire', a site of memory or a repository of what the author clearly views as peculiarly Welsh customs, values and beliefs. And it is evident that the novel, set as it is in the late 1850s, is intended as a wake-up call to those Welsh people who have turned their back on their heritage, becoming Anglicized and leaving the Nonconformist denominations for the greater security and social status of the Anglican Church. Despite the underlying 'message' of the novel, which occasionally rises to the surface in some overt didacticism, the novel is also shot through with humour and a lively, idiolectal use of language. In the figures of Angharad and her mother, Luned, the two principal female characters, there is also a concern with women's social roles and influence. What passes as female education is dismissed as trivial, though the novel falls short of suggesting a solution to the limited possibilities open to able women. The extraordinary abilities and ambitions of Angharad are, in the end, rather in the manner of those of Dorothea Brooke in George Eliot's *Middlemarch*, dissipated in a subsidiary role as helpmeet to the narrator, Bob, who becomes a politician.

Just as George Eliot's decision to set *Middlemarch* in a period about half a century before the publication date of the novel gave her an opportunity to comment on the social changes which had occurred between 'then' and 'now', so Gwyneth Vaughan takes the same opportunity, in this case in order to belabour the contemporary Welsh for their lack of patriotism, their Anglicization, their secularization and their aspirations to gentility. She contrasts the wooden bowls used by the forefathers with the dainty lace tablecloths of today. The agricultural community she describes is one which nestles perfectly into its landscape, the cottages melting into the background in such a way as to highlight the human inhabitants' interdependence with the land. The shepherd-poet, Dewi Wyn, knows all his sheep individually and they know his whistle. Yet Vaughan's description of the community is not idyllic – there is real poverty, and drunkenness, and some old women are shunned on suspicion of being witches. Sir William, the local squire, is a figure of fun who speaks hilariously bad Welsh, but there is also an edge of protest in his characterization. Sir William does not understand the religious revival sweeping the countryside and complains to his neighbour, Robert Fychan, who tries but fails to explain the phenomenon to him, 'everyone go mad, Robert ... my head spinning, Robert, you worse than House of Commons; me sleeping there fine like in bed and leave peoples to do business like they chooses' ('pobol ty pawb o'u co's, Robert . . . ' a pen fi troi, Robert; ti cwaeth na House of Commons; fi cysgu fano noble fel yn cwely, a cadel i pobls gneyd business fel nhw dewis [*sic*]' – the Welsh is deliberately ungrammatical).[52] As the local MP, Sir William, with his penchant for a good snooze, is clearly less than effective.

Interestingly, Vaughan links the strength of religious belief to the landscape. In the ideology presented here, one is more likely to be a believer if one is familiar with mountains: 'On the mountaintop the Divine Presence descends again like it did in former days' ('Ar ben y mynydd mae'r Presenoldeb Dwyfol yn disgyn eto fel y dyddiau gynt').[53] Connected with this is the novel's celebration of the peat gathered on the mountain heights, as opposed to the coal which lurks in the depths beneath:

> Nid yw gweithio ganoedd o latheni o dan y ddaear, mewn tywyllwch dudew ... yn tueddi i ddyrchafu dynion chwaith: rhydd gwaith dyn ddylanwad ar ei gymeriad a'i gyraeddiadau heb yn wybod iddo, a gresyn fod yn angenrheidiol cadw miloedd o'n cyd-ddynion mewn tywyllwch, bron ar hyd ei hoes, er codi'r glo o galon y ddaear, yn danwydd o'r fath a hoffir oreu, neu er cyfoethogi y gwr bia'r cyfalaf. Pa un yw y rheswm cryfaf, tybed? Un peth a wyddom oll, sef fod aml i lecyn fu yn brydferth fel Paradwys yn myned yn ddu fel bro marwolaeth a distryw, a'i fwg yn dyrchafu yn ddibaid, nes pardduo gwybr a daear, a'r ardaloedd megis heint-leoedd, lle y cyrcha pob aderyn aflan.[54]

> [Working hundreds of yards underground, in the pitch-black darkness ... does not tend to exalt men either: a man's work influences his character and his achievements unbeknownst to him, and it's a pity that it's necessary to keep thousands of our fellow-men in darkness almost throughout their lives in order to bring coal up from the heart of the earth as the fuel of choice or to increase the wealth of the man who owns the capital. Which is the stronger reason, I wonder? One thing we all know, that some little places which were as beautiful as Paradise are now becoming as black as the kingdom of death and destruction, their smoke rising ceaselessly until it stains heaven and earth, leaving these areas like places afflicted by plague, to which all the unclean birds flock.]

This passage is both a lament for the beautiful rural landscapes polluted and destroyed by industrialization and, at the same time, a social critique and questioning of the motives of those behind that industrialization, which certainly transformed parts of the land-scape of Wales between the 'then' of the novel (1859) and the 'now' of its publication (1905). Other elements of social critique also enter the novel, for example when Dewi and Bob, the narrator, go to Oxford and find most of their fellow-students living lives of idleness and debauchery, when many young Welsh boys longed to get such an education but were denied it, owing to poverty. Although Angharad, the main female character, later acquires a European education, there is no explicit mention of the impossibility of her being sent to Oxford, which had no women's colleges at the time.

Instead, Angharad is closely associated with the landscape of Wales in a quasi-mystical way. This trope is repeated in a number of contemporary works in both languages, such as Allen Raine's *Queen of the Rushes* (1906) and Eluned Morgan's *Dringo'r Andes* (1904). Both Morgan and Vaughan use the phrase 'plentyn Natur' (child of Nature) to describe the female figure in the landscape, though Morgan also applies this epithet to the native Indians of South America. Angharad also 'reads' her native landscape in allegorical terms, identifying certain well-known spots with places in Bunyan's *Pilgrim's Progress*, a text which echoes throughout the novel. Although Sir William is not ousted from his estate, there is a suggestion that the true Welsh heirs regain their birthright at the end of the novel, when Dewi Wyn inherits the old Wyn estate from the dastardly half-Englishman who had cheated his family out of it in the first place. Significantly, the old harp is still standing in the corner of the living-room when Dewi once more takes possession of the house. Outside, the estate is compared to 'the garden of Eden before the coming of the serpent' ('ardd Eden cyn i'r sarph ddod o hyd iddi').[55]

O Gorlannau y Defaid (1905) and Allen Raine's novel *A Welsh Singer* (1897) share some narrative features, which suggest that, despite the difference in language, Allen Raine and Gwyneth Vaughan had a surprisingly similar vision of Wales and Welsh identity. The main female character in Raine's novel begins as a sunburnt shepherdess on the west coast of Wales; similarly, one of the two main male characters in *O Gorlannau y Defaid*, as the title suggests, begins life as a shepherd in the Welsh mountains, looking out over Cardigan Bay. Both characters experience a transformation in their lives, effected by some traditional devices of the romance genre: Mifanwy travels to London and becomes a world-renowned opera-singer, before returning to west Wales in triumph to reveal her true identity and be reunited with her childhood sweetheart, who by this time has become suitably gentrified. Dewi also heads east, as far as Oxford, to acquire a university education and a fortune from an unexpected benefactor before returning to his birthright in an old Welsh country house. Dewi does not acquire a Romantic happy ending, however, finding his apotheosis instead in devoting his life to religion and a new translation of the Bible, which omits all the morally dubious parts.

Another female writer inspired by the religious concerns of her age was Sara Maria Saunders, who wrote stories and essays in both Welsh and English-language periodicals around the turn of the century. Her writing in Welsh is particularly vibrant, and full of humorous sketches of gender politics in rural west Wales. The popularity of her work is reflected in the fact that her stories were collected and published in two volumes, namely *Y Diwygiad ym Mhentre Alun* (The Revival in Pentre Alun, 1907) and *Llithiau o Bentre Alun* (Essays from Pentre Alun, 1908). All the stories are connected with the 1904–5 religious revival led by Evan Roberts and reveal the effects of the Revival on a series of sleepy west Wales villages, with occasional forays into evangelical work in the large towns of south Wales. Saunders herself was a native of Llangeitho in Carmarthenshire, and she renders west Wales speech in her stories in an authentic and appealing style. Indeed, authenticity is important to Saunders's aesthetic, since she refers to her stories as *ysgrifau* (essays) and announces in the foreword to *Y Diwygiad ym Mhentre Alun* that 'the aim of these essays is to record . . . some of the facts of the Revival' ('[a]mcan y rhan fwyaf o'r ysgrifau hyn yw cofnodi . . . rai o ffeithiau y Diwygiad').[56] Fortunately, the contents of the volume are much more interesting from a literary point of view than this drearily worthy purpose suggests.

All the stories have a first-person speaker who is a member of the community, usually the mild-mannered Griffri Roberts or Ifan Cadwgan, but occasionally the more acerbic female voice of Mrs Watkin Jones. All reveal the dramatic and powerful effects of the religious revival on their communities; true to the authenticity to which Saunders aspires, she shows that women have a very promi-nent role to play in the Revival. Indeed, the chapel ministers themselves appear very much in the background, while strong female characters such as Mrs Powel Ty'nrhos, nicknamed 'etholedig arglwyddes' (elected lady), the sharp-tongued chapel caretaker Sarah Thomas and the evangelical Martha Jones, who works in the slums of the city of 'Caerfor', play prominent roles. When the wife of the old preacher Mr Griffis experiences her conversion, he complains: 'the wife back home has got the better of me' ('mae'r wraig acw wedi mynd yn drech na fi').[57] When the eminently sensible Mrs Powel experiences her conversion, she is seen by others as going mad – an interesting parallel to Allen Raine's *Queen of the Rushes* (1906), which also associates religious conver-sion with female madness.[58] However, Saunders's account of the

Revival is enthusiastically positive, unlike Raine's more sceptical approach. Nevertheless, Saunders emphasizes the intensity and extremity of people's behaviour at this time: 'Mrs Powel confessing in public! She had been the last woman in Pentre Alun who would have taken part in a public meeting' ('Mrs Powel yn dweud ei phrofiad! Y wraig olaf yn Pentre Alun i gymeryd rhan mewn cyfarfod cyhoeddus').[59] As she stands up among the congregation, her face is shining like that of Moses and she compares the immensity of her own sin to the mountains of Wales: 'On my right hand was a huge Snowdon of my sin; behind me a huge Cader Idris of my sin; on my left hand a huge Plinlimon of my sin . . . and there wasn't even a narrow path between them, where I could escape' ('Ar fy neheulaw yr oedd Wyddfa fawr o'm pechod; tu ôl i mi, Cader Idris fawr o'm pechod; ar fy aswy Plinlimon fawr o'm pechod; . . . a doedd dim hyd yn oed llwybr cul rhyngddynt, lle y gallaswn ddianc').[60] Mrs Powel gets into a preacherly *hwyl* as she describes how the Welsh mountains of her sin are eventually cleansed by a river of blood. The whole congregation is impressed and there are many converts. However, the narrator himself retains a slightly sardonic tone at times; he is surprised that there are quite so many sinners in Pentre Alun who suffer from quite such mountainous burdens of sin. Although the overall tone of the stories is pious, there is a strong undertow of humour, largely as a result of the female characters' mockery of men's pretensions. Griffri Roberts urges his sister, Mrs Watkin Jones, to tell her story and not worry about making too many mistakes; the latter repays her brother's patronizing of her by reflecting 'these men – even the best of them are extraordinarily self-important' ('rhai hynod o hunan – dybus yw'r gwŷr yma, hyd yn oed y goreu o honynt').[61] Sarah Thomas, meanwhile, has had a series of husbands, none of whom has been totally satisfactory; she claims that at the critical point of the marriage service, she coughs instead of promising to obey.[62] The fact that Sara Maria Saunders herself was the wife of a Calvinistic Methodist minister adds a soupçon of extra daring to her portraits of New Women in turn-of-the-century Wales.

A common topos unites Allen Raine's *Queen of the Rushes* (1906), Sara Maria Saunders's *Y Diwygiad ym Mhentre Alun* (1907) and Gwyneth Vaughan's *O Gorlannau y Defaid* (1905), namely the Welsh chapel and populace swept up in religious revival. Admittedly, Gwyneth Vaughan's novel purports to be an historical novel, set in the 1859 Revival, though she remarks in her foreword that she little expected the country to be caught up in another Revival before she came to publish her work in book form. Nevertheless, all three writers figure Wales as a land ripe for religious revival; both Welsh-language writers clearly support Revivalism, while Allen Raine presents a more sceptical view of it. The short-lived but widespread Revival led by Evan Roberts, a charismatic young former collier from Loughor (Casllwchwr), in 1904–5, appears to have had a more significant role in Welsh women's writing of this period than is perhaps warranted by its historical importance. Far from being an ephemeral phenomenon over-shadowed by more substantial and far-reaching events, such as the election of the first Labour MP, the 1904–5 Revival clearly held a symbolic, even one might say an allegorical importance, for Welsh women writers which far exceeded its historical weight.

One might argue that this exaggerated importance of the Revival in women's writing is accounted for by the prominent role played by women themselves in its development. Many contemporary commentators were shocked by the way in which girls and very young women accompanied Evan Roberts on his missionary journeys around Wales and England, even taking part in the preaching in the chapel, thus usurping traditional male roles. As Deirdre Beddoe remarks: 'Eight of Roberts' team of ten followers on his first missionary journey were women who, far from being besotted religious "groupies", as male versions of history frequently depict them, in fact, played a key part in organizing meetings and preaching.'[63] Others might argue that the Revival's main significance lay in its being led by a young working-class man, a former collier with little formal education. Moreover, the Revival certainly had a nationalist dimension, assertive of Welsh difference at a time when the Welsh language was losing ground to English, there was wide-spread population movement, and traditional customs and ways of life were beginning to disappear.

Gwyneth Vaughan's later novel, *Plant y Gorthrwm* (1908), is more overtly political than *O Gorlannau y Defaid*, focusing on the General Election of 1868 and its consequences in a corner of rural Wales. In her note to the reader, the author states her aim in writing the novel as being the education of Welsh children about their country's past and the fight for freedom from political and cultural oppression. She emphasizes the *factual* nature of the suffering represented in the novel, and this claim to documentary truth is

re-emphasized at the close of the novel, which focuses on a com-
memorative plaque on a chapel wall in rural Merioneth, which can
still be seen: 'if my dear reader wishes to see the plaque, it remains to
this day in the old rural chapel in the "county of the white gloves"'
('os myn fy narllenydd hynaws weled y tabled, erys hyd heddyw yn
yr hen gapel gwledig yn "sir y menyg gwynion"').[64] The material
appearance of the book also adds to the impression of authenticity,
since the text is set out in two columns per page, thus resembling a
newspaper.

The plot of the novel revolves around the General Election of
1868, in which the Liberals under Gladstone defeated the Tories
under Disraeli; in Llangynan, the rural Welsh setting of the novel,
the Tory landowner's agent, the villainous Mr Harries, attempts to
bully and blackmail the local men into voting for Tattershall, the
Tory candidate. However, the Liberal candidate, Mr Edwards, is
returned, and reprisals follow. These reprisals take the form of
evictions, a recurring trope in Welsh women's fiction, one which
suggests an allegorical dimension, in that the native Welsh are
ousted from their ancestral lands by oppressive and manipulative,
quasi-colonial, foreign, often absentee, landowners. The political
polarization between Liberal and Tory also corresponds with cultural affiliations: the Tories are seen as Anglicized, gentrified and
churchgoing, whereas Liberalism is identified with the Welsh-
speaking, chapelgoing *gwerin*, (the ordinary people). Tellingly, the
only sympathetic squire-figure, old Syr Tudur Llwyd, decides at the
last minute to vote Liberal, for the first time in his life.

The fruitful land around Llangynan is divided into two great
estates, one belonging to Syr Tudur and the other to an absentee
landlord, who has brought in the odious, chapel-hating Mr Harries
to manage his land. There is a duality to the whole landscape, where
there are two of everything – rivers, shops, cobblers, smiths,
chapels, and even drunks! Again, this spatial division bears ideological meaning, in that there is a stark difference in the experience
of the people who live on Syr Tudur's land, in comparison with
those unfortunate enough to occupy the land ruled by Mr Harries.
In a sense, Vaughan is delineating spatially the difference between
slavery and freedom. It is no accident that the dominant textual
allusion in this novel is to Harriet Beecher Stowe's *Uncle Tom's
Cabin*, rather than to *The Pilgrim's Progress*, which underlies *O
Gorlannau y Defaid*. On several occasions Vaughan makes an
implicit comparison between the oppression of the common Welsh

people in the mid nineteenth century and the enslavement of African people in the New World. She points out that the Welsh translation of *Uncle Tom's Cabin, Caban F'ewyrth Robert*, was one of the most popular books in Welsh homes in those days.[65] The identification between the oppressors of the Welsh and the slave-owners is hinted at when the dubious origins of English land-owners' fortunes is mentioned: 'it was whispered that some gained their wealth through catching negroes in Africa and selling them in America' ('chlywid sibrydion distaw i rai fyned yn gyfoethog trwy ddal negroaid yn Affrica a'u gwerthu yn yr America').[66]

Another aspect of the increased politicization of this novel is the explicit reference to women's rights to education and suffrage. When Rhianon, the heroine, and her sister Olwen see a political meeting at a crossroads, Olwen is reluctant to join the crowd because there are no other females there; Rhianon's reply is forthright: 'The sooner we get there the better, then, if that's the case; there's plenty of need for women to help these men to set things to rights' ('Gore i ni pan gynta' i fynd yna, os felly mai hi, mae digon o eisiau merched i helpu'r dynion yma i drin tipyn ar betha').[67] The message about women's suffrage becomes even more explicit towards the end of the novel, when the supremely capable Mrs Meyrick takes over the estate from Mr Harries and begins to set things to right after the suffering and injustice of the evictions: 'Mrs Meyrick, if she'd been born a man, would have made one of the best Chancellors of the Exchequer ever to be a member of any Administration' ('Gwnaethai Mrs Meyrick, pes ganesid hi yn ddyn, Ganghellydd y Trysorlys gyda'r goreu fu erioed yn aelod o un Weinyddiaeth').[68] Meanwhile, the precocious little girl, Dyddgu, receives a proper education and grows up to dedicate herself to feminism.

There are two significant 'lieux de memoire' in the text: the blacksmith's forge and three ancient white standing stones. The standing stones, called *trioedd* (triads), are reminders of an ancient Celtic past which binds the *gwerin* to their land; at the same time, these pagan symbols are endowed with a Christianized ideology, since Olwen, in the opening scene of the novel, christens them 'Hope, Patience, Love' ('Gobaith, Amynedd, Cariad'),[69] and it is these virtues which allow the oppressed Welsh to win out in the end. The forge, presided over by the smith, Huw Huws, is a meeting place for the local men, a place of political debate and clearly, in metaphorical terms, the forge of the new ideas about freedom and cultural independence.

There are many similarities between the characters of Vaughan's two novels: the good-hearted old squire speaking comic Welsh, the freedom-loving young heroine, the idealized parents, the wise old woman, the good preacher, the precocious little girl, the devious agents of Anglicization. Despite this formulaic characterization, Vaughan's skill at using direct speech is always in evidence and her characters often speak in lively, authentic-sounding dialectal voices, except when they are quoting the Scriptures (which they are, sadly, wont to do with great frequency), when the prose becomes cloyingly didactic. One interesting character who is not formulaic is Elin, the mad girl. Elin wanders the countryside singing and asking questions; she is also subversive, in that she sabotages the people she dislikes, such as Mr Harries by tripping his horse in the dark. She is searching for Jesus Christ because all her neighbours are constantly talking of him and she, taking their words literally, is keen to meet this prodigious personage. Elin is an interesting character because, despite the political rhetoric of the 'good' characters, such as Nisien Wyn, who dedicates himself to rid his people from the yoke of Toryism, she is the only one to take direct action against her enemies. Elin is also an alter ego of the heroine, Rhianon, in some ways, since Rhianon also quests and questions; there is a point in the novel where she is also threatened with incipient madness, after the loss of her parents and sister. Boba, the idealized old woman who spins socks and wisdom, manages to save Rhianon from that fate, however: 'the poor old woman calmed . . . Rhianon's sensitive mind gradually but surely' ('arweiniodd yr hen wraig dlawd . . . feddwl tyner Rhianon yn araf ond yn sicr i ymdawelu').[70]

It is clear that Gwyneth Vaughan's novel is a political call for a 'Cymru Rydd' (Free Wales), and yet it falls far short of radicalism. Though the novel is anti-Tory, the happy ending is nothing more than a return to benevolent feudalism. There is apparently nothing wrong with the squirearchy in Vaughan's ideology, as long as it speaks Welsh and is paternalistic. Her freedom-fighters are curiously passive, perhaps because there is a tension between the passionate nationalism enshrined in the texts and the equally passionate religious conviction which is also pacifist. When a Vaughan hero is required to do something great in order to follow his vocation, as Dewi Wyn does in *O Gorlannau y Defaid*, he sets about preparing a 'clean' version of the Bible. Bowdlerization, nowadays at least, does not appear to be a particularly heroic activity. Part of Vaughan's difficulty is her struggle with form: her novels are uneasy hybrids of romance and various kinds of political propaganda.

Although Allen Raine's struggle with form is less overt than that of her contemporary, Gwyneth Vaughan, it is nevertheless present, even in some of her most accomplished and successful romances. The texture of the writing makes it clear that Raine resorts to easy cliché when she is narrating the love-story formulae of her novels, which nevertheless have to be present in order to conform to the conventions of the romance genre. This is the aspect of Raine's work which has alienated some readers, and which is, undoubtedly, empty sentimentality. However, when Raine is sketching in the background to the love-story plot, her art becomes much more individual, richly textured and convincing. Indeed, it is to do Raine a disservice to describe her creation of a fictional world as a 'sketching-in of background', since it is the landscape of west Wales and its inhabitants that give substance and energy to Raine's eleven novels.

'Allen Raine' was the pen-name of Ada Puddicombe, neé Evans, a solicitor's daughter from Newcastle Emlyn, on the border of Cardiganshire and Carmarthenshire. Apart from *Hearts of Wales* (1905), a historical novel set at the time of Owain Glyndŵr's rebellion in the fourteenth century, all of Allen Raine's novels, published between 1897 and 1910, are set contemporaneously on the south-west Cardiganshire coast, with occasional forays into other areas of Wales, notably to the industrial valleys of Glamorganshire in *A Welsh Witch* (1902), and to London in *A Welsh Singer* (1897).

Early reviewers of her novels assumed that 'Allen Raine' was a man; the reviews are extremely positive. The *Daily Mail*'s reviewer, referring to *A Welsh Singer*, comments:

> Wales has waited long for her novelist; but he seems to have come at last in the person of Mr. Allen Raine who, in his perfectly beautiful story ... has at once proved himself a worthy interpreter and exponent of the romantic spirit of the country.[71]

Nor was it only English publications, such as the *Daily Telegraph*, *Punch*, the *Pall Mall Gazette*, *Vanity Fair* and the *Athenaeum*, which provided Raine with ecstatic reviews; the *Western Mail* praised her work as reflecting 'the inner life of rural Wales'.[72]

34

Traditional accounts of the development of 'Anglo-Welsh' literature, such as Gwyn Jones's *The First Forty Years*,[73] tend to dismiss
Allen Raine as a trivial romantic novelist who, in Jones's notorious
phrase, constructed a sandcastle dynasty – presumably on the beach
at Tresaith, where she spent her last twenty years. Dismissive critics
suggest that Raine's fictional world is impossibly idyllic and clichéd,
but this is to ignore the fact that Raine actually includes and
comments upon a wide range of distinctly un-idyllic aspects of rural
life. In the opening pages of her first published novel, *A Welsh
Singer* (1897), for example, Mifanwy the shepherdess lives in fear of
her cruel master, John Powys, who beats her regularly and pays her
a pittance of 2*d* a day (while her fellow shepherd, Ieuan, gets 3*d* by
virtue of his maleness). In other novels, Raine repeatedly addresses
such taboo subjects as madness, witchcraft, domestic abuse and
religious frenzy. Moreover, as Sally Roberts Jones has pointed out,
Raine is the earliest Anglo-Welsh novelist to represent – in a realistic
manner – a coal-mining disaster.[74] In *A Welsh Witch* (1902) the
protagonists, Goronwy and Walto, are trapped underground for
four days by a pit explosion; the description of their interminable
wait in the pitch darkness to be rescued is made all the more sinister
by 'the rats, now bolder and more numerous, [which] approached
closer and closer'.[75] One of the trapped men, David Humphreys,
goes mad and suggests killing one of their smaller companions,
Will, and eating him; however, Will dies of natural causes and is
greedily devoured by the waiting rats, while David Humphreys is
saved but is immediately sent to the lunatic asylum. This is hardly
the wishy-washy romance writing which Raine is caricatured as
producing; in fact, it is a good deal closer in its macabre naturalism
to Zola's *Germinal* or to the work of Caradoc Evans, though it
pre-dates *My People* by thirteen years. Neither does Raine represent
rural village life as unremittingly idyllic; Catrin, the 'Welsh witch' of
the title of Raine's 1902 novel, is whipped by her father and cruelly
persecuted by the entire village for her 'uncanny ways'.[76] Indeed,
any form of deviation from the norm tends to lead to public
disapproval or even physical abuse in Raine's west Wales villages;
even the *meistr*, Gildas Rees, in *Queen of the Rushes* (1906), is
ostracized and suspected of murder because he refuses to join in the
frenzied behaviour of the religious revival, which sweeps over
everyone else in the village. Meanwhile, Valmai, in *By Berwen
Banks* (1899), is evicted from her home, expelled from the chapel
and generally vilified when she becomes pregnant while (apparently) unmarried.

In representing 'the inner life of rural Wales', then, Raine does not ignore the negative aspects, but she does present a complex portrait of a cultured and distinctive people. The Welsh language is used extensively and accurately in Raine's novels, frequently with English glosses in footnotes; mention is also made of literary and musical culture, folk customs, eisteddfodau, religious festivals, and peculiarities of dress and habit. Interestingly, Welsh culture is seen as springing directly from the world of nature; in more than one sense, the characters are shaped and moulded by the landscape in which they live and which they, in turn, shape to their own uses. Mifanwy, the 'Welsh singer' of Raine's 1897 novel, is heard early on in the narrative singing

> one of the old pathetic hymns of her nation, that must surely have been caught by her ancestors from the sound of the wind as it whistled over the bleak moors, or sighed through their deep forests in the early ages, so closely do some of their melodies imitate its weird and mournful tones.[77]

Similarly, her companion, Ieuan, is a naturally gifted sculptor, whose stone carvings come literally out of the land itself. Raine frequently personifies the landcape, and prominent topographical features recur from novel to novel; one of these is 'ogo wylofen', a cave in the cliffs which emits human-like cries: 'then came a panting and a sobbing that swelled into a sound of weeping and wailing, so like the cry of a human being in distress, that it was almost impossible to believe that the cave held nothing of living misery'.[78] The same cave features as the refuge of Catrin, the 'Welsh witch', since no other living creature ventures to enter the cave, which is littered with wreckage and skeletons. In *A Welsh Witch*, when Goronwy travels to north Wales to find Catrin, he is guided by old man Snowdon, referred to as 'that old fellow' with a 'rugged head'.[79]

Another way in which characters are formed by their environment is that several of Raine's heroines are distinguished by their deep suntans, acquired through their work and, indeed, life out of doors. Raine makes much of the prejudice shown towards these brown-skinned girls, whose tan presumably is seen as a badge of low social status, but may also be seen as Raine's veiled commentary on racial prejudice. Ieuan's aunt comments disparagingly on Mifanwy: 'I never saw such a little brown-faced monkey.'[80] Certainly, Mifanwy's 'swarthy' skin appears to mark her out initially as inferior, and subsequently as foreign, when she attains success as 'la belle Russe', the singer on the London stage. The suggestion here that to be Welsh is to be perceived as racially, as well as culturally, other is an interesting one.[81] It is also noteworthy that when Mifanwy goes to England she gradually becomes whiter, even before she enters high society. This symbolism invites a post-colonial reading of the text, in which Raine is subtly suggesting the way in which Wales has been colonized and designated as racially inferior by its powerful neighbour. The plot is subversive, in that it shows the racialized other infiltrating into the heartland of the colonizing power and 'conquering' them with the cultural superiority of her song. Even Mifanwy's pseudonym can be seen as conveying covert meanings, since it is a pun for Welsh readers – the French phrase 'belle Russe' being a corruption of her acquired Welsh name 'Belle Roose' – and can also suggest 'ruse', in the sense of trickery or subterfuge. The Welsh shepherdess, scorned for her supposed class, cultural and racial origins, triumphs over the English and Anglicized Welsh gentry, but she eventually returns to Wales to assert her true identity, joining together her two selves, Mifanwy and Belle Russe. The final union of Mifanwy and Ieuan takes place in the 'broom-parlour', a natural formation in the hillside, flanked by broom bushes and topped by a rock ledge.[82] The reinsertion of the characters into their rightful place in the Welsh landscape could not be more clearly indicated.

The heart of Raine's map of rural Wales is a little coastal village called variously Abersethin, Mwntseison, Treswnd or Aberlaswen in the novels, and there are common references in them all to the nearby small market-towns of Caer Madoc and Tregarreg, and to the offshore island, Ynysoer. Like Hardy's Wessex, Raine's west Wales is a fully realized fictional world which bears striking similarities to the actual landscape on which it is mapped. Most of her novels begin with a detailed topographical description of the coastal landscape, which is often recognizable as Tresaith and the surrounding area, where Raine lived and wrote during the last twenty years of her life. All these little villages conform to Lefebvre's concept of the 'appropriated' landscape, that is, they are modest, home-built dwellings which blend into the land itself and are suited to the farming and fishing activities of the inhabitants. In *Torn Sails*, (1898), for example, the village of Mwntseison is described as 'look[ing] like nothing more than a cluster of white shells left by the storm in a chink of the rocks'.[83] Similarly, the cottage of 'Sara Sbridion' in *Garthowen* (1900) is described as:

> almost hidden by the surrounding gorse and heather for, according to the old Welsh custom, it had been built in a hollow scooped out behind a natural elevation, which protected it from the strong sea wind; in fact, there was little of it visible except its red chimney-pot.[84]

These 'appropriated' landscapes contrast strongly with the 'dominated' landscape of the collieries of Glamorganshire, as represented in *A Welsh Witch*, where Mr Jones has risen through the ranks to become a coal-owner himself, and his dwelling reflects his new-found social status:

> On the side of a rocky hill, overlooking one of the most romantic valleys in Glamorganshire, stood the residence (for we dare not call it a house) of Mr and Mrs Jones. A snug, old-fashioned farmhouse when it came into the rich coal-owner's possession, Glaish-y-dail had been added to and improved out of all recognition. The front door had been enlarged, and a massive portico, with pillars of stucco, adorned it. The lawns were trim and soft, the gravel on the drives immaculate, foreign shrubs and trees stood stiffly where they had been planted. No trailing branches, no moss-grown stumps, were permissible in the grounds of Glaish-y-Dail . . .[85]

She also describes the pollution of the valley by the 'works' of copper and iron.

Contrasting with these contemporary-set novels is *Hearts of Wales*, Raine's only attempt at an historical novel, and it is certainly not one of her best works. It is set during the Welsh uprising against the English Crown led by Owain Glyndŵr between 1400 and 1416. Interestingly, although notions of national identity and patriotism are addressed throughout the text, Glyndŵr's uprising is presented as doomed from the start. Instead, the more politically neutral battle between robbers and good people is substituted for a national rebellion. The novel is hampered by Raine's attempts to use archaic language, and she also tries to convey the atmosphere of a more violent and ruthless age – there are murders and maimings in this novel, as there are nowhere else in Raine's oeuvre. Nevertheless, certain motifs occur here as elsewhere in her work, notably the figure of Malen Ddu the witch, and the doubling of characters, here Eleri and Indeg, almost identical cousins.

Duality of identity is a recurring theme in Raine's novels, albeit rendered in different ways. It is expressed most overtly in the novel she wrote first, *Ynysoer* (published posthumously as *Where Billows Roll*, 1909), as identical twins, a trope which recurs in *By Berwen Banks* (Valmai/Gwladys), then as a single person with a dual identity (Mifanwy/La Belle Russe in *A Welsh Singer*). Valmai in *By Berwen Banks* (1899), the daughter of Welsh Patagonian missionaries, now an orphan in Wales, has multiple identities; as she reflects: 'Well, indeed, I don't know what have I grown up! Welsh, or English, or Spanish, or Patagonian! I am mixed of them all, I think.'[86] Later, different characters tend to be paired, as representing alternative fates for an individual, with similar backgrounds or appearance. Frequently, two female characters are paired as sane and mad: Gwladys and Gwen in *Torn Sails*, Nance and Gwenifer in *Queen of the Rushes*. *Torn Sails* is a particularly poignant representation of female madness, which, as the authorial voice states in the narrative, 'is no uncommon thing to see in a small village . . . the dread of the asylum hangs like a cloud over the scene that appears such a picture of rustic happiness'.[87] When Gwen's baby sickens, she consults the witch, 'Malen hysbys', who recommends a 'roasted mouse' as a cure.[88] After the baby's death, Gwen becomes increasingly distracted; however, some of her questioning is surprisingly lucid: 'God indeed! What sort of a God must he be who gave me a little baby . . . and then tore him cruelly away?'[89]

The concern both with madness and with duality may relate directly to Allen Raine's own experiences. In later life, when she began to write her novels, her husband, Beynon Puddicombe, was suffering from bouts of madness which regularly necessitated his being taken away to a private asylum. Clearly, Raine had first-hand experience of this suffering; as she puts it elsewhere in the novel, 'alas! Life does hold out to us sometimes a cup of so much bitterness that imagination even would hesitate to picture it . . . We drink it to the dregs and we survive it.'[90] Similarly, Raine's novelistic obsession with duality may not only be a reflection of her own personal experience as the dual figure of respectable Mrs Beynon Puddicombe, banker's wife, and the ambiguous romantic novelist, 'Allen Raine', but might also connote a dualism in terms of national and class identity. Despite the novels' championing of Welsh culture and the working classes, there are moments in the texts where the authorial voice becomes both self-consciously Anglicized and gentrified. When she asserts, for example, that 'morality amongst the unmarried peasantry lays itself open to reproach',[91] Raine appears to be endorsing the Anglicized and colonial viewpoint of the authors of the 1847 Blue Books. Elsewhere, however, Raine is vigorously opposed to Anglicization, as in her comment in *By Berwen Banks*:

> Gwynne ... endeavour[ed] to express himself in his mother-tongue [Welsh] but with that hesitation and indistinctness common to the dwellers in the counties bordering upon England, and to the 'would-be genteel' of too many other parts of Wales, who, perfectly unconscious of the beauty of their own langauge, and ignorant of its literature, affect English manners and customs.[92]

Raine's own rare representation of English characters tends to have them exclaiming 'By Jove!' a great deal and evincing harsh class and racial prejudices.[93] Some of her west Walians think that Glamorganshire is populated by English people: Goronwy is despatched by his father to 'get Yshbel home at once from those Saeson.'[94] Goronwy gently corrects his father and finds that the Welsh people of Glamorgan are kind to him; his landlady welcomes him with the exclamation, 'Oh, a Cardi! . . . we have plenty of them here.'[95] Goronwy becomes a heroic collier, embodying the bravery and self-sacrifice which 'kindles a glow of pride in every Welsh heart'.[96] Meanwhile, Catrin travels with her gipsy kindred northwards to 'the Cribor Mountains, . . . just beyond the Snowdon range'.[97] Thus, Raine displays a sense of a diverse Wales beyond the confines of the rural west, and suggests a sense of historical change in reflecting the internal migration of workers from the rural west to the industrialized south-east and further afield. In her later novels Raine emphasizes a sense of Welsh national identity which transcends locality, though it is based on cultural and historical, rather than political, allegiance; at the eisteddfod described in *On the Wings of the Wind* (1905), the whole audience responds positively to the song of an old woman at her spinning-wheel: 'the maidservant home from her service in London, the shopman who had timed his holiday so as to take in the Eisteddfod, the raw ploughboy, the Glamorgan collier – to each and all came some tender reminiscence of long ago'.[98]

Duality is also represented in the church–chapel rivalry which occurs in most of the novels. Raine herself was a member of the Anglican Church, but her own religious family background also included strong links with Unitarian Nonconformity. Raine's engagement with the religion which played such a prominent part in many Welsh people's lives at the turn of the century is, consequently, not sectarian, but relatively even-handed. Several novels present the dwindling congregations of the Anglican Church and, conversely, the huge open-air *Sassiwn* of the Methodists. Chapelgoing characters, such as Mali and Stivin in *On the Wings of the Wind*, are contemptuous of the church's 'old Devods'.[99] The Methodists come in for some mild criticism: 'No one who has not spent a Sunday afternoon in a Methodist household can really have sounded the depths of dullness.'[100] And there are touches of humour: when Jos Hughes in *Garthowen* makes his public confession in the chapel, he cannot forget his work as a shopkeeper: 'I was as dry as – a paper bag! . . . I have received the "Invoice" of good things to come'.[101] Nevertheless, the great appeal of the chapel in contrast to the moribund church is acknowledged: the congregation in Penmorien chapel look forward to the sermon, which 'possesses for the Welsh the intense charm of a good drama . . . denied to them through the medium of the forbidden theatre'.[102] *By Berwen Banks*, which is the novel most centrally concerned with religious conflict, shows that narrow-mindedness and prejudice are not the sole preserve of any sect: both the Anglican Revd Meurig Wynne, the 'Vicare Du', (the black vicar) and Essec Powell, the Methodist preacher, show prejudice and dogmatism, but they are finally reconciled and united, realizing that they are both antiquarians at heart![103]

Apart from *Queen of the Rushes* (1906), which deals with the 1904–5 religious revival, engagement with specific historical events in Wales is rare in Allen Raine's work. However, she certainly engages with social issues such as poverty and madness, as mentioned above; another prominent concern for Raine is the issue of eviction, which again aligns her with her Welsh-language contemporary, Gwyneth Vaughan. Characters in Raine's novels are constantly threatened with eviction from their homes and often suffer actual homelessness. Given the way in which dwellings are characteristically described in Raine as an organic element of the landscape and their inhabitants as 'belonging' in a profound sense to these dwellings, eviction presents not just a social and economic threat to the individual, but an existential one. Characters' identities are closely bound up with their homes in a way which Raine presents as typically Welsh; this is reflected partly in the habit of characters being named after their homes or their environments, as Raine remarks in *Under the Thatch* (1910): 'His name was Philip

Lloyd, but he was familiarly known as "Phil-y-Velin" or "Phil of the Mill"; the name tripped off the tongue, and it distinguished him from the many other Lloyds of the neighbourhood.'[104] Similarly, in her story 'Ana "Pwr Thing!"', the eponymous Ana acquires the name 'Pwr Thing!' by virtue of the loss of her home, Pantgwyn, after her father's death. Another story from the same collection, *All in a Month* (1908), addresses the issue of homelessness in an even more poignant way: 'Home, Sweet Home: A True Story' is a very moving account of an old woman being ejected from her farmhouse home by her callous son and placed, against her will, in the local workhouse.[105] It tells us a great deal about the operation of the Poor Law in rural Wales at the turn of the century, and it offers a stark expression of an old woman's powerlessness in the face of the patriarchal structures which oppress her. She enacts an escape at the end of the story, but it is a triumph only in death, a trope of martyrdom and self-sacrifice which is common in female-centred writing, even in the twentieth century. Raine pulls out all the stops as a sentimental novelist to ensure that readers both sympathize and identify with Nancy Vaughan, the protagonist. But the sentiment is used for a political and, arguably, for a feminist purpose. Nancy is at the centre of her story: her distress, loneliness, anguish and alienation, are also ours; when she lies down on the comfortless hard bed of the workhouse and cringes away from the poor mad woman who lies beside her, we understand what the statistics of the history of pauperism in Wales mean in human terms.

Examination of statistics shows that Raine's representation of Nancy Vaughan's plight is by no means unhistorical, but it may not necessarily be entirely typical. Even the story itself makes clear that Nancy is, to some extent, an exceptional case, for whom some concessions are made within the workhouse. Historians also inform us that so-called 'outdoor relief' was actually statistically much more prevalent in Wales than in other parts of the United Kingdom. Raine's sentimental representation of a clearly 'deserving' and respectable widow in such dire straits may be regarded as a political point made as part of an increasingly voluble outcry around the turn of the century against the plight of the elderly poor under the workhouse system. It is fitting, perhaps, that Raine's story was published posthumously in 1908, the year when old age pensions were finally introduced, spelling the end of the old workhouse system and the beginning of the Welfare State.

Allen Raine's critical acclaim and phenomenal popularity ensured that she had many imitators and followers. One of these was Edith Nepean whose first novel, *Gwyneth of the Welsh Hills* (1917), betrays the strong influence of Allen Raine, with a rather incongruous dash of Caradoc Evans. Nepean, born in Llandudno but married into the English aristocracy, dedicates her first novel to David Lloyd George, but also includes an acknowledgment for the encouragement of 'her fellow-countryman, Caradoc Evans, on writing this, her first book'.[106] The convoluted plot, involving several sets of star-crossed lovers, owes much to Allen Raine, while the satire on Nonconformity is a mild version of Caradoc Evans's full-blown satirical attack in *My People*, published only two years previously. One of the main protagonists, Davydd Owen, known as 'Pharaoh', is a Methodist deacon, whose 'knee was ever bowed in worship of the Golden Calf'.[107] The minister, the Reverend Peris Roberts, is equally in thrall to Mammon; Jane Rhys relates that when she tells him of her fears that her foster-daughter, Gwyneth, is dead, 'he asked me if her life was insured, look you, when she was a baby. Pity now that I did no such thing, said he. If she is dead the money would have been useful for Capel Siloh. A new Bible cushion Siloh wants.'[108] However, these are barbed moments in a novel which is largely what Sally Roberts Jones might rightly call 'sentimental slush',[109] suffused with patriotic clichés about Wales and Welshness, such as that 'the Celt is inseparably connected with a deep love of music'.[110] The Welsh are gallant, proud, overemotional, deeply patriotic and given to running away with the gypsies. Nevertheless, Nepean clearly found favour with the reading public, since she followed *Gwyneth of the Welsh Hills* with no fewer than thirty-four further novels, a number of which continue to use Wales as a picturesque and exotic backdrop for romance. Reading Edith Nepean brings home the relative sophistication and subtlety of Allen Raine, particularly in her creation of a believable fictional Wales, for Nepean's Wales is never more than a flimsy painted backdrop for the melodrama of her plots. If Raine represents an important step forward in the creation of an autonomous Welsh literary tradition in the English language, Nepean can be regarded as a step back towards pre-twentieth-century romances which simply use Wales as a conveniently exotic elsewhere. As Sally Roberts Jones points out, Allen Raine 'wrote from within, of "*our* land", "*our* national character" and never, as did many later novelists [including, I suggest, Edith Nepean] . . . from the standpoint of an English audience'.[111]

Clearly, the phenomenon of Edith Nepean and her thirty-five romantic novels is by no means unique to Wales. Romantic novelists tend to be prolific, partly because they use the same formula for every text. To look further afield, Edith Nepean's productiveness is dwarfed by the achievement of her contemporary, Hedwig Courths Mahler (1867–1950), the German authoress of romantic novels, who published no fewer than two hundred and eight novels in her lifetime, beginning with *Die wilde Ursula* (Wild Ursula) in 1912. Indeed, *Die wilde Ursula* and *Gwyneth of the Welsh Hills* share many features, despite being set ostensibly in completely different settings. In German, such novels are sometimes categorized as *Trivialliteratur*, and it may be that the similarities of the romance formulae of *Trivialliteratur* vastly outweigh the authors' apparent attempts to portray cultural and geographical specificity.

In contrast to the authors of *Trivialliteratur*, Allen Raine was important because, although she used the formula of the romance genre, she gave fictional life to a landscape, a way of life, a culture, which had not been adequately depicted from the inside in English-language fiction before. The Caribbean poet Derek Walcott has spoken of the prodigious sense of excitement, which was also a terrific burden of responsibility, which he felt as a young poet growing up in St Lucia in the 1930s and 40s. He felt that this was a virginal territory, a landscape which had not in a sense been made real by being consecrated in art or literature; he felt charged with 'Adam's task of giving things their names'[112]. Rural Cardiganshire was Raine's St Lucia: she gave it life, she animated it, and she went even further: she justified it, she defended it, she spoke up for a Welsh identity which had been diluted and denigrated by a late-imperialist notion of Britishness. And she was certainly not speaking into a vacuum: she became very popular, each novel selling hundreds of thousands of copies, so that rural Cardiganshire became real in the minds of all her avid readers. She was mapping the territory, putting names on the map. Moreover, though she herself was a solicitor's daughter from Newcastle Emlyn, she took as her heroes and heroines ordinary working-class people.

Fortunately, not all of Raine's followers were pale imitations, like Nepean. In 1913, a collection of short stories entitled *Picture Tales from Welsh Hills*, by Bertha Thomas, was published simultaneously in Chicago and London. Thomas was an experienced author, but this was the first time she had turned to her native Wales for material for her fiction. The opening story of the volume, 'The

Madness of Winifred Owen', is a first-person narrative told by a spinster taking a cycling tour through Wales in 1899. This is a characteristic opening: the figure of the cycling spinster immediately indicates that this is 'New Woman' fiction of the turn of the century, but what is interesting is the encounter between the 'New Woman' and a Wales which is immediately recognized as 'Other'. On the first page of the story, the narrator asserts that: 'Wales, the stranger within England's gates, remains a stranger still.'[113] The brash narrator listens to the story of Winifred Owen and is left feeling admiration for this humble but resourceful woman; at the end the speaker feels 'commonplace and middle-class',[114] an interesting and unusual pairing. Similarly, in the second story, 'The Only Girl', the spinster and her companion, Edith, are left feeling slightly inadequate and wrong-footed by their experiences in Wales. Notably, Edith, who is a 'eugenist', opines that Catrin, the 'feeble-minded' daughter of Issachar Jones, would be 'better dead',[115] but after the girl's death everyone realizes how much they depended upon and loved her. Here, contemporary 'progressive' ideas are held up to judgement against Welsh values and are found wanting. The longest story in the volume, 'The Way He Went', is particularly illuminating for its juxtaposition of England and Wales, and its portrayal of the way in which English education alienates Welsh children and cuts them off from their roots. The latter is a trope which recurs in later Welsh writing in both languages and by writers of both genders.[116] In Bertha Thomas's story, Elwyn Rosser is sent away from Trearvon, his widowed mother's Welsh 'farmstead' to Llanwastad College, a school 'run on English public school lines', and thereafter wins a scholarship to Oxford. (Again, this is a pattern which will be repeated by many Welsh writers in English, especially male, but it is interesting to note this early example by a female autor.) Trepidation greets Elwyn's news that he is to go to Oxford, since the Welsh people of the neighbourhood regard England as a dangerous place; as Bertha Thomas's narrator puts it:

> In every European country but Elwyn's the English are well known for a terribly serious-minded nation – puritanical, taking their very pleasures sadly . . . the land of prudish, dowdy women . . . compulsory church-going . . . rigid respectability . . . In Elwyn's native circle a contrary conviction prevailed . . . There, across the border, was the land of Play – or worse . . . That England spells the world, the flesh and the devil was a time-honoured doctrine none cared to call into question.[117]

When Elwyn survives and succeeds at Oxford, he comes to the realization that he can 'never be at home in his real home again'.[118]

As the title of Thomas's volume indicates, there are many pictorial descriptions of Welsh scenery and dwellings in *Picture Tales from the Welsh Hills*; indeed, at times the narrative appears to become a travelogue, aimed primarily at the American reader. However, there is some astute commentary on the picturesque nature of Welsh topography. 'An Undesirable Alien', for instance, begins with two contrasting views of the same cottage: ' a labourer's roughcast, two-roomed thatched cottage . . . that you, in passing, would have condemned because of its narrow window-space and lack of water supply', and 'the witch cottage of a fairy tale, or the dwelling of some hermit of old, where the Knight Errant of Romance, riding up one of the five cross-roads that here meet in the shade, would rein in and sue for rest and refreshment'.[119] These two alternatives are succeeded by a third, in which the cottage is seen as 'like a beehive in a grove, sheltered and shadowed by a semicircle of fir and ash'.[120] Such a description is echoed in 'The Only Girl', where the farmhouse of Glascarreg is compared to 'a fox's hole or a bird's nest'.[121] All these descriptions, like Allen Raine's pictures of Cardiganshire cottages, evoke a gentle, organic, appropriated landscape, suggestive above all else of a sense of rightness, of belonging. Even the 'undesirable alien' of the story's title, an English tramp named Tim Brady, is outwitted by Martha, the inhabitant of the picturesque beehive, and sent on his way without the bag of savings that he had thought to steal.

Another alien, in the form of Eustace Smart, a cockney boy from a reformatory school sent to Wales to work the land and mend his ways, is the first-person narrator of 'Comic Objects of the Country: Being the Impressions of an Industrial School Boy'. Although the dialectal comedy of this story is not invariably successful, it does afford some interesting outsider's views of Wales. Eustace is resigned, for example, to the constant attempts of the livestock to escape; as he reflects 'Guess they can't help it, bein' Welsh, an' longin' for to show their independence'.[122] He also makes fun of the Anglicized lady landowner, Miss Durden: 'I said I thought I'd get used to Welsh folk in time, an' pointed out as I'd learnt more of their lingo in six months than she in as many years.'[123]

Pandering perhaps to the American readership of the volume, one of the stories has an American narrator, Ivy Harvey, who is from Kansas and spending a sightseeing holiday in Wales. Ivy writes in travelogue style, being particularly taken with the picturesqueness of Carreg Cennen Castle, until she gets lost and impatiently wishes to meet 'a white man with an English tongue in his head'.[124] Again, as elsewhere, the implication is that the Welsh are racially Other; given that Ivy is American, her use of the phrase 'white man' might additionally suggest an identification between the Welsh and the native American Indian.[125] Despite Ivy's exasperation, when she does find shelter in a Welsh country house, she is impressed by its antiquity: '"Those fixings were sawn before ever the Mayflower set sail," she thought enviously.'[126] The volume ends on a similar note to that on which it began, emphasizing the continuing strangeness of Wales and its possible dangers to the unwary traveller: Jaques Robinson, described as an experienced Alpinist, gets lost and almost killed on the Welsh mountains; he reflects 'Mont Blanc, the Ortler, the Matterhorn, seemed places of public amusement by comparison'.[127]

Most of the stories in this volume are set in and around the same fictional south-west Wales town, Llanffelix. Sara Maria Saunders, in her *Y Diwygiad ym Mhentre Alun*, uses a similar structure of a series of short stories loosely linked by unity of place. Even Winnie Parry's *Sioned*, ostensibly a novel, is more like a series of short stories linked by place and narrative voice, as indicated in its subtitle *Darluniau o Fywyd Gwledig yng Nghymru* (Pictures of Rural Life in Wales), which echoes Bertha Thomas's *Picture Tales from Welsh Hills*. Arguably, later Welsh women writers in both languages, such as Kate Roberts, Eigra Lewis Roberts and Dorothy Edwards, as well as male writers like Gwyn Thomas and D. J. Williams,[128] use a similar generic structure. Interestingly, place is the linking element in all of these writers' short story collections, suggesting that place is perhaps more important as a distinguishing feature of Welsh fiction even than language or gender.

The final writer discussed here, Elizabeth Mary Jones, who wrote under the pseudonym of 'Moelona', like 'Allen Raine' came from southern Cardiganshire. But Moelona emerged from a Welsh-speaking farming community and did not, ostensibly, experience the duality of identity evident in the life of Allen Raine. Like Raine, Moelona was encouraged to write by that most Welsh of routes – winning an eisteddfod competition. However, it is important to note that Moelona was born in the late 1870s, some forty years later than Raine, and that her fictional representations of Wales not unnaturally reflect a more modern political and social sensibility.

Since Moelona's published fictions span the period 1907 to the late 1940s, her early works will be considered here and later ones discussed in the following chapter.

Moelona's earliest published works were *Rhamant y Rhos* (The Romance of the Moor) and *Dwy Ramant o'r De* (Two Romances from the South), in 1907 and 1911, respectively. The latter consists of two separate novellas, namely *Rhamant Nyrs Bivan* (Nurse Bevan's Romance) and *Alys Morgan* (Alice Morgan).[129] As these titles suggest, these novels are written in the romance mode which had already proved so fruitful for Allen Raine, and which was considered 'suitable' for a female author. Moreover, Moelona writes in a note to the republished edition of her earliest novel that her aim is to provide Welsh reading material for young people, that is, there is a didactic and, implicitly, a linguistically nationalistic motivation to her work. Examination of the texts themselves, however, suggest that feminism is, if anything, a more dominant ideology in these early works. This is unexpected, to say the least, in texts which appear to be conventional romances. *Rhamant y Rhos* (1907), her first published novella, is a first-person narrative told by Meinir Huws of 'Bwlchyrhos' in south Cardiganshire. Ostensibly, the plot concerns Meinir's love for her childhood sweetheart, Alun, their separation, her courting by another suitor, Jâms, and the final happy union of Meinir and Alun. However, much of the text is a discussion of female education and vocation. Meinir is fond of reading but has to do so surreptitiously because her parents disapprove. As she reads *David Copperfield*, her mother chides her and her father expresses the view that she reads too many novels. Jâms Lewis spoils his chances with Meinir by agreeing with her parents: 'No good will come of these novels, Huws ... and reading them won't bring bread and cheese to anyone' ('Sdim daioni yn y novels ma, Huws, ... a ddaw i darllen nw ddim â bara chaws i neb').[130]

A similar theme is explored in a more elaborate and sophisticated narrative in *Alys Morgan* (1911), one of the two novellas in *Dwy Ramant o'r De* (Two Romances from the South). Another first-person narrative told by the eponymous protagonist, the text engages more fully and more provocatively with the contemporary issue of women's rights. From early on in the text Alys, a farmer's daughter in south Cardiganshire, longs for education and fulfilment. When her friend Harri teases her for being a girl and therefore not studying geography or doing hard sums, she reflects sorrowfully 'I wish I were a boy' ('leicwn i 'swn i'n grwt').[131] Later, Alys does get a place in the grammar school, but her education is interrupted when her mother dies and she has to return home to look after her father. (This is a motif which recurs in several of Moelona's works and is a reflection of her own experiences.) Alys's future hangs in the balance between forces of conservatism (her new stepmother and other women of the village) and liberalism (the Reverend Llewelyn Parri and his wife). Mrs Morgan and Mrs Parri have a long debate about female education, the former arguing that it is purposeless and counter-productive in that it makes girls less marriageable, while the latter puts the case for female emancipation. The Reverend Parri even discovers John Stuart Mill's *The Subjection of Women* and has his own eyes opened to the extent of women's enslavement in a patriarchal society. Again, as in *Rhamant y Rhos*, the would-be suitor, Mr Philips the exciseman, is an implacable opponent of female suffrage. His view is that 'Indeed I think that they [women] get treated far too well and that's why they dare to stir things up and go on about their rights' ('Wir wy'n meddwl taw cal 'u trin yn rhy dda ma nhw [merched], 'na pam ma nhw'n beiddio aflonyddu a sôn am 'u hawlie').[132] Alys is rebellious, but still tempted to give in to pressure and marry the 'good match', Mr Philips; the author herself interrupts the narrative at this point with the reflection:

> Druan o Alys! Nid hi oedd y gyntaf na'r olaf o'i rhyw i deimlo fod y cyffion, o'u gwisgo mor hir, wedi dod yn bethau cyfarwydd iawn, ac fod treio ymsymud hebddynt yn beth anghyfarwydd, ac anhawdd, ac amhleserus iawn ar y dechreu.[133]

> [Poor Alice! She was not the first nor the last of her sex to feel that the fetters she wore had become very familiar, after wearing them for so long, and that trying to move without them was an unfamiliar and difficult and uncomfortable thing to do at first.]

However, Alys manages to escape the restrictive clutches of Mr Philips, and in the second part of the novella, set ten years later on the shores of Lake Geneva, we see Alys as a successful and independent writer, who publishes novels under the male pseudonym of Guy Lee. Eventually, however, Alys does marry – the little boy who first provoked her into a sense of gender inequality, Harri, returns a grown man from America, and the two fall in love. Interestingly, Alys and Harri finally get married and return, not to Wales, but to America, where the two are united in suffrage campaigns on behalf of women. In this novella, Moelona's Welsh nationalism, very evident elsewhere in her oeuvre, is subordinated to her feminism, a fact which may well be seen to reflect the politics of the period, when the women's suffrage campaign was at its most intense, before the granting of the first concessions in the legislation, which took place in 1918, and subsequently were extended in 1928.

The other novella in the volume, *Rhamant Nyrs Bifan*, remains located in Wales virtually throughout (with one excursion to London) and is more concerned with Welsh identity, although female vocation remains an important issue. The narrative is set, not in Moelona's native Ceredigion, but in an industrialized valley in Glamorganshire:

> Yn un o lecynnau mwyaf rhamantus Sir Forgannwg – un o'r cymoedd afrifed lechant yng nghilfachau ei mynyddoedd moelion, saif yr ardal boblog a adnabyddir yn yr hanes hwn wrth yr enw Y Fronddu. Du yn wir yw y rhan fwyaf o bethau yno. Y mae yr hen fynyddoedd talgryf wedi colli eu gwyrddlesni er's llawer dydd, ond ymgodant i fyny mor feiddgar a safant mor ddiysgog ag erioed. Du yw llwch yr heolydd, a ffrydiau terfysglyd y nentydd. Du hefyd yw gwedd allanol llawer o'r preswylwyr, eithr o'r tu mewn i'r duwch i gyd, cura calonnau o wynder diail, a blodeua cymeriadau nad oes eu tecach mewn unrhyw ran o Walia Wen.[134]

> [In one of the most romantic corners of Glamorganshire – one of those myriad valleys nestling between its bare mountains, lies the populous area known in this story by the name Y Fronddu (Black Hill). Black indeed is the colour of most things there. The old stout mountains have lost their blue-green colour long ago but they still rise up as defiantly and stand as unbending as ever. Black is the dust in the streets and the turbulent waters of the streams. Black too is the outer appearance of many of its inhabitants, but underneath all the blackness there beat hearts of paramount whiteness, and as lovely characters flower there as can be found in any other part of White Wales.]

While Moelona is well known for beautiful descriptions of rural west Wales, it is clear here that she has a political point to make about the unity of Wales and the persistence of Welsh values and character, even in an industrialized, 'desecrated' landscape. The Rhondda remains a Welsh ethnoscape, despite the pollution, because the Welsh, like their mountains, are indomitable. The plot of the novella reflects the championing of the Glamorganshire

Welsh, too, since Mai Bifan, the female protagonist, when faced with the choice between her long-lost love, Hywel, now a successful doctor in England, and the local collier and choirmaster, Jenkin Morgan, chooses the latter. It is also notable that Moelona attempts to render the dialect of Glamorganshire in the direct speech of this text, as she does the Cardiganshire dialect (which would have been more familiar to her) in her other works.

Bugail y Bryn (The Shepherd of the Hill, 1917) differs from Moelona's earlier romances in that it has a male protagonist, Owen Elis, who is the new minister of the chapel at Cwmgwynli in Ceredigion. He is the *bugail* (shepherd) of the title. Moelona sets this novel in the past, in the period of the tithe wars (like Gwyneth Vaughan's *Plant y Gorthrwm*), but the text is rather less interested in the injustices of tithes than in the religious and moral struggles of the principal character. Somewhat like Mai Bifan, who sacrifices her own happiness in order to care for her elderly father, Owen Elis represses his own love for Gwen and forfeits his legitimate claim to wealth and property in order to follow his religious vocation wholeheartedly. Gwen, the main female character, is courted by no fewer than three men but eventually dies, Ophelia-like, by drowning in the local river. Owen is left alone to fulfil what is suggested to be a higher purpose: 'he continues onwards cheerfully and peacefully on his lonely path, with a light from heaven on his face. Some prophesy an even more astonishing future for him' ('â yntau ymlaen yn siriol dangnefeddus ar hyd ei lwybr unig, a goleu o'r nef ar ei wyneb. Proffwyda rhai iddo dyfodol mwy rhyfedd fyth').[135] Possibly, this novel's representation of Wales as a deeply religious land, where idealistic and self-sacrificing ministers like Owen Elis shepherd their flocks, is a direct rebuttal of the satirical caricature of Wales and its chapels published by Caradoc Evans in *My People* only two years previously.

Moelona's *Teulu Bach Nantoer* (The Little Family of Nantoer, 1912) is a publishing phenomenon in Welsh; it was popular from the time of its first publication and, according to Roger Jones Williams, was the best-selling of all children's novels in Welsh, achieving sales of over 30,000.[136] It is another example of a hybrid genre which appears to have been much used by Welsh-language women writers during this period: a novel which is ostensibly for children, and yet which was evidently much read by adults and which contains an ideology relevant to both adults and children. We have seen that Saunders Lewis is contemptuous of this hybridity, but the practice can be seen more positively as a deliberate strategy of women writers, often forced into the role of 'children's writer' by society's gender expectations, attempting to subvert the restrictions of the juvenile fiction genre. Certainly *Teulu Bach Nantoer*, which is now available to all in an online edition, can be seen to embody the author's own political ideology in the guise of an innocuous children's fable.[137]

Teulu Bach Nantoer is, as the title suggests, the story of a family, rather than an individual. The widow Gwen Owen and her four children are so poor that they depend partly on parish relief, as well as on Gwen's sewing and the produce of their one cow; they are penniless because their drunken father, who died the year before, spent all their money. This setting is clearly not idealized in the sense of excluding painful realities, but the narrative is overtly didactic in the way that it shows the family overcoming poverty and adversity. 'Nantoer' itself is a tiny thatched cottage but is described in terms which emphasize its unassailability:

> Er yn fychan, yr oedd y bwthyn yn hynod o glŷd a diogel. Pan chwythai yr ystorm arwaf dros eangder digysgod y rhos, ni siglid ei furiau cedyrn, ac o'r braidd y medrai y gwlaw trymaf beri clywed ei sŵn drwy y tô diddos o wellt.[138]

> [Though it was small the cottage was extraordinarily cosy and safe. When the storm winds blew strongest over the unsheltered expanse of the moor, its solid walls did not shake, and the heaviest rain could not make itself heard through the watertight roof of straw.]

There is an implicit link between the heroic stability of 'Nantoer' and the strength and determination of its inhabitants; indeed, since the text is described as a *ffug-chwedl*, or mock-fable, it may not be too far-fetched to suggest that Nantoer and its inhabitants stand as a microcosm of Wales itself.[139] In a school speech-day, a patriotic speech addressed to the children is a nationalist polemic; as Mr Puw informs the pupils: 'Wales is today on its feet again, awakened, and we'll have different books in our schools before long' ('Mae Cymru heddyw ar ei thraed, wedi deffro, ac fe geir llyfrau gwahanol i'w hysgolion cyn hir').[140] He goes on to warn them: 'No Welshman will become great by trying to become an Englishman' ('Ddaw'r un Cymro byth yn fawr wrth geisio troi'n Sais').[141] The children of Nantoer take this and their mother's moral teachings to heart, and become, variously, a member of parliament, a ship's captain and a teacher. The central event of the plot, in which the youngest daughter, Eiry, is kidnapped by a childless Englishwoman and brought up in Bermuda as her own child, ends in redemption as Eiry returns to Nantoer as a grown woman, announcing poignantly: 'Ieuan, I'm Eiry, your little sister, and I've come back' ('Ieuan, fi yw Eiry, dy chwaer fach, wedi dod nôl').[142] There is undoubtedly something powerfully attractive in Moelona's apparently simple little story for children. It appealed to children because of its aspirational quality and its use of suspense and adventure and to adults because it reflected truthfully some of the poverty and frustration of their own lives, and perhaps embodied their hopes for a better future. The motif of the return of the lost child, with its biblical echoes of the Prodigal Son, may be seen as an allegory for the 'awakened' Wales, whose sons and daughters are returning to her, having been 'kidnapped' by the foreign interloper.

These first two decades of Welsh women's writing in the twentieth century show clearly how their literary production was affected ideologically by the aftermath of the Blue Books Report of 1847 and the subsequent campaign to redeem Wales, and the Welshwoman particularly, from the condemnation expressed in that Report. Different women writers defended their land and gender in differing ways, but all show the influence of contemporary social and political developments, such as the movements for home rule, temperance and suffrage, all of which are reflected in these writers' works from a distinctively female point of view. One writer, Eluned Morgan, is distinguished from the others by her focus upon the Welsh colony in Patagonia, which nevertheless conforms closely to the notion of an ancestral Welsh 'ethnoscape', as adumbrated by Anthony D. Smith. Wales and 'new' Wales are constructed alike in the writing of this generation of women as a culturally, spiritually and politically Other place, which they position squarely at the centre of their fictional worlds. For many, Wales is seen as the land of redemption, a sacred space in which women had a particularly important and transformative role to play. At the same time as Wales contains within itself the potential for redemption, it is also sometimes viewed anthropomorphically as a suffering, humiliated female in need of redemption. Many of these writers express a strong political message, aimed at their fellow Welsh people to resist Anglicization, assert their Welsh identity, speak Welsh, and retain the distinctiveness of Welsh religious feeling and practice. Writers in both languages perceive Wales as a sacred place, already threatened with desecration by forces such as Anglicization, industrialization and urbanization. These threats, together with the depredations of the First World War will also emerge in the transformed landscape of Wales represented in the work of the next generation of Welsh women writers.

2 Fallen Place: 1921–1945

The immediate post-war world was, inevitably, a place of mourning and regret for Welsh women; at the same time, great pressure was placed on them to return to the domestic roles which the exigencies of the First World War had forced many of them to abandon. Soon, these demands were succeeded by the more urgent struggle of the Depression, which blighted Wales from the mid 1920s virtually until the outbreak of the Second World War. Many regard the 1930s as the heyday of the Welsh industrial novel, written by men such as Lewis Jones, Gwyn Thomas, Rhys Davies, Gwyn Jones and others. It is striking that no Welsh women writers are considered among this group, with the exception of Kate Roberts, whose novel *Traed mewn Cyffion* (Feet in Chains, 1936) is sometimes seen as an industrial novel of the same type, despite being set in north Wales. In fact, the male industrial novelists do not form such an homogenous grouping as is often suggested: Rhys Davies's grotesque and often subversive comedy, for example, is hardly in the same mode as the quasi-documentary realism of B. L. Coombes. Similarly, Welsh women's literary production in this period is characterized by its diversity of style and perspective, though all share an interest in issues of belonging and identity, in the land of Wales, and in the changing expectations and experiences of women and girls.

In 1918, many women over thirty gained the franchise, but it was not until 1928 that the Equal Franchise Act extended the vote to women over twenty-one. Unsurprisingly, a number of Welsh women writers engage directly with the continuing struggle for equality, notably the Welsh-language novelist, 'Moelona', who, as we have seen, had already begun publishing her work before the War. Women were also politically active during the period in protesting against injustices such as unemployment and means testing, and in peace movements, which sought, as it turned out in vain, to prevent the outbreak of another war. Mass migration changed the face of Wales yet again, as it had during the heyday of the industrial revolution, but this time the migration was out of Wales: almost half a million people left south Wales between 1921 and 1940. From the end of the First World War, Welsh nationalism grew and home rule aspirations, temporarily laid aside during the war, finally became enshrined in the foundation of Plaid Cymru, the Welsh Nationalist Party, in 1925. Meanwhile, the south Wales coalfields were increasingly radicalized, as is reflected powerfully in the novels *Cwmardy* (1937) and *We Live* (1939) by Lewis Jones.

Despite being born and raised in Ogmore Vale and educated in Cardiff, the fictional world of Dorothy Edwards seems a million miles away from the world of Lewis Jones. One of the oddest and most intriguing of Welsh women writers, Edwards published only two volumes of work, *Rhapsody* (1927) and *Winter Sonata* (1928), before her tragically early suicide in 1934. Only one of her short stories has a recognizably Welsh setting, while the other work exists in a strange kind of limbo world, which is as if Turgenev's characters have been transported into an English upper-class milieu. Edwards herself was – at least in 1931, when she wrote an adulatory letter to Saunders Lewis – an ardent Welsh nationalist and revolutionary.[1] Her stories appear to reflect nothing of this, though one story in *Rhapsody*, namely 'The Conquered', does engage directly with the Welsh landscape and Welsh identity.

I and others have argued elsewhere[2] that English-language Welsh writers of this period were forced often to pander to a London-based publishing world. It is unsurprising to find Dorothy Edwards's writing acclaimed by English critics such as Arnold Bennett, who praised her 'subtle and intriguing talent',[3] and bracketed with contemporary English women writers, such as Virginia Woolf and Vita Sackville-West. In a sense she may be said to be performing an act of literary ventriloquism; only in 'The Conquered' are there hints of that repressed revolutionary and nationalistic zeal which is so carefully excised from the artificial literary world of her other works.

'The Conquered' has a first-person English male narrator, Frederick Trenier, who is urbane, cultured and egocentric. 'I have been nearly everywhere', he declares smugly in the opening paragraph.[4] He spends his summer holiday with his aunt and cousins on the Welsh border, and there meets Gwyneth, 'a very charming Welsh lady', possessor of a country house and a voice of equal loveliness.[5] To the extent that Gwyneth has a Welsh name and is a singer who is also very fond of the natural world, she could be any one of a recognizable line of heroines, not unlike Nepean's 'Gwyneth of the Welsh Hills' or Allen Raine's 'Belle Russe'. Her house stands in a historicized landscape, which bears a Roman road and a hill 'where the ancient Britons made a last stand against the Romans, and were defeated'.[6] Gwyneth differs from earlier avatars of the Welsh heroine, not in her gentrification, but in her identification with 'the conquerors'. She admires the Romans and is proud of her family ancestry, which has connections with the English royal family. She also refuses to sing Chopin's 'Polens Grabgesang', a song of defeat and defiant Polish nationalism, because it is, in a sense, against her pro-imperialist nature. Inscribed within this story is a subtext relating to Wales's 'conquered' position; implicitly identified with the ancient Britons and the Poles, the Welsh are a defeated people who have been stripped of their language and their pride. Gwyneth represents the spoils of the collaborator; in repudiating her own people and identifying with the victors, she is a traitor, but a very happy and successful one. As Frederick's cousin, Ruthie, laments: 'Gwyneth is so rich it is hard to think of something to give her.'[7] Edwards's English readership in 1927 can hardly have been expected to understand the subtext of this story but, once it has been grasped, it is difficult to read Edwards's other stories as anything other than parodies of British imperialist attitudes.

If Dorothy Edwards can be described as conveying her views of Wales in the not-said and the gaps of her texts, 'Moelona' is the opposite type of writer, one whose instinct is towards the didactic and who has the teacher's urge to spell things out. Elizabeth Mary Jones, known as 'Moelona', has already been introduced in chapter 1. However, the bulk of her work was published between the 1920s and the early 1940s. Both *Cwrs y Lli* (The Course of the Stream, 1927) and *Breuddwydion Myfanwy* (Myfanwy's Dreams, 1928) are novels for young adults, and their didactic purpose is clearly indicated, not only in the texts, but in the fact that both have 'Exercises' and lengthy vocabularies at the end. The stories take their young Welsh protagonists on adventures abroad to France and to Australia; *Breuddwydion Myfanwy* is particularly rich in shipwrecks and allusions to Robinson Crusoe. However, beneath the moderately rollicking adventures, the authorial ideology is plainly seen: Moelona teaches the value of education for both sexes, the worth of European culture, and fervent Welsh nationalism. In *Cwrs y Lli*, for example, the story of the Swiss national hero William Tell is retold and characters reflect on its pertinence to Wales:

> 'Wel, yn wir,' ebe Mr Wyn ymhen tipyn, 'mae gan y Swisiaid rywbeth i ddysgu ini'r Cymry. Gwyddant hwy y ffordd i gadw eu harwyr ar gof gwlad o genhedlaeth i genhedlaeth.'

> 'Gwyddant, yn wir. Yng Nghymru, hanes arwyr y Saeson a ddysgir yn yr ysgolion, ac iddynt hwy y codir cof-golofnau,' ebe Mr Owen.

> 'A ninnau'r Cymry yn dioddef ein sarhau felly o hyd!" ebe Mr Herbert, "Onid yw'n bryd i ni ddeffro?'[8]

> ['Well, really,' said Mr Wyn at length, 'those Swiss have something to teach us Welsh people. They know how to keep their heroes in their national memory from generation to generation.'

> 'They certainly do. In Wales it's the history of English heroes that's taught in schools, and it's to them that memorials are built,' said Mr Owen.

> 'And we Welsh still suffer ourselves to be humiliated like that!' said Mr Herbert, 'Isn't it time for us to awake?']

Ffynnonloyw (Bright Spring, 1939) is different from these earlier, didactic textbooks, however; it is Moelona's most ambitious novel. It has a tripartite structure, set in the 1880s, in 1906 and in 1925, respectively. Focusing on two sisters, it charts the changing experiences of Welsh women during that revolutionary period. It is the novel which shows most clearly Moelona's own political commitment to women's suffrage and in which Welsh women's involvement in the liberation movement is effectively dramatized.

In Part 1, which deals with the childhood of Nan and her sister Mimi, brought up on a farm in south Cardiganshire, the ideology of the novel is immediately made clear. In contrast to their brothers, whose education is taken seriously and who are pampered and indulged, Nan and Mimi's education is considered unimportant. The family is ready to make financial sacrifices for the sake of the boys' education, but the girls have to struggle hard and make an unladylike fuss in order to obtain what they feel they deserve. These opening chapters also discuss the consequences of mis-education: one of the older sisters, Marged, is sent away to be educated as a lady, and returns to Wales full of petty affectations and apparently no longer able to speak Welsh. Similarly, Lewis, one of the brothers, is also affected and Anglicized; Moelona relishes mocking him:

> Gwisgai Lewis fwstash main, llaes, tywyll ei lliw, a chymerai cryn gofal ohono, er y gallesid tybio weithiau y byddai'n rhyddhad iddo gael ymadael ag ef. Ond rywfodd, ni ellid dychmygu am Lewis ar wahân i'w fwstash. Siaradai yn yddfol a phendant ar bob pwnc, fel petai o flaen dosbarth, a dywedai 'Very well, then' bob hyn a hyn wrth adrodd rhywbeth. Ef oedd ysgrifennydd Eglwys Saesneg yr Annibynwyr yn y lle, a chlywid ganddo yn fynych rywbeth am 'our pastor', 'my fellow deacons' . . . 'our precentor', a thermau eglwysig eraill.[9]

> [Lewis wore a thin, limp, dark moustache, of which he took great care, though you got the impression sometimes that it would be a blessed release for him to be rid of it. Yet, somehow, you couldn't imagine Lewis apart from his moustache. He spoke deeply and definitely on every topic you cared to mention, as if he were standing in front of a class, and he said 'Very well, then' periodically whatever he was talking about. He was the secretary of the English Congregational Chapel there, and you'd often hear him refer to 'our pastor', 'my fellow deacons' . . . 'our precentor' and other churchy terms.]

Unsurprisingly, it does not take long before Nan gives her brother a piece of her mind, and she then moves on to greater battles with patriarchal authority:

> Yng Ngwanwyn a haf y flwyddyn honno bu Mudiad y Bleidlais i ferched bron a chymryd lle Mudiad yr Iaith ym meddwl Nan . . . Ennill y Fôt mewn ffordd heddychol trwy rym rheswm oedd nod y Gymdeithas honno. Ni theimlai Nan . . . eu hunan yn ddigon dewr i ymuno â'r fyddin a geisiau eu hawliau mewn ffordd arall, er y cyfrifai . . . yn arwresau y rhai hynny a geisiau dynnu sylw at eu cais trwy dorri'r gyfraith mewn gwahanol ffyrdd.[10]

> [That Spring and Summer the Votes for Women movement almost took the place of the Language movement in Nan's mind . . . The society's aim was to win the Vote in a peaceful way through the power of reason . . . Nan did not feel brave enough to join that army of women who were trying to gain their rights through other means, though she regarded them as true heroines . . .]

Not many of Nan's friends join in the struggle, however. Her sister, Mimi, simply sighs and shrugs her shoulders, regarding it as yet another of Nan's many enthusiasms. Yet both sisters have come under the influence of the 1904–5 Revival, which appears to intensify Nan's nationalism and to prepare her for the suffrage struggle to come.[11] Nan's brother, Davey Henry, warns her not to go too far while Miss Ryle, the headmistress of the school where Nan teaches advises her to 'get married, my dear. It's the best life after all.'[12]

It is clear that Nan is a fictionalized version of the author herself. Interestingly, Nan witnesses the scene which took place in reality at the Albert Hall in London in the summer of 1909, when suffrage campaigners heckled and disrupted the National Eisteddfod. Moelona had herself been present at this occasion. Unlike Nan, who is simply an onlooker, Moelona was actually taking part in the proceedings on that day – she was being accepted and honoured as a member of the Gorsedd y Beirdd. Her two identities, as ardent Welsh Nationalist and equally committed suffragist, therefore came into conflict with one another in a highly public way. Nan's reactions to the event may reflect the author's: at first she is joyful because she sees:

> twrw Llundain yn distewi i beri clywed llais Cymru! Ni bu Nan erioed yn falchach mai Cymraes ydoedd. Cafodd yr ail orfoledd pan welodd o'r llwyfan ferch yn codi o ganol y dyrfa fawr a gweiddi rhywbeth i dorri ar draws araith Mr Lloyd George . . .[13]

> [the hustle and bustle of London being hushed to hear the voice of Wales! Nan had never felt so proud of being a Welsh woman. She soon had her second joyful experience when she saw a woman stand up in the middle of the audience and shout something to interrupt Lloyd George's speech . . .]

Shortly afterwards, Nan accepts a proposal of marriage from the charismatic preacher, Harri Herbert. However, it turns out that Herbert disdains to speak Welsh, and his views on suffrage become clear when he reacts with horror to news that his fiancée has made a speech on the topic in a public meeting:

> Pa fath wraig y fyddai hon iddo? . . . dyna hi wedi ymuno a'r haid o ferched gwyllt a ffôl a oedd yn destun chwerthin a chas bob dyn call, ac i wneud ffŵl pellach ohoni ei hun dyna hi'n siarad o'u llwyfan.[14]

> [What sort of wife would she be to him? . . . There she was, having joined that flock of wild and foolish women who were the object of hilarity and scorn to every sensible man, and to go so far as to make a fool of herself on a stage, in public!]

This patriarchal recoil from women speaking in the public arena is
directly reminiscent of Gildas's reaction to hearing his wife praying
vociferously in the Revival meeting in Allen Raine's *Queen of the
Rushes* (1906). The upshot of patriarchal disaproval is very different in the 1939 novel, however; when Harri Herbert thunders his
disapproval, Nan promptly returns his ring and shows him the
door.

Part 3 of the novel begins with the death of the matriarch of the
family, Mali, in 1925. The family returns for the funeral to the farm
where they were born, Ffynnonloyw, evidently based on Moelona's
own birthplace, Moylon, in Rhydlewis, Cardiganshire. This allows
Moelona to demonstrate how women's lot has changed since the
opening of the novel, some fifty years previously. One of Nan's
nieces, Pansy, who has a car and lives in her own flat, also has a
camera, and she insists on taking photographs of the quaint Welsh
women in the village, who are wearing their funny, old-fashioned
clothes: 'O Daddy! Do look . . . I must have a snap.'[15]

The novel also contains a poem, entitled 'Y Delyn ar yr Helyg'
(The Harp on the Willow), composed by Moelona but supposedly
entered by Nan for an eisteddfod competition, where it is ridiculed
by the judges:

> Mae 'nhelyn ar yr helyg,
> Oes rhywun ofyn pam?
> Sut medr merch roi miwsig
> A hithau'n cael fath gam?
> Y dyn, medd ef ei hunan
> Yw'r bod o werth, bid siwr,
> Ni oes i'r wraig un amcan
> Ond ceisio boddio'i gŵr.
>
> Pa bryd ca merch ei hawliau?
> Pa bryd daw'r fôt i'n rhan?
> Nyni wna drefn ar bethau,
> Nawr anrhefn sy 'mhob man.
> Ond O! Ar ffordd ein llwyddiant,
> Cyndynrwydd dyn a roed,
> A dyna pam mae'm telyn fach
> Yn segur ar y coed.[16]
>
> [My harp is on the willow,
> Does someone ask me why?
> How can a woman music play
> When she's gravely wronged today?
> Man, in his own opinion,

    Is the only human to rate,
    For woman has no ambition
    But to try to please her mate.

    When will woman gain her rights?
    When will we win the vote?
    Now chaos reigns, and see no light
    But come the day, we'll steer the boat.
    But oh dear! on the way to success
    We find man's stubbornness,
    And that's why my harp still hangs low
    From the branches of the willow.]

The poem is a very open political statement and yet at the same time is both lyrical and skilfully crafted. The Welsh cultural context is made explicit by Moelona, not only in her use of the Welsh language but also in her adoption of the central image of the harp. The harp symbolizes Welsh poetic utterance: the speaker is a would-be poet, but her way ahead is barred by a patriarchal literary regime. At the same time, the harp stands for woman's voice more generally: silenced, ignored. The deliberate echo of Psalm 137, in which the exiled Jews hang their harps on the willows, underlines women's role as the chosen, yet despised, ones. Potentially harmonious, Welsh women's voice remains unheard. Her harp hangs on the willow tree, symbol of mourning and grief. And yet, of course, the poem itself is a quite explicit political statement, a challenge. She does not need her harp to accompany this message – perhaps the implication is that the time for lyricism and art for its own sake will come, but only when the political battle is won.

In the context of the novel, the battle for suffrage is not yet won but progress has been made. Nan herself does compromise by accepting marriage, but only to an older man who adores and obeys her. They recreate the 'Ffynnonloyw' of her childhood in their comfortable town-house. The emphasis in the final pages of the novel is on the power of education and the need to undo the Anglicization of the system up to this point. In the mid 1920s, Moelona's characters are getting involved with the new political nationalism in Wales, soon to be incorporated in the founding of Plaid Cymru. But this allegiance by no means takes the place of feminism; as Nan discovers in the Albert Hall in 1909, and as Moelona clearly suggests, it is possible to be both proudly Welsh and proudly a woman.

'Proudly Welsh' is certainly a description which applies to a slightly younger and equally prolific contemporary of Moelona, namely the novelist Hilda Vaughan. Born in Builth Wells, Vaughan rejoiced in her family's descent from the great seventeenth-century poet, Henry Vaughan. During this period, Hilda Vaughan published no fewer than nine novels, two novellas and two co-authored plays. *The Battle to the Weak* was her first published volume, appearing in 1925, but her reputation was really established with *The Soldier and the Gentlewoman* in 1932. Her novels are set wholly or partly in the eastern counties of Wales, Breconshire and Radnorshire, where she herself had her roots, or in rural Carmarthenshire.

One of Vaughan's most accomplished works is the novella *A Thing of Nought* (1934). It is representative of her fiction in the symbolic prominence of its Welsh rural setting, and its concern with familial and marital relationships, gender and religion. The importance of place to Vaughan as a writer is indicated by her own account of the genesis of this story; at first she believed that she had invented the whole narrative, but then she remembered seeing a particular place, which had evidently sown the seed of the story in her mind. Travelling in a remote area of Wales, she recalls:

> Suddenly, around a bend in the road, I came across one isolated farmhouse. It was whitewashed – the only white object in a vast green landscape. Facing it, upon the other side of the stream, was a gaunt square chapel, built of grey stone, with the caretaker's cottage clinging to its side – as a little shell might do to a strong rock. Something about those two lonely dwelling-places and that chapel ... stirred my imagination.[17]

These three places are the central images of the novella and in a sense the scene might be taken as archetypally Welsh, a setting which recurs time and time again in the work of twentieth-century Welsh women writers. The colour contrasts are indicative of the moral polarities between which the action of the narrative takes place: the gaunt greyness of the chapel connoting the fanatical and austere Calvinism of Rees Lloyd the preacher, and the whiteness of the farmhouse (Cwmbach) connoting the purity and innocence of Megan, who becomes Rees's wife against her will. Megan loves Penry Price throughout her life, but is prevented from marrying him when he goes to Australia to try to make his fortune. Megan has a baby with the blond hair and blue eyes of Penry, which the whole neighbourhood, including her furious husband, believes is the fruit of adultery. However, Megan is innocent and the child is explained as the creation of Megan's intense desire. There is some mystical, inexplicable mystery surrounding the child, which finally forces Rees to call his own rigid beliefs into question. Nevertheless, in the end both he and the child die, leaving Megan to live on to old age to tell her story to the unnamed female narrator of the text. At one point in the story, Megan stands outside the chapel caretaker's cottage where she lives unhappily with Rees Lloyd, 'gaz[ing at] a point where, at a bend in the valley, the road was lost to sight. Something about that lonely road, leading away into a world she had never seen, fascinated her.'[18] Like the white farmhouse and the grey chapel, this lonely road is another recurrent element in the topography of Welsh women's writing, reflected for example in Kate Roberts's autobiography, *Y Lôn Wen* (*The White Lane*,1960), and, later still, in Gillian Clarke's *Letter from a Far Country* (1982). In the latter:

> A stony track turns between
> ancient hedges, narrowing,
> like a lane in a child's book.
> Its perspective makes the heart restless
> like the boy in the rhyme, his stick
> and cotton bundle on his shoulder.
>
> The minstrel boy to the war has gone.
> But the girl stays. To mind things.
> She must keep. And wait. And pass time.[19]

As Megan Lloyd gazes at the lane, she descries Penry Price, the 'minstrel boy' returned from his travels, walking wearily towards her. Megan's frustration that he has returned like this, too late, indicates the frustrations of the person who is condemned, by gender expectation, to 'wait' and 'pass time'. Nevertheless, as the frame narrative of this reverberant little novella shows, Megan Lloyd is also an emblem of quiet patience and resignation; she has 'minded things' throughout her life and, as she nears death, provides a saintly model for the impatient youthful narrator. This echoing between a text of 1934 and one of 1982 is not uncommon in Welsh women's writing, suggesting that there is a women's literary *tradition* in Wales which has so far been largely neglected and ignored.

In other novels, Hilda Vaughan addresses the clash between Wales and England, as well as gender conflicts. Her 1932 novel *The*

Soldier and the Gentlewoman returns to the aftermath of the First World War to explore issues of belonging and property rights which, as we have seen, were already established as typical concerns of Welsh women writers. The relationship between the Welsh woman and the land of Wales is presented in this novel as superseding all other allegiances and loyalties; Gwenllian, the main character in the novel, asserts that: 'Better than gold, we [the Welsh] love music and song, poetry and rhetoric, the history and traditions of our race, and, above all, our land.'[20] Meanwhile, Dick, the English incomer in the novel, who will inherit the estate rather than Gwenllian, since she is not male, is initially not impressed by his female cousins – he finds them 'tall and dark . . . too foreign, too much what you expected of the Welsh . . . those almost Italian features with so little flesh upon them, suggested bad temper, or worse, fanaticism. He shouldn't wonder if they were rabid teetotallers, or religious, or something of the kind.'[21]

In direct contrast to the saintlike Megan Lloyd, Gwenllian Einon-Thomas is a fierce and monomaniacal character, who eventually turns into a murderer. The estate, Plâs Einon, means everything to her and she is willing to sacrifice anything to ensure its survival in the family. The plot echoes that of an earlier novel by Vaughan, *The Invader* (1928), in which the English incomer and inheritor of the estate of Plas Newydd is a woman, Miss Webster, and her antagonist is the Welshman Daniel Evans; however, the earlier novel takes the form of a comedy, rather than the tragedy of *The Soldier and the Gentlewoman*. In the latter novel, Gwenllian marries the feckless Dick and bears two sons, who ensure that the estate will remain within the family. However, the estate is endangered by Dick's reckless extravagance, and Gwenllian takes the final step of deliberately ignoring the doctor's instructions in the care of the ailing Dick, with the result that he dies. Here Dick, though not an admirable character, is certainly the victim; he is a survivor of the Great War but has returned not fully healed, either physically or mentally, from that terrible experience, only to be killed by a vengeful, angry and fervently patriotic woman. Despite the melodrama of some scenes in the novel, it clearly touched a chord for readers in the 1930s, since it became a bestseller and was even adapted as a stage play. In terms of its representation of Wales, it exposes the proverbial pride in ancestry which is supposed to characterize the Welsh (and which is also explored occasionally by other woman writers, such as Elena Puw-Morgan and Allen Raine).

The relationship with the land here is so close that it becomes pathological; possibly this is so because it occurs in a different class dimension from other texts by Vaughan, though there are echoes of it too in *Her Father's House* (1930). The Einon-Thomases in *The Soldier and the Gentlewoman* are, precisely, Welsh *gentry*, and their mania for possession and immortality through inheritance is seen as a terrifyingly destructive force.

Iron and Gold (1942), the only one of Vaughan's novels to have been republished in recent years, differs from her other work in being based quite closely on the Welsh legend of the lady of Llyn y Fan.[22] Although the novel uses mythical material and is written in a style more laden with imagery than is characteristic of Vaughan's work, the novel's concerns are actually with marital and familial relationships and gender roles, rather than with the supernatural. Spatially, the novel is interesting because it juxtaposes the 'tamed' environment of Owain's farm with the wild landscape in which he meets and captures his fairy bride, Glythin. Through enclosure of the mountain and the felling of trees, Owain appropriates more and more of the wild landscape, just as he domesticates and socializes his wife. Ultimately, though, Glythin returns to the lake and Owain disappears, suggesting in a proto-ecological manner, perhaps, that proper regard for Nature is linked with the female, and that the male – even a poet like Owain – tends to be tempted to exploit and possess both the natural world and women.

Iron and Gold is a rare example of Welsh mythical material being used by Welsh women writers of this period. Later on, certainly, some Welsh legends appealed powerfully to the imaginations of Welsh women writers[23] and to a few male writers of this period, such as Saunders Lewis, whose play *Blodeuwedd* dates from 1948, but generally female contemporaries of Vaughan tended to eschew the mythical in favour of the realistic.

One exception to this trend is Kate Bosse-Griffiths, a German incomer to Wales who settled here, married, learned Welsh and wrote fiction in her adopted language. Her 1944 short story 'Fy Chwaer Efa' (My Sister Eve) is a highly unrealistic feminist allegory.[24] It is a story of competing ideas, a dialectical story, betraying the author's intellectual, Germanic and academic background. Kate Bosse was born in Wittenberg in 1910 of half-Jewish parentage, had a brilliant academic career as an Egyptologist and was fortunate to escape Hitler's Germany in the late 1930s. Though she herself escaped persecution, her Jewish mother did not: she died in Ravensbrück concentration camp. Given this background, it is not surprising to find Kate Bosse-Griffiths writing a pacifist polemic which is strongly female-centred. It is a story which bears comparison both with the Welsh-Jewish writer Lily Tobias's *Eunice Fleet* (1933) and with another feminist attack upon war dating from the same period, namely Virginia Woolf's *Three Guineas* (1938). Interestingly, both Bosse-Griffiths and Woolf identify the destructive warlike impulse with a crass masculinity, and call for a kind of moral revolution based on the rediscovery and the resurrection of the neglected female.

'My Sister Eve' is also, as the title indicates, an interrogation of Christianity. Just as post-colonial writers have rewritten canonical texts in order to tell the other, untold side of colonial history, so Bosse-Griffiths boldly sets out to rewrite the most canonical text of them all, namely the Bible. The names of the sisters in the frame story, Mary, Martha, Magdalen and Eve, are overt echoes of their biblical namesakes. Unlike the latter, however, these sisters come together to support one another, not as followers of a male Messiah. The occasion of their coming together is a hinted-at personal loss of Eve's: the sisters' aim is to effect Eve's recuperation, which can be understood on several levels. At an allegorical level, the recuperation of Eve means a refusal to accept the version of Eve presented in Genesis as the mother of all our woe. Significantly, when we first see her, Eve is numbed and grieving, a mother who has lost her child. In the context of the time, this Eve is Everywoman, every mother who has lost a child to the war. Given the particular family circumstances of the author, the attempt enacted in the story to recover and heal a mother has a special poignancy.

The method used by the sisters to try to heal Eve is a shared storytelling session, returning to a favourite story made up by them jointly in their childhood. The feminist emphasis here is clearly on cooperation, rather than antagonism, and there is a communal attempt to create a wholeness of identity, to heal up the breach between the adult woman and the girl child each once was. The recuperative method also succeeds in suggesting the healing potential of art and, in a story which is predominantly intellectual, it extols the creative power of the imagination.

The sisters' story is a feminist appropriation with a vengeance. Their heroine – who is clearly a composite female figure representing all four of them – is Maia, no less than a female Christ. She is a gentle questioner; the sisters' stories about her are simple parables which nevertheless point to some uncomfortable and perhaps unresolvable tensions within Christian dogma. Kate Bosse-Griffiths was born in the city where Luther nailed his ninety-five theses to the church door; arguably, she is performing a similar protest in this most radical of stories.

As the story passes from sister to sister, we hear different voices and viewpoints in the text. The women perform for one another, provoking and teasing, but ultimately all with one purpose: to waken Eve out of the torpor of her depression. After the dreadful vision of the altar, evidently an allegorical picture of the contemporary world, bathed in the blood of war, Eve finally awakens and ends the story optimistically. The miraculous recuperation, has, it seems, occurred, though the author is careful to leave the ending open, with a question.

Maternity is a constant concern in the story. We turn from Eve's bereft maternity to the relationship between Maia and her mother, her later attempts to help a woman in childbirth, to the grieving mothers at the sacrificial altar. In the course of the story, motherhood itself is resurrected and revalued. It is as if the tender concern of motherhood and the relationship between mother and child is being held up as an example to a world gone mad and unnatural, bent on a warlike and negative course identified as crudely masculine. It is significant, however, that the story shies away from essentialism by making clear that the spirit of negativity who tempts and almost defeats Maia is not *necessarily* masculine: 'she met her opponent. For the sake of simplicity, I'll refer to him as "He"' ('cyfarfu a'i gwrthwynebydd. Er mwyn bod yn syml, cyfeiriaf ato fel "Ef"').[25]

Kate Bosse-Griffiths's story is wholly allegorical and driven by moral questions and ideas. Its landscape, such as it is, is not Wales but the world in which human beings live out their lives and make their choices. And yet Bosse-Griffiths's ideology is tacitly driven by the pacifism and religious convictions of the group of Welsh writers, 'Cylch Cadwgan' (Cadwgan's Circle), based in Pentre, in the Rhondda Valley, to which she and her husband, the poet and scholar J. Gwyn Griffiths, belonged. Her work is comparable to that of her contemporary, Lily Tobias, another Welsh-Jewish writer, whose construction of Wales is very much at the service of her intense political and social convictions.

Bosse-Griffiths's 1941 volume *Anesmwyth Hoen* (Uneasy Joy) is a paradoxical text, in that it is a novel of ideas which deals quite daringly with female sexuality. It won a competition set by the publishing company Llyfrau'r Dryw, judged by the novelist E. Tegla Davies, whose adjudication reveals that he awarded the prize to Bosse-Griffiths reluctantly because he was uncomfortable with the subject-matter. Indeed, he even suggested toning down the content before publication, in case it were to find its way into the hands of the young and impressionable.[26] The novel deals with Megan, a young Welsh girl who goes to university in London and then to Munich to teach English. The setting of the novel is largely outside Wales, then, but we see Megan struggle to adjust her rather puritanical Welsh moral upbringing to the modern urban world outside Wales and to her own feminist ambitions. In London she has a sexual encounter with one of her history lecturers; it is this section probably which aroused Tegla's anxieties, for the novel is quite forthright in describing Megan's sexual enjoyment: 'Waves of heat pulsed through her body' ('Ai tonnau o gynhesrwydd drwy ei chorff').[27] However, the evocatively named Peter Wilde proves an unsatisfactory lover, and Megan leaves London for Munich. Despite the Nazi government and the dark political clouds which are looming over the city, it is here that Megan begins to find a sense of her own autonomy; in a concert at 'Llys y ffynnon' (recognizable as the *Brunnenhof* in the *Residenz* in Munich city centre) she reflects:

> aethai i ffwrdd oddi cartref er mwyn ei chanfod ei hun . . . Hyd yn hyn bu rhyw anniddigrwydd mewnol yn ei gyrru, rhyw ofn y byddai bywyd yn prysuro heibio heb adael iddi afael yn ei rhan . . . Yma, ymhell oddi cartref, ar ôl clwyf siomedigaeth fawr, darganfu ei chyfoeth mewnol ei hun.[28]

> [she had left home in order to find herself . . . Up to now some inner dissatisfaction had driven her, some fear that life would hurry by without letting her grasp her own part to play . . . Here, far from home, after being wounded by a great disappointment, she had discovered her own inner wealth.]

Although the author is careful to reverse her own situation, that is, her protagonist is a Welsh woman in Germany, rather than a German woman in Wales, it is tempting to suggest that these words express Bosse-Griffiths's own experience of 'finding herself' in a situation of exile which nevertheless offers her a peculiar feeling of personal fulfilment.

If Kate Bosse-Griffiths is primarily a serious and intellectual novelist, her contemporary Jane Ann Jones explores similar gender issues largely through the mode of ironic comedy. Jones's *Storïau Hen Ferch* (A Spinster's Stories, 1937) consists of seventeen short stories, set largely in seaside towns in mid and north Wales. Her narrators vary widely, though she particularly excels at adopting the voice of a male first-person speaker who unwittingly displays his own prejudices and limitations, particularly with regard to gender. In this regard, the tone of Jones's wholly neglected work is not dissimilar to that of Dorothy Edwards's stories, which use a male narrator. Characters such as Fred Lloyd in 'Ofer Ichwi Fore-Godi' (No Need for You to Get Up Early) are also reminiscent of the satirized figure of Stanley Burnell in Katherine Mansfield's New Zealand stories, the self-satisfied paterfamilias who is blissfully unaware that all the womenfolk in his house breathe a sigh of relief when he leaves the house. Some of the stories are fantastical in mode, such as 'Fel Angylion' (Like Angels), which traces Sera Jones's ascent to heaven – she takes her umbrella along with her, just in case. However, she finds heaven a little embarrassing because she's expected to take off all her clothes in order to bathe away all her feelings of hatred and envy; an angel chivvies her along, however, and gives her a tub of 'Cariad Brawdol – i'w Rwbio ar ôl Ymolchi' (Brotherly Love – to Rub in after Bathing) to anoint herself with after her bath.[29] Jones clearly enjoys satirizing Welsh Nonconformist prejudices and narrow-mindedness, as well as aspects of Welsh culture. In heaven, for example, the poets and singers are all running about naked in an idyllic landscape, except for members of the Gorsedd, who are still wearing their long robes and get on God's nerves because they are still obsessed with competition.[30] Despite the comic tone, these stories often have an edge of sadness and an unmistakable feminist critique of a Welsh patriarchal society. Men tend to be represented as smugly authoritarian – as Ann Morris in the story 'Porthi Nwydau' (Feeding Desires) discovers, after seven years of marriage to John:

[roedd hi] wedi rhoi'r gorau i geisio ei ddarbwyllo mai rhydd oedd i bawb ei farn. Fel y gwyddai, barn John Morris oedd yr unig farn ddiogel, ac ni chaech lonydd tan y deuech, o flinder ysbryd, i gyfaddef hynny.[31]

[she had given up trying to persuade him that everyone's entitled to their own opinion. As she knew by now, only John Morris's opinion was really sound, and you had no peace until you came to acknowledge that fact, from sheer exasperation.]

Yet Ann, and the other female characters in Jones's stories, are quietly subversive: 'He [John]would have had a fit if he'd known that Ann had voted for the Labour Party in the last Election and him a true blue Tory – like his father and grandfather before him' ('Cawsai ffit pe gwyddai fod Ann wedi rhoi ei phleidlais i'r Blaid Lafur yn yr Etholiad ddiwethaf ac yntau yn Geidwadwr – a'i dad a'i daid o'i flaen').[32] In addition to married women and patriarchs, Jones's stories – as the volume's title suggests – also addresses the lives of spinsters. These are among the saddest of the stories – a character such as 'Miss Williams' in the ironically named story 'Taledigaeth y Gwobrwy' (The Payment of the Prize) has sacrificed herself all her life for others and for the chapel, and her payment in old age is to be confined to the paupers' ward in the madhouse by a distant male relative.[33]

A very different Welsh-language author of this period, who nevertheless also draws attention to women's experiences in Wales, is Elena Puw-Morgan, who, despite the paucity of her published work, is one of the most accomplished of twentieth-century Welsh women writers. Indeed, her novel *Y Graith* (The Scar, published 1943, written in the late 1930s) is one of the greatest novels of the century, though it has been shamefully overlooked by critics and has yet to be translated into English. Despite her own relatively privileged and sheltered background as the daughter of a Nonconformist minister and his wife, brought up in isolation in Corwen, north-east Wales, Puw-Morgan's fiction is notable for its imaginative and powerful focus on female servants living in conditions of extreme poverty and deprivation. *Y Graith* is particularly memorable for its harrowing and intensely drawn representation of the physical abuse and neglect of a child by its mother.

Puw-Morgan published three novels for adults, beginning with *Nansi Lovell* in 1933. This short novel takes the form of a fictional autobiographical letter written by an old Welsh gypsy woman to her granddaughter, who is the heiress of the local great house. Like her later novels, *Nansi Lovell* immediately reveals Puw-Morgan's strong sympathies with outsiders and downtrodden female figures, as well as the supple beauty of her language. It also reveals her interest in ancestry and heredity, which is explored with more subtlety in the later novels. Romany language and customs are shown here in a sympathetic way, though Nansi's pride in her 'pure' Romany blood is seen as analogous in some ways to Lord Madog's arrogant pride in his rank and ancestry. Nansi's experiences of the clash of cultures is particularly interesting, for she lives through a double alienation when she is sent away to Blackdene House, an English girls' boarding school; here she is required to suppress both her Welsh and her Romany identities, but she rebels against this attack upon her selfhood and runs away. Similarly, her marriage to Lord Madog eventually fails because she refuses to suppress her Romany origins completely, as he requires. She returns to her people; when Madog attempts to reclaim his wife, she spurns him: '"What on earth are you thinking of, Nansi, to behave like this? You know that I won't permit . . ." but I interrupted: "I can do without your permission from now on . . . I am free."' ('"Beth ar wyneb daear yw'ch meddwl chwi, Nansi, yn ymddwyn fel hyn? Mi wyddoch ni chaniatâf i . . ." "Gallaf hepgor eich caniatâd mwy," meddwn wrtho ". . . yr wyf yn rhydd"').[34] Despite its interest, though, compared with the later works, this novel is somewhat melodramatic and awkward in terms of structure.

Elena Puw-Morgan's 1939 novel, *Y Wisg Sidan* (The Satin Dress), is probably her best-known; it was also the first work by a woman to win the newly established Prose Medal at the National Eisteddfod in 1938. It is a historical novel set in rural Wales in the late nineteenth century, revolving around the experiences of Mali Meredur, the central female character. She inherits a beautiful, wine-red satin dress from her mother, and this object of desire is her only comfort in a life of dire poverty, exploitation and deprivation. After escaping from her cruel brother, Mali spends most of her life as 'third servant' in the large farm of Plas-yr-Allt, where the 'Master' seduces and then ignores her. Mali has an illegitimate child, whom she abandons on the doorstep of a manse. Despite his treatment of her, Mali continues to idolize Tim Huws, the Master of Plas-yr-Allt. In terms of plot, structure and style, this novel is complex and sophisticated; told largely from Mali's point of view, there are extended passages of free indirect discourse, which sometimes shift to the point of view of Tim Huws. One key episode in the plot – where Mali and Tim first meet at the fair – is in effect narrated twice, from both, contrasting points of view. Both gender and heredity are important concerns in the novel. Mali in a sense conforms to gender expectations in her frequently infuriating passivity and self-sacrifice, and yet she also exhibits extraordinary resilience and loyalty. Saro, a strong older woman who is the local herbalist (known to some as a witch) suggests that 'the Master there is one of those who always *takes* and you are one of those whose fate it is always to *give*' ('un o'r rheini sy'n *cymryd* ydi'r Meistr acw, a thithau'n un o'r rhai a dynghedwyd i *roi*').[35] Yet Mali is not particularly maternal, though she is entranced and perplexed by icons of femininity, primarily the red dress, but also by mirrors. She herself is an 'ugly creature' ('creadures diolwg')[36] according to Tim, and she is mesmerized at the age of seventeen when she goes to the fair for the first time and sees some dolls on display: 'She failed completely to understand the dolls – she called them pictures of babies in her own mind except that they were a lot prettier than real babies' ('Methai'n lan â deall y doliau – lluniau babanod y galwai hwy yn ei meddwl ond eu bod yn llawer tlysach na babanod iawn').[37] Her confusion at the sight of the dolls is suggestive of the deprivation of her own childhood, her lack of maternal instinct and her vague sense of her own inadequacy to fill a gender role which requires doll-like beauty. Despite the suffering she experiences, ultimately the plot of the novel traces a trajectory of empowerment and vindication for Mali. Only late in life does she learn, slowly and painfully, to read and write, but learn she does and, at the same time, she accumulates savings and acquires a home. The final scene of the novel depicts Mali burning the red dress in order to look after her dying idol, Tim Huws. The image is suitably ambiguous for a novel of this complexity: it could be interpreted as an emblem of Mali's continuing, foolish admiration for what Saro calls an 'unworthy object' ('gwrthrych annheilwng'),[38] but it could also indicate the end of Mali's 'curse' of bad luck, always associated with the dress and the illicit desires it represents.

Although *Y Wisg Sidan* depicts a life of great hardship, Puw-Morgan's last novel, *Y Graith* (The Scar), is even more extreme in its representation of a female character who is treated sadistically by her own mother, and goes on to experience further exploitation and injustice. Chronologically, this novel is set later than *Y Wisg Sidan*, spanning a lengthy period from the last decade of the nineteenth century up until the 1930s. This gives scope for Puw-Morgan to show the social and political changes happening in Wales during the first decades of the twentieth century, coinciding, of course, with the author's own lifespan to that date.[39] The opening chapters show Dori Llwyd as a bright, intelligent eleven-year-old, eager to keep her place at the top of the primary-school class. She and her classmates struggle because the language of instruction is English, a foreign tongue to them, yet Dori's lively intelligence and curiosity bring her success. Her life at home is very different: she has to labour constantly under the critical eye of her mother and suffer the lash of her tongue and, regularly, the leather strap. When Dori and her younger sister dare to go to the church to see Mrs Powell the vicar's wife play the organ, instead of going to chapel, Gwen Llwyd beats them mercilessly. She beats Dori so badly that she is ill in bed for many days, and has a permanent scar above her eye where the belt buckle wielded by her mother almost put her eye out. This scar, which gives the novel its title, is both a physical mark of her mother's brutality and an emblem of the psychological scarring that such an upbringing will have on Dori's life. Flatly refusing to allow her to stay on at the school as a pupil-teacher, her mother packs her off as a maidservant to a middle-class family house in the 'Crescent', Liverpool. By this time Dori has been literally browbeaten into submission; even the appalling conditions she suffers at the 'Crescent' are not so severe as those she suffered at home under her mother's tyranny.

Dori's experience as a maid-of-all-work in the 'Crescent' can be seen as representative of the fate of thousands and thousands of Welsh women in the early years of the twentieth century. Deirdre Beddoe notes that 'the census of 1901 records that 50.7 per cent of the Welsh female workforce was in service, compared with 40.3 per cent in England'.[40] Beddoe goes on to quote a letter from a young female maidservant to the *South Wales Daily News* in 1912: 'I consider I am treated more like a slave than a human being . . . driven from 6.00 a.m. until eleven and twelve at night, eating my own meals while running about waiting on others.'[41] This drudgery, not far removed from slavery, is certainly what we see Dori experience in her employment at the Crescent, exacerbated even further by abysmal wages, constant humiliation and racist abuse from her English fellow-workers.

Puw-Morgan renders Dori's sense of displacement and alienation with great skill: everything in Liverpool, from the train, the traffic, the ferry and the English vernacular to the domestic mores of the 'Crescent', is completely unfamiliar to her. The domestic work she has to carry out is chronicled, not in documentary detail, but with a tangible sense of physical experience that forces the reader to empathize with Dori. For example, 'She hated [washing the front steps] because it meant rubbing them afterwards with a kind of light stone to whiten them, and the scraping of the stone against stone caused an unpleasant sensation in her chest' ('Casai [golchi'r grisiau cerrig] . . . am y golygai iddi rwbio'r rheini wedyn â math o garreg olau i'w gwynnu, a chodai rhygniad y garreg ar garreg rhyw ymdeimlad annymunol yn ei brest').[42] The other domestic servants mock and humiliate her, calling her 'Taffi' and a 'country bump-kin'.[43] She is unable to attend any of the Welsh chapels in Liverpool because they are too far away and she gets almost no time off. Most of her minute salary is sent home to her mother. The ineffectual and ailing father whom she resembles dies and Dori returns for the funeral, only to be threatened with physical violence again by her mother. What is extraordinary about the characterization of the mother, Gwen Llwyd, is that she is totally believable, even though her behaviour might mark her out as a cardboard villain from a melodrama. On the contrary, several passages in the novel are seen from her point of view and we can see that she is the product of a curdling resentment against everyone and everything, a resentment which must find an outlet in sadistic behaviour towards her daugh-ter and, while he was alive, her husband. The second half of the novel chronicles Dori's adult life, when she is married off, has children of her own, and begins to develop the personality and strength that her mother had earlier beaten out of her. By the closing stages of the novel, one of Dori's grown sons is campaigning for the 'Blaid Genedlaethol' (Plaid Cymru),[44] a political party that neither Dori nor her mother-in-law knows anything about. The family acquires a motor car and electric light in their home; the children go to the cinema to see 'George Formby', and finally Dori's daughter insists that she will go to college, like her brother. Dori, having vowed to be as unlike her own mother as possible, always gives in to her children's wishes. The ending is somewhat sad, both for Dori, who is left alone with her mentally disabled son, and for the land, since she will be forced to sell it as a site for summer houses for people from the towns in order to fund her daughter's education.

Elena Puw-Morgan's fiction is markedly different from the work of Welsh women writers of the first two decades of the century, in that it seems to lack a nationalistic conception of Wales. By virtue of being written in Welsh and concerned with a naturally Welsh-speaking community, clearly her work is 'about' Wales, and yet in political terms it appears to be much more concerned with class, gender, heredity and economics. The Cymru Fydd/Young Wales movement had, by the time Puw-Morgan was writing, lost its impetus, arguably under the pressure of more urgent political concerns related to the Depression and the aftermath of war. Kate Roberts had sketched the economic realities of ordinary Welsh women's lives in works such as *Traed mewn Cyffion* (Feet in Chains); what Elena Puw-Morgan achieves, in her creation of her two main female protagonists, Mali Meredur and Dori Llwyd, is to give that economic and social reality considerable psychological complexity.

One motif which was prominent in some Welsh women's writing in the earlier decades is also a recurrent concern in the work of Elena Puw-Morgan, though, and that is the motif of madness. In all three of her novels for adults, characters who have various mental afflictions play prominent roles, but the exploration of the subject becomes increasingly complex and troubling in each book. Alana Lee, in *Nansi Lovell*, is a gipsy woman who has been abandoned before her wedding, and she spends the rest of her life afflicted by a monomania of revenge. Similarly, Seimon Meredur, Mali's brother in *Y Wisg Sidan*, becomes obsessed with the mistaken idea that he is actually the son of the local squire; he takes to roaming the fields at night dressed up as a gentleman. The neighbours want to send him to the local 'gwallgofdy' (asylum), but Mali shudders at the thought of the shame of this. Several characters in this novel are, to various degrees, obsessed with the notion of their noble blood, though the novel reveals quite clearly that nobility of blood is quite unrelated to nobility of character. Saro's words in describing her former lover, Syr Meurig, indicate that such pride of ancestry is potentially evil when she says: 'The same man still . . . kind enough, but as proud as Lucifer when his own ancestry's involved' ('Yr un o hyd . . . yn ddigon caredig, ond cyn uched â Lwsiffer lle bo'i dras o yn y cwestiwn').[45] In *Y Graith*, some characters have innate mental defects, while others are 'scarred' by their environment and upbringing into developing traits of madness. Gwen Llwyd suffers from a kind of persecution complex which builds in her an un-assuageable frustration and anger; bizarrely, she also takes pride in her manifestations of piety, seeing no contradiction in her devotion to the chapel and her sadistic treatment of her child. The danger throughout the novel is that Dori will begin to repeat the pattern of frustration, anger and abuse manifested by her own mother. On several occasions she is in danger of doing just this, especially when she loses her temper with her mentally disabled son, Nathan. When this occurs, the scar on her forehead begins to throb and she has to exert great strength of will to resist the temptation to lash out: 'Oh God . . . [she prays,] give me the grace to stop me from scarring my children as I myself was scarred' ('O Dduw,' 'dyro ras i mi . . . i ymgadw rhag creithio fy mhlant megis y'm creithiwyd i').[46] I have discussed elsewhere the importance of the trope of female madness in Welsh writing;[47] Elena Puw-Morgan's work demonstrates that further, and moreover continues the association between female madness and religion, already established in Allen Raine and continued later by Kate Roberts in the novella, *Tywyll Heno* (Dark Tonight, 1962).

Both mental illness and physical deformity are concerns Puw-Morgan shares with her contemporary, Kate Roberts. The latter's early story 'Y Man Geni' (The Birthmark, 1925) has three genera-tions of children in the same family marked with the same facial deformity, a prominent birthmark.[48] Clearly, both writers are using the facial mark symbolically; in Roberts's case there is a suggestion that the mark is connected with birth itself – to come into this world is to be marked out for suffering and death. But, typically, Roberts's story is culturally specific to Wales. Death in this family is likely to occur in the nearby slate quarry, where all the menfolk work. The title in Welsh, moreover, can mean both a birthmark and a place of birth, perhaps suggesting that to be born in this place – Wales – is to be marked out especially for a life of hardship and disappointment.

Another shared concern of Elena Puw-Morgan and Kate Roberts (together with Margiad Evans) is with women's labour. Back-breaking domestic work, such as washing the quarryman's work-clothes, or the endless tedium of knitting and mending, is given detailed and unwonted attention in the fiction of these Welsh women writers. Raymond Williams has suggested that men's work, such as coal-mining, in the Welsh industrial novel is not simply an economic activity but is itself *formative*;[49] a similar assertion could be made with regard to women's work in these Welsh female writers' literary production.

In stark contrast to the way in which *Y Graith* reveals how childhood experiences can maim and scar, and the way in which Kate Roberts suggests that the Welsh are marked out for suffering, *Dew on the Grass* (1934), a novel by Eiluned Lewis, an exact contemporary of Elena Puw-Morgan, lovingly describes how an idyllic childhood can shape the adult and stay with one forever in nostalgic memories. Though one author wrote in Welsh and the other in English, there are many similarities in the two authors' representations of rural Wales in the early years of the twentieth century. The novels share a female child's perspective, and deal with country life, religion, gender and Welsh culture and identity, as well as with class, work and family structures. However, the class perspective is markedly different, and can be seen as responsible for some of the poignant differences between these two stylistically distinguished works.

Dew on the Grass opens with the following topographical description:

> A stranger, crossing the valley from north to south, searching for ford or footbridge over the young Severn, would come suddenly upon Pengarth and might wonder – if his sense of direction were confused – to which point of the compass the river was flowing. For it so winds and wanders, looping the fields and threading the tangled trees with S-shaped curves, that it seems in two minds whether to make its way into England or return to the hills. Embracing the last inch of orchard and hayfields, it turns at length reluctantly towards the east, the widening valley and the fat water-meadows.[50]

This scene establishes the setting in the border country between England and Wales; unlike *Y Graith*, which in a sense has no need to emphasize its Welsh setting because it is written in Welsh, Lewis must spell out the setting's cultural specificity. The opening description also underlines a sense of disorientation and uncertainty, an appropriate opening for a novel which focuses on childhood with all its unanswered questions. The river Severn itself is described as 'young', like the children who will take centre-stage in the novel; the river, like the children, is not a purposeful, rational being but a wanderer, a meanderer in the landscape, turning back on itself and inscribing its S – the initial letter of its name – on to the land. Both children and river seem reluctant to leave Wales. Later in the opening chapter, the four children of the Gwyn family – Delia (eleven), Maurice (six), Miriam (three and a half), and the central character, Lucy (eight) – also have their identities carved into their environment when Beedles, the coachman, records their varying heights 'on the stable door of stout oak'.[51]

The introduction of the travelling stranger in the opening paragraph functions both as a mediating and as an authenticating device, while the relationship between Wales and its neighbour, England, is mentioned twice on the first page. The succeeding description of the homestead of Pengarth emphasizes its ancient, rambling nature – it seems like an untidy, organic outgrowth of the land itself. The house is full of nooks and crannies and low ceilings, suggesting not only its age but also, symbolically, a place of childhood – 'no-one above the age of ten could stand up in the [rooms]'.[52] More sinisterly, 'between the walls were spaces, large enough to hide a dozen men, where birds entered and flapped dismally in the dark'.[53] This detail suggests the house's involvement in historical conflicts of the past – so that priests, kings or politicians might have hidden in these commodious walls – but now that space is given over to nature. One reading of this trope might be that history now – the 'now' of Lucy, aged eight – has come to a stop. Certainly the arresting of time may be linked to that gesture of inscribing the children's heights on the stable door. Moreover, when Beedles is carrying out this act, he is forced to flatten down Lucy's curls, which 'grew upright', making her appear a little taller than she is; Beedles's gesture predicts accurately the somewhat unruly and precocious nature of this female child who will be the novel's central consciousness.

Given that the title of the novel is an echo of a biblical verse and that the whole text is littered with religious references and quotations, it would be tempting to see Lewis's novel as a representation of a sacred place, a locus of salvation or a 'soteriological landscape', in Dorian Llywelyn's terms. However, the text from Proverbs which gives the novel its title – 'The king's wrath is as the roaring of a lion; but his favour is as dew upon the grass'[54] – conjures up the extremes of the child's world: Lucy and her siblings live in a Welsh rural environment which seems blessed with the favour of the Creator, whose generosity and beneficence is rendered in the image of dew upon the grass. It seems like a landscape of salvation but the other – unquoted – element of the verse suggests the ever-lurking danger of incurring the wrath of the Old Testament God, who is as dangerous and destructive as the marauding wild beast. It is between these extremes of beatitude and terror that the child's life is lived. There is also the strong suggestion that the Edenic aspects of the rural world which Lucy sporadically experiences come to an end with the passage from childhood to adulthood.

Lucy's family, the Gwyns, are Anglo-Welsh landed gentry; the Gwyns' estate appears to be extensive, including a number of farms and cottages with dependent tenants, and Pengarth, the 'home-farm', is run by a large complement of servants. Lucy and her three siblings have a formidable Welsh nursemaid, Louisa, and there are at least two housemaids, a parlourmaid, a cook, a stableboy, farm labourers, a gamekeeper and a coachman. Thus, this novel offers a view of servants' lives from a very different class perspective from that offered in the work of Elena Puw-Morgan or, indeed, Kate Roberts. The Gwyn family has a close and friendly relationship with the servants but there is a definite sense of social hierarchy, reflected for instance in the fact that Denis the hay-cutter refers to the children deferentially as '*Miss* Daylia and *Miss* Lucy'.[55] Lucy is largely unaware of class distinctions, however, living as she does in perpetual fear of retribution by her stern nurse, Louisa. There are indications that poverty and want exist in this society but, interestingly, these occur towards the end of the novel, reflecting Lucy's growing awareness of the adult world around her. In chapter 16, for example, the Gwyns visit Martha Hamer and her seven children in their tiny cottage, 'which smelt hot and damp, like the ironing room at Pengarth'.[56]

Lucy has a number of encounters with figures who lie on the margins of the class system and, interestingly, she identifies with them and seems to be acknowledged by them as a kindred spirit. She meets the gipsy, Ned Lovell, who teaches her how to fish and for whose 'heady companionship' she is willing to suffer 'retribution – Louisa and dry bread for supper'.[57] Later, she meets Billy Bennett the poacher, who carries a ferret in a bag and is allegedly looking for 'oonts' (moles); he kindly gives her the mushrooms he has picked, to replace the blackberries she has managed to spill while falling into a bog. These poacher characters actually disrupt the system on which the Gwyn estate is built, but Lucy is fascinated by these outsiders and their life of freedom. There is certainly no critique of the class system in the novel, but, through Lucy's consciousness, there is a sense that some of its rigid demarcations of 'good' (Louisa) and 'bad' (Billy Bennett) are at least questionable.

Most poignant of all, in terms of Lucy's encounters with outsiders in the novel, is her meeting with the unnamed tramp near the end of the novel. She and the rector's son, David, are playing in the cemetery, where there is a newly opened grave, and they are interrupted by the arrival of a strange man. Echoes of the opening chapter of Dickens's *Great Expectations* are inevitably created as the man asks for food and boots, but the menace created by Magwitch never materializes here, and the man is seen, through Lucy's eyes, as a pitiful and poignant figure. It is a tangible irruption of history into the timeless world of Pengarth, for the tramp is a refugee from the industrial unrest and poverty of the south Wales valleys. As he himself says, bridling at the rude label of 'tramp' that David assigns him:

> 'Oh, it's tramps, is it? . . . What right 'ave you got to call me names, I'd like ter know, if an honest man can't get work? Why don't you blame the rotten country? 'Aven't I walked all the way from Cardiff? And the bloody Unions taking it out of a chap till you might as well be dead, I tell you, dead and rotted and shovelled away in there.' He nodded at the grave.[58]

In a rather inadequate gesture of sympathy, Lucy gives the man a slice of bread and treacle and he goes on his way. Yet the encounter remains in Lucy's mind as a disquieting omen that she will soon be entering that adult world of injustice and pain.

Lucy and her siblings, despite their youth, are connoisseurs of sermons, showing a decided preference for the *hwyl* of the chapel minister's Welsh over the dull dutifulness of the Anglican vicar's English, although they can scarcely understand the language of the former. Lucy herself 'was always expecting God to call her, as He had called the Infant Samuel'.[59] Her early ambition is to be a hymn-writer, surely a very Welsh choice of vocation for a little girl. She is entranced by biblical language, which echoes through her active imagination, though she often has at best a hazy idea of the meaning of the words themselves. Thus, the phrase 'carnally minded' appeals to her ear, though ironically she has as yet no conception of what the phrase denotes. Lucy is drawn to theological speculation; her favourite pastime is to lie in a hammock and think about death and religion.

Lewis's characters usually define themselves as Welsh and significantly different from their English neighbours. The mother of the family is a Welsh-speaking Pembrokeshire woman, as is the grandmother, who visits and teaches the children verses in Welsh. Moreover, aunt Shân lives in a west Wales seaside resort recognizable as Aberdovey, where the children are immersed in a more intensively Welsh-speaking environment for part of the summer. Characters and places are marked by their distinctively Welsh names, even if sometimes rendered in an Anglicized form, such as 'Twm the Weeg' ([G]*wig*, 'wood'). Nevertheless, the Gwyns are typical Anglo-Welsh gentry of the period (*c*.1908), in that they ensure that their children receive a thoroughly English education. Before they are packed off to boarding school in England, the children are subjected to the ministrations of Miss Crabtree, who 'came on a bicycle three mornings a week to teach arithmetic, grammar and the Kings of England'.[60] This curriculum calls to mind Moelona's repeated complaints that Welsh children are taught an English syllabus which succeeds in alienating and Anglicizing them. Yet Louisa, the Gwyns' nursemaid, is clearly a Welsh-speaker and a devout chapelgoer. The text is sprinkled with approximations of her Welsh exclamations, such as 'caudle' (*cawdel*, 'mess') and 'nem-o-dear' (presumably a corruption of 'yn enw Duw', in the name of God). Other servants and tenants are also Welsh-speakers, such as Davey John, the farm-worker, who calls the children 'bach' and is fond of the exclamation 'Jowks' (a version of the Welsh swear-word *diawl*, meaning 'the devil'). But this is the time of the heyday of the British Empire, as evidenced in Delia's pencil-box, which bears 'a picture of Lord Kitchener on the lid',[61] and they all intone 'a prayer for the King'.[62] The children's father recites Gray's 'Elegy' to them, while aunt Shân's house in Aberdovey contains just four books: 'two bound volumes of the *Ladies' Magazine*; Dickens's *Christmas Carol*; *Tristan and Iseult* in green suède, and *Scenes from Clerical Life*'.[63] This is indistinguishable from a bourgeois English house-hold of the period, and yet the girls are bewitched by the fact that in Shân's house, 'after you had gone to bed you could hear the swish and slap of waves, and the noise of people walking to and fro and talking in Welsh'.[64] The children have a copy of *Little Arthur's England* in the nursery and a painting of 'An English Farm Yard' hanging in their bedroom in Shân's house.[65] And yet Lucy, when she holds forth to Davey John about the probability that 'Henry VII . . . came through this field on his way to the Battle of Bosworth', urges 'wouldn't you like to have been there, marching into England with a Welsh army?'[66] Lucy's political allegiances, such as they are, are clear. Similarly, when the traditional Welsh harpist, John Roberts, comes to play on their lawn, Lucy responds intensely to this 'different music: it came from everywhere, and yet from nowhere . . . and at the same time it came from inside Lucy's own head, so that she knew that this was the music for which she had always been waiting'.[67] The music the harpist plays is Welsh folk music, such as 'Hob-y-deri-dando', 'Bugeilio'r Gwenith Gwyn' and 'David of the White Rock'.[68]

The Gwyns' Wales is defined by its rurality and by its relatively static social hierarchy. South Wales is, for the Gwyn children at least, an alien place. Lucy is startled by the tramp from Cardiff because he speaks differently and displays an anger at injustice which is new to her. When the family travels to aunt Shân's house in west Wales, they hear the porters in the railway station shout 'Change here for South Wales!' and Lucy reflects wonderingly that 'there actually is a train waiting to go to South Wales – that unknown country – and people strolling unconcernedly to catch it'.[69]

Dew on the Grass, then, presents an ostensibly contradictory representation of Welsh identity. While the Welsh language and aspects of Welsh culture such as music, poetry and religion are certainly presented in a positive way, these markers of Welshness are incorporated within a dominant social identity defined by Britishness and class allegiance. There are, moreover, indications that the new sense of working-class identity which was historically crystallizing in the south Wales valleys at the time is viewed as something threatening and alien. Lucy is acutely aware that the tramp's accent sounds 'quite different from the voices of the people who lived in Pengarth'.[70] This 'difference' has underlying political implications which, as it were, force themselves into a text which is trying to avoid them; while the Welsh servants and tenants of Pengarth are apparently content with their station, the tramp's voice is the rumbling murmur of social change which will soon threaten and destroy the stable world of Pengarth forever, and will, at the same time, lead to a new, and politicized, form of Welsh identity.

Lewis's second novel, *The Captain's Wife* (1943), is set in Pembrokeshire during the late nineteenth century and is based largely on the memories and stories of the author's mother and grandmother. Like *Dew on the Grass*, it has an episodic structure and the child's point of view is privileged. However, the central consciousness of the novel is Lettice Peters, the sea captain's wife of the title. The main setting is St Idris, 'the village that boasts itself a city',[71] which is recognizable as the cathedral 'city' of St David's. Matty is the principal child character and many of her experiences and perceptions are similar to those of Lucy in Lewis's earlier novel. However, this novel engages more centrally with a Welsh-speaking culture, and religion plays a prominent role. As the narrator observes, 'religion in this country is native as the rocks taken hence to be the sacred stones of Stonehenge'.[72] Matty's family visits Rehoboth, a Carmarthenshire chapel in the ministerial care of her

Uncle Simon and the description of the place might be taken as the archetypal Welsh Nonconformist chapel:

> [Uncle Simon's] father had built it on his own land, and the date 1784 stood over the sturdy, whitewashed porch. . . . within the chapel was austere . . . High-backed seats flanked both sides of the pulpit and on these sat the Cefnmawr family; the rest of the space was filled with backless wooden benches. A 'set fawr' (big seat) for the deacons stood under the pulpit, and behind it, written on the wall in two languages, Hebrew and Welsh, were the words 'Cry Aloud and Spare Not'.[73]

The Hebrew–Welsh coupling is clearly suggestive of the Nonconformist appropriation of the Jewish notion of the sacred land and chosen people;[74] elsewhere in the text, however, the encroachment of English is evident. An advertisement on the wall of a west Wales railway station, for example, offers 'Cyflawnder o Raincoats Mewn Stoc Ac Overcoats' ('A Wealth of Raincoats in Stock And Overcoats).[75] Similarly, Miss Lloyd of Pwllglas wonders why all the railway guards announce their marital status on their peaked caps, since they bear the word 'GWR', meaning husband in Welsh but, unbeknownst to her, actually standing for 'Great Western Railway'.[76] In general, this novel is also infused with a nostalgia for a Welsh Wales of the past, associated here with extensive family networks (the novel is bristling with aunts), and embodied in a cultural landscape intimately known and mapped out by its inhabitants.

Eiluned Lewis published two slim volumes of verse, as well as three novels. Her poetry is written in a mode reminiscent of the Georgian poets of the early twentieth century, notably W. H. Davies. The verse is lyrical and song-like, almost invariably expressing a sense of loss, nostalgia or longing; tonally, then, it is similar to *Dew on the Grass*. However, very few of the poems refer specifically to Wales; rather, the identity projected by them is a *rural* identity which seems to take precedence over any cultural specificity, as expressed most memorably in the poem called 'The Birthright':

> We who were born
> In country places,
> Far from cities
> And shifting faces,
> We have a birthright
> No man can sell,
> And a secret joy
> No man can tell.

For we are kindred
To lordly things,
The wild duck's flight
And the white owl's wings;
To pike and salmon,
To bull and horse,
The curlew's cry
And the smell of gorse.

Pride of trees,
Swiftness of streams,
Magic of frost
have shaped our dreams:
No baser vision
Their spirit fills
Who walk by right
On the naked hills.[77]

The use of the first-person plural voice here is telling. The voice speaks for a communal rural identity which apparently transcends class and national allegiance, although the reference to the 'naked hills' in the final line is suggestive of a Welsh landscape, rather than the more lush topography of south-east England, where Eiluned Lewis settled in later life. The allusion to birthright and kinship also suggests a concern with ancestry and family associations with the land which we have seen as being characteristic of certain types of Welsh women's writing. Nevertheless, in class terms the poem is subversive, in that the 'lordly things' extolled by it are not associated with the possessions and mores of the gentry but, rather, with untamed, wild Nature. Similarly, the 'right' to walk the 'naked hills' is not endowed by title deeds and wealth but by a sense of belonging, which borders on the mystical.

Another border writer who uses the Welsh landscape in an emblematic way in her work is Margiad Evans. Her first published work was *Country Dance* (1932), a historical novella set in 1850. Structurally, it is interesting in that it has a frame narrative in which Margiad Evans masquerades as the editor of a found manuscript: the 1850 diary of Ann Goodman, which constitutes the main body of the text. Ostensibly, the narrative concerns the rivalry between Gabriel Evans, an English shepherd, and Evan ap Evans, a Welsh landowner, for the love of Ann, who is the daughter of a Welsh mother and an English father. In the end, the frame narrative informs us that Ann was murdered by her rejected lover, Gabriel, though local gossip pins the blame for the crime on Evan. However, the core of the narrative is Ann herself; the editor sets out to recuperate Ann from oblivion and to reinstate her voice at the centre of a story in which she has been reduced to silent victimhood.

Ann's story is about her search for identity and autonomy, primarily with regard to national belonging – Ann initially defines herself as English and is scornful of the Welsh, but ends by recognizing and accepting her Welshness. Space and place play key roles in this text, which is set in the border-lands and presents characters continually criss-crossing, country-dance-like, between Wales and England. In this way, Margiad Evans complicates the simple binary opposition between the two countries, for Welsh people are found inhabiting English soil, and vice versa. Beneath the apparently simple narrative, rigid demarcations regarding both national and gender identity are being radically questioned. Although Ann eventually adopts a Welsh allegiance, it is the border itself which is celebrated in the text; it forms a third space where oppositions and antagonisms can be resolved, as occurs in the scene where a potentially violent situation at a supper party at Tan y Bryn is defused:

> Gwen has put out her blackberry wine; it sets the men to singing reckless words from 'Men of Harlech', despite [Gabriel's] mutters and angry looks.
>
> One of them jumps up from his place shouting:
>
> 'I drink to Wales!'
>
> Gabriel roars:
>
> 'And I to England!' and stands facing the other across the table. Megan and Margiad clap their hands; Mary looks serious.
>
> 'There'll be trouble in a minute, the men are hot as coals,' she whispers.
>
> Gwen purses up her lips.
>
> 'I give the Border,' she says, very quiet.
>
> We all drink it down . . .'[78]

The landscape itself plays a large role in the narrative, not only because virtually all the characters are agricultural workers but also because certain places are endowed with symbolic resonance. The

Welsh landscape is infused with both history and myth, as suggested by Ann's question of Gabriel: 'Have you seen the Roman soldiers marching through Craig Dinas and the White Lady that drowned herself in Llyn-tro (the turning pool)?'[79]

Margiad Evans herself, like Ann Goodman, had an in-between identity. Born in England and brought up near Ross-on-Wye (probably the 'Salus' that features in both *Country Dance* and her second novel, *The Wooden Doctor*) she defined herself as a border writer, though by adopting her Welsh grandmother's surname instead of her real name, Whistler, for her writing, she was often regarded as a Welsh author. She complained of this in a 1946 letter to Gwyn Jones, where she asserts 'I'm not Welsh . . . I am the border – a very different thing', though she does add 'I'm glad of my drop of Welsh blood and I'd never want to move out of the range of the Welsh voice'.[80]

Ann Goodman's first-person, present-tense narrative is prompted by her lover Gabriel giving her the book and instructing her to write all she does in it, 'for him to see, until we shall be married'.[81] In retrospect, the opening sentence is ominous, suggesting Gabriel's possessiveness and need for surveillance. Soon, however, Ann's book becomes her own and she records her thoughts, feelings and experiences in it for herself, not for Gabriel. Like Mali Meredur in Elena Puw Morgan's contemporary work, *Y Wisg Sidan*, Ann Goodman is a young girl much browbeaten by a tyrannical father and still searching for confirmation of her identity; like Mali, she examines her own reflection in order to try to recognize herself. In Ann's case she sees her reflection in the landscape itself: 'there is my face staring back at me out of the brown water among the weeds, almost like a person drowned'.[82] Sadly, this search for recognition results only in a poignant foreshadowing of her own death. Ultimately, however, despite the silencing of Ann, her book resurrects her and places the experience of an overworked country girl from the border country at the centre of a vivid construction of the land of Wales and its relationship with its powerful neighbour.

Evans's next published work, *The Wooden Doctor* (1933), concerns Arabella Warden, a girl from the English side of the Welsh border, whose early life is blighted by the alcoholism of her father. The novel develops into a complex account of Arabella's mysterious illness, which is assuaged but not cured by the ministrations of the local doctor, an Irishman. The illness is personified as a 'fox' which 'out of the darkness . . . sprang with flaming feet and famished jaws, rending, biting, tearing'.[83] The illness is obscurely connected with sexuality and Arabella's terrible desire for the unresponsive 'wooden' doctor, who is both sexual object and father substitute ('Papa-doctor').[84] In Part III of the novel, Arabella goes for a recuperative stay to a farm in north Wales. Initially, she is unimpressed by the landscape but gradually its bleakness begins to reflect her inner self: 'I heard the murmuring water in the darkness and it spoke of measureless desolation encompassing this kitchen comfort, of wet and solitary fields, of bare, windy mountains, of black pools reflecting the stars, and bending sighing rushes.'[85] Arabella finds that the only reading matter to be had at Bodgynan is the novels of Allen Raine, but she rejects these as 'unrealistic sentimentalities'.[86] When Arabella returns to Salus she finds that the wooden doctor has married a young girl. Despite the sadness of the ending, Arabella's journey into the land of Wales has enabled her to finish her novel and, arguably, to grasp a sense of agency and identity once more, wresting it away from from the jaws of the 'fox'.

Evans's next two novels, *Turf or Stone* (1934) and *Creed* (1936), have few connections with Wales. Neither does her *Autobiography* (1943), although the latter, written largely during the war years when she was separated from her husband and living in a cottage in Llangarron, near Ross, is remarkable for its intense personal response to the natural landscape of the border country. Technically, it is quite experimental, attempting to capture the moment, the lived experience of 'now', rather than constructing a narrative of the author's life. As P. J. Kavanagh observes, 'in the ordinary autobiographical sense it gives us hardly any information at all. But of what it was like to be Margiad Evans, to live inside her skin, it tells us as nearly as possible everything.'[87]

If Margiad Evans grew increasingly mystical in her later work, before her early death in 1958, such an accusation could never be made of Kate Roberts, whom few would deny was the most important Welsh female novelist and short-story writer of the twentieth century. Despite the fact that there is a considerable hiatus of some twelve years in the middle of her writing career, she produced a large oeuvre extending over a period of more than half a century. She was, moreover, an influential critic, journalist, editor and publisher, not to mention a political activist and one of the founder members of Plaid Cymru, the Welsh Nationalist Party, or BB (Bloody Blaid), as she affectionately referred to it.

Roberts's first collection of short stories, *O Gors y Bryniau* ('From the marsh of the hills', 1925), draws strongly on her own background in the village of Rhosgadfan in Snowdonia, a mixed area of slate-quarrying and small farming. No fewer than eight of the nine stories in this early volume deal with the lives of the quarrymen of the Caernarfonshire slate quarries, while five of them refer to deaths or accidents in the industry. Roberts renders with palpable authenticity the lives of hardship and poverty struggled through by people in this north-west corner of Wales. The stories offer a vivid confirmation of the statistics of the industrial historian: the hazards of the quarryman's work meant that his profession was actually more dangerous even than that of the coal miner in the south Wales valleys at the time. As R. Merfyn Jones states in his standard history of the north Wales quarrymen:

> The open slate quarries, in which the majority of the slate quarrymen worked, remained . . . outside the scope of any effective legislation (unlike the coal mines). They were lethal places in which, between 1883 and 1892, out of a workforce of only some 8,500, 116 men lost their lives in accidents.[88]

The overwhelming impression of Kate Roberts's early short stories, with their looming threat of death or mutilation in the quarry and their vivid depiction of the economic and emotional consequences of such accidents in the domestic sphere, bears out the historian's assertion. But clearly Kate Roberts's stories are worth a great deal more than simple documents corroborating historians' accounts. Roberts creates a poignant, human, touchable world. In the story 'Newid Byd' (Changing World) we are presented with an old man who, like Allen Raine's protagonist in her story 'Home, Sweet Home', is suffering from *hiraeth*, both for his old home and for his old occupation in the quarry. Despite the dirt and danger of the quarryman's life, William Gruffydd now longs for it as a salve for his loneliness. He wants to reclaim that quarryman's identity which he has lost through retirement; he longs to go back. And one morning he can resist the temptation no longer: he dons his workboots and he really does go back to rejoin his old companions in the quarry. The story centres on his feeling of disappointment when he finds that he cannot turn back the clock and that there is no space, no role for him in his old *caban* at work. In this regard, of course, the story can be seen to articulate what might be called elemental human emotions: the sadness of loss, the melancholy of old age, the inevitability of time passing and the coming of mortality, but it manages to articulate these in an exceptionally moving, and culturally specific way.

The story is deeply rooted in its time and place; set during the First World War, it includes a brief conversation among the quarrymen about a politician they call 'Y Mawr' (the Great One), which is clearly a reference to Lloyd George:

> 'Beth wyt ti'n feddwl o sbitsh y Mawr?' ebe Dafydd Rolant heb gyfarch neb yn neilltuol.

> 'Tydw i'n meddwl dim ohoni,' ebe Wiliam Gruffydd.

> 'Sut felly?' ebe Morgan Owen.

> 'Wel, does dim yn dangos yn well na'r sbitsh yna 'i fod o wedi troi'i gefn ar y werin. . . . mi fasa'n rhyfadd iawn gin i feddwl ma'r dyn fu'n siarad am hawliau'r gweithwyr gyda'r fath hwyl ers talwm fasa'n gweiddi am hel 'u plant nhw i'r Rhyfal', ebe Wiliam Gruffydd . . .[89]

> [What do you think of the Great One's speech?' said Dafydd Rolant to nobody in particular.

> 'I think nothing at all of it,' replied William Gruffydd.

> 'Why's that?' asked Morgan Owen.

> 'Well, nothing shows more clearly than that speech that he's turned his back on the ordinary people . . . I'm very surprised to think that the man who spoke so eloquently about workers' rights in the past should now be calling on them to send their children to the War', remarked William Gruffydd . . .]

William Gruffydd's disillusionment with Lloyd George and his silencing by the younger, more reactionary and pompous Morgan Owen shows the direction history was moving in. Yet it is crystal clear that authorial approval lies with the point of view of William Gruffydd. Writing in the early 1920s, when Lloyd George was viewed as the apostle of peace at Geneva, Kate Roberts here reveals a palpable political agenda. She is calling attention to the bankruptcy of Liberalism and its claim to speak for the interests of the *gwerin* of Wales. After all, 1925, when *O Gors y Bryniau* was published, was also the year in which Plaid Cymru was founded, partly in reaction to the disillusionment of Welsh nationalists with

Lloyd George, the failed Home Rule movement and, overwhelmingly, with the First World War. Plaid Cymru was the political party that Kate Roberts came to see as the way forward for the ideals that had been betrayed by Lloyd George, and she dedicated most of her adult life to fighting for the nationalist ideals embodied in the new party.

But there is another, more profoundly human, concern in the story, and that is with the losses of the war itself. Kate Roberts stated several times that the experience which made her into a writer was the desolating one of losing her brother in the First World War. This experience is partly rendered in the devastating ending of *Traed mewn Cyffion* (Feet in Chains), discussed below, but it was a memory which never left Kate Roberts and spurred her on to write again and again of human experiences of loss and alienation. When William Gruffydd perceives in his cruel epiphany toward the end of the story that the gaps left by people are only temporary ones, soon filled by others, the reader makes the link with what is going on at the Front, where the dead soldier's place is soon filled by another, and another, and another, all sons of workers like himself. One hears an echo also of the biblical ending of Hilda Vaughan's 1934 novella: 'Man is like a thing of nought; his time passeth away like a shadow.'[90]

Kate Roberts's second volume, *Rhigolau Bywyd* ('The Ruts of Life', 1929), contains eight short stories, including well-known and much-anthologized ones such as 'Y Golled' (The Loss) and 'Rhwng Dau Damaid o Gyfleth' (Between Two Pieces of Toffee). 'The Loss' figures, largely in spatial terms, Annie Williams's disillusionment with marriage and her 'loss' of a lover in acquiring a husband. Annie manages to persuade the unromantic Ted to take a bus-trip into the mountains on a Sunday, in hope of rekindling some of their earlier affection. The landscape fulfills her expectations:

Eisteddent ar eu lled-orwedd ar lan y llyn. O'u blaen yr oedd mynyddoedd mawr yn sefyll fel ceiri rhyngddynt â'r awyr, porffor y grug a melyn yr eithin yn ymdoddi i'w gilydd arnynt . . . Wrth eu traed yr oedd dŵr y llyn yn llepian yn gyson fel cath yn taro ei phawen ar eich glin o hyd i gael eich sylw. Golygfa i'w hyfed ac nid i'w disgrifio ydoedd; golygfa i'ch meddwi ac i'ch gwneuthur yn ben-ysgafn.[91]

[They sat reclining on the lake shore. In front of them great mountains stood like fortresses between them and the sky, on their sides the purple of the heather and the yellow of the gorse melting together . . . At their feet the lake-water lapped regularly like a cat pawing your knee constantly to get your attention. It was a view to be drunk in

with the senses and not to be described; a view to intoxicate you and
make you light-headed.]

Clearly, Annie's romantic expectations are colouring the landscape,
but her carefully resurrected world of romance is shattered at the
end of the story when the prosaic Ted wishes he had spent the day in
his favourite place, the chapel. Here the basic juxtapositions of
inside and outside, the freedom of the mountainside and the
confines of the chapel, are used very skilfully by Roberts to represent the tragically opposed world-views of husband and wife. Ted
espouses a small-town Nonconformist Wales, while Annie longs for
a more socially unrestricted, wilder place.

The landscape of Caernarfonshire plays an important role in
Roberts's early fiction. Its bare hillsides and rocky mountains,
dotted with slate quarries, present a scene of austerity and bleakness, often symbolic of her characters' inner lives. Roberts never
resorts to the picturesque, for her landscape is always peopled; the
land is significant in people's lives because they have to wrest a
living from it. Nevertheless, her characters often experience a
scarcely articulated enjoyment of the beauty of the natural world.
Jane Gruffydd, for example, rushes to finish her many household
and farm tasks in order to be free to take her babies for a walk on
the hillsides in Roberts's 1936 novel *Traed mewn Cyffion* (Feet in
Chains). The walk has no practical purpose, but it is clear that Jane
needs it psychologically in order to carry on with her daily struggle.[92]

The two World Wars loom large in the experience and the
literary production of Welsh women of this period. As historians
have reminded us, the First World War particularly had a paradoxically cataclysmic and formative effect on Welsh women's lives.[93]
Although it features only in the last five chapters of Kate Roberts's
1936 novel *Traed mewn Cyffion*, the First World War is nevertheless central to the book's conception and impact. Roberts herself
stated that the catalyst for her becoming a writer in the first place
was the loss of her brother, who was killed in that war. The
experience of that loss is given fictional form in the novel. Her
writing, then, springs from a sense of loss and disillusionment
(*siom*); the novel may be regarded as an attempt at personal
catharsis and as a commemoration of the dead and their lost world.

Opening in 1880, the novel initially presents a highly atmospheric picture of an apparently unchanging, traditional Welsh

ethnoscape. An open-air Methodist prayer-meeting on an oppressively hot June afternoon is the backdrop for Roberts' introduction
of her main character, Jane Gruffydd, the new bride at Ffridd Felen.
Roberts skillfully conjures a vanished world, a people entranced by
the velvet voice of the preacher and the crackling of the gorse in the
intense heat, only to reveal how this past is jolted into self-
consciousness by the advent of the War.

At first, the people of Moel Arian regard the war as something
distant and incomprehensible: 'they did not understand its causes;
they believed in what the papers said, that Great Britain was going
to the help of smaller nations' ('Ni ddeallent yr achosion, ond
credent yr hyn a ddywedai'r papurau, mai myned i achub cam
gwledydd bychain a wnaeth Prydain Fawr').[94] The family at Ffridd
Felen connect it initially with the Boer War, which they remember as
'the headmaster . . . ma[king] them march through the village in
procession with their banners flying when Mafeking was relieved,
but it had not meant anything to them' ('fel y gwnaeth prifathro'r
Ysgol Elfennol iddynt gerdded mewn orymdaith fanerog i fyny
trwy'r pentref pan ryddhawyd Mafeking, ond ni olygai hynny ddim
iddynt').[95] The wars of the British Empire are clearly of no interest
to these people, neither do they admire the warrior hero – the local
militiaman is an object of scorn rather than awe. They are, at best,
indifferent colonial subjects, unaware of their own subject status or
their own stake in the colonial enterprise. However, the novel
demonstrates how an awareness of subjection begins to grow in the
general consciousness, and it is the War which, unexpectedly, effects
this political awakening.

When Twm, one of the sons of Ffridd Felen joins up, his family is
at first shocked by his dereliction of familial duty: 'here was Twm
playing such a shabby trick! When he could be sending a little
money home each month, he had gone and joined the army' ('A
dyma Twm yn gwneud tro mor wael! Pan allasai anfon ychydig
arian adref, yn mynd at y soldiwrs').[96] Such a reaction underlines
the people's naivety, since at this point they still believe that the war
will soon be over and that there is no danger of any of the local boys
who join up actually being required to fight. Life goes on as usual
on the smallholding, disrupted only by Bet, one of the daughters,
who 'kept saying she would like to go away to work in an
ammunition factory' ('Swniai . . . am gael mynd i ffwrdd i waith
cad-ddarpar').[97] Soon, though, the shocking news comes that Twm

is to be sent to France. His mother, Jane, consoles herself by sending him two packages of home-made food every week; Roberts is an astute observer of her people's reactions – generally taciturn and often unable to articulate their emotions verbally, the women at least have an outlet in the ability to express love by means of food. Gradually, the people of Moel Arian begin to awake from their stoical quietism:

> A dechreuodd y bobl oedd gartref eu holi eu hunain a holi ei gilydd beth oedd ystyr peth fel hyn . . . Ni chredent o gwbl erbyn hyn mai achub cam gwledydd bychain oedd amcan y Rhyfel, ac mai rhyfel i orffen rhyfel ydoedd . . . daethant i gredu bod pobl ym mhob gwlad oedd yn dda ganddynt ryfel, a'u bod yn defnyddio eu bechgyn hwy i'w mantais eu hunain. 'Y bobol fawr' yna oedd y rhai hynny, yr un bobl a wasgai arnynt yn y chwarel, ac a sugnai eu gwaed a'i droi'n aur iddynt hwy eu hunain. . . . Siglai eu ffydd mewn pregethwyr a gwladweinwyr . . . Ond âi'r Rhyfel ymlaen.[98]

> [They began to ask what was the meaning of it all . . . They did not believe at all now that the war was being fought to save the smaller nations, or that it was a war to end all wars . . . They came to realize that, in every country, there were people who regarded war as a good thing, and were taking advantage of their sons to promote their own interests. These were 'The Ruling Class', the same who oppressed them in the quarry, who sucked their blood and turned it into gold for themselves . . . their views began to change. Their faith in preachers and politicians was shaken . . . But the war continued . . .]

The climax of the novel occurs when the mother, Jane Gruffydd, receives an official letter informing her of the death of her son, a letter which she cannot understand because it is written in English. Kate Roberts's writing here is deceptively simple and emotionally explosive. The experience of Jane Gruffydd is intensely personal, and yet the whole episode is emblematic of the experience of many Welsh people during World War I. Roberts' realist technique, focusing on the materiality of the object, 'rhyw bapurau Saesneg' ('sheets of paper, written in English), in which Jane recognizes only Twm's name and his army number, forces the reader into sharing her bewildered, panicky incomprehension.[99] At the same time, the political undercurrent of the scene is unmistakable: Welsh-speaking Wales is being sacrificed for an alien cause by an imperial power which is both ruthless and insensitive.

The family's period of shock and mourning after the bereavement is memorably evoked: 'time stood still in Ffridd Felen . . .

There was no tomorrow. There remained only yesterday' ('yn y Ffridd Felen safasai amser . . . Nid oedd yfory i edrych ymlaen ato. Nid arhosai dim ond ddoe').[100] The loss caused by the war in a way consecrates the past; this is a feeling shared by Kate Roberts herself, who said in a 1961 letter to Saunders Lewis, referring to the 'rootless' young people of the day: 'the past isn't important to them at all. It means everything to me' ('nid yw'r gorffennol yn bwysig iddynt o gwbl. Y mae'n golygu popeth i mi . . .').[101] This period of numb suffering after the death comes to an end in the novel with the visit of a military pensions officer, who smugly informs Jane and her son, Owen, that he reduced a neighbouring widow's pension when he discovered that she earned some money by selling eggs. The self-congratulation of this representative of the British state is soon dispelled, however:

> Y munud hwnnw daeth rhyw deimlad rhyfedd dros Jane Gruffydd. Ers pymtheg mis o amser, bu rhyw deimladau yn crynhoi yn ei henaid yn erbyn pob dim oedd yn gyfrifol am y Rhyfel, yn erbyn dynion ac yn erbyn Duw; a phan welodd y dyn blonegog yma yn ei ddillad graenus yn gorfoleddu am dynnu pensiwn gwraig weddw dlawd i lawr, methodd ganddi ddal. a dyma hi'n cipio'r peth nesaf i law – brws dillad oedd hwnnw – a tharo'r swyddog yn ei ben. 'Cerwch allan o'r tŷ yma, mewn munud,' meddai.[102]

> [At that moment a strange feeling came over Jane Gruffydd. For fifteen long months, a deep resentment had been gathering in her very soul against everything that was responsible for the war, against men and against God. And when she saw this plump man in his immaculate clothes preening himself on the fact that he had reduced a widow's pension, she lost control of herself. She grabbed the nearest thing to hand – a clothes-brush – and struck him on the head with it. 'Get out of this house at once,' she shouted.]

The final vision of the novel is that of Owen, who belongs to Kate Roberts' own generation; he climbs the mountain and has a vision of 'great cities with countless streets, and they had Mod Arian slates on their roofs . . . and his eyes were opened to the possibility of doing something instead of simply enduring like a dumb animal' ('trefi mawrion a rhesi dirifedi o dai â llechi Mod Arian ar eu to . . . ac fe agorwyd ei lygaid i bosibilrwydd gwneud rhywbeth, yn lle dioddef fel mudion').[103] The novel shows a nationalist and a socialist consciousness being born in the people of one corner of Wales as a direct result of their bitter experience of war. Historians of Plaid Cymru, founded in the 1920s, concur that war experiences greatly influenced the nationalist feeling which gave rise to the party. Particularly galling for many was the idea that the war was allegedly fought, as the novel puts it, to 'help the small nations', a slogan which naturally encouraged many young Welsh people to join up. Gradually, like the characters in the novel, the people who would go on to found and support Plaid Cymru realized not just the falsity of the claim, but the oppressive weight of the colonial edifice which that political banner concealed. Thus, Kate Roberts's novel is an eloquent expression of political protest. Emblematically, as we have seen, the archetypal Welsh Mam takes up her brush, not to scrub and scour, but to attack the representative of the oppressive British state, which extends its tentacles even as far as her own domestic hearth. At the same time, the enchanted, timeless land enters into the flux of history.

Kate Roberts's next publication after *Feet in Chains* was the volume of short stories *Ffair Gaeaf* (Winter Fair) in 1937. Like her first volume, this one contains nine stories, several of them, such as 'Y Condemniedig' (The Condemned) amongst the best-known and most poignant in the Welsh-language literary tradition. One of these, 'Y Taliad Olaf' (The Last Payment) focuses on a central female character who has lived a life of economic hardship, struggling to make regular payments to a local shopkeeper. It is a story, like many of Roberts's, about money, poverty, the raw economic facts of life, but it also focuses readers' attention on gender roles and on the repressed or neglected desires of the female. Not unusually for Kate Roberts, the male characters are depicted negatively, as unimaginative, insensitive, incommunicative. Desire and imagination appear to be the prerogative of the female, yet the story is hardly celebratory in tone. Rather, it is about death and the inevitability of defeat and disappointment in Welsh women's lives.

Over and over, in her stories and novels, Roberts represents the determining and constricting pressure of gender in close and traditional Welsh communities. Although Roberts cannot be categorized straightforwardly as a feminist writer,[104] as, for instance, Moelona can, she certainly foregrounds female experience and draws attention to the way that gender roles are constructed and performed in society. As Judith Butler has persuasively argued: 'there is no core gender identity behind the expressions of gender ... identity is *performatively* constituted by the very "expressions" that are said to be its results'.[105] Many of the women writers represented here draw attention to this restrictive social construction of gender, even in childhood: for example, both Lucy and Matty, the girl protagonists of Eiluned Lewis's first two novels, discussed above, feel and bemoan the restrictions placed on them by their gender.[106]

'Y Taliad Olaf' turns to a woman in old age, however, emphasizing Ffani Rolant's isolation: 'This was further proof that it was with herself alone that she was best able to communicate. No-one could understand her thoughts, none of her neighbours and not even her husband' ('Yr oedd heno'n brawf pellach iddi mai gyda hi ei hun y gallai hi ymgyfachrathu orau. Prin y gallai neb ddeall ei meddyliau, neb o'i chymdogion na'i gŵr hyd yn oed').[107] Her husband is indifferent, the male shopkeeper equally so. She is an old woman, looking towards death, displaced in a new house without roots, without responsibilities, finally without debts. Emptiness echoes throughout the text. The road to the shop is, Ffani muses, her own biography: fifty years of Friday payments. The emphasis is on futility, monotony – what was the point of it all? The last payment, which is the final emblem of triumph over a lifetime of poverty, is, ironically, not triumphant or ecstatic in any way. She hesitates to make the last payment because it seems to set a seal on that futility. All she gets in return for her final payment is an erasure – her name wiped out of the book. No longer possessing an account, she herself is no longer of any account. It is almost as if it is the debts which have kept her yoked to life, as if the shopkeeper's weekly inscriptions conferred an identity upon her. This ostensibly simple story is reverberant with a theme found repeatedly in Welsh women's writing of this period: the way in which economic pressures mould and, in a sense, create working-class female identity. It is potently evident in the work of Elena Puw-Morgan, Dilys Cadwaladr, Margiad Evans, Hilda Vaughan – regardless of language, many Welsh women writers share a similar vision. As Kate Roberts put it: 'Someone has said about me that I have too much to say about money in these stories. That's not it exactly, but you have to have money to live, and it was a source of great suffering to them' ('Mae rhywun wedi deud amdana i mod i'n sôn gormod am arian yn y storïau yma. Nid dyna yn hollol ydi o, ond mae'n rhaid i chi gael arian i fyw, ac mi roedd o'n boen mawr iddyn nhw').[108]

Suffering and survival are also prominent concerns in the work of Hilda Vaughan during this period. Yet, in comparison with Kate Roberts's unequivocally nationalist response to war in *Traed mewn Cyffion*, Vaughan's novels reveal an interesting dual sensibility in regard to Wales, Britain and both World Wars. In *Pardon and Peace*

(1945) which actually deals directly with both World Wars, Wales is figured as a beautiful, timeless place to which the wounded First World War soldier longs to return, in order to heal himself of his physical and psychological wounds. Yet, paradoxically, Mark Osbourne is not a native returning to his homeland, but an Englishman who has visited rural Wales only once, fleetingly, before the war. Nevertheless, the memory of 'Cwm Tawel' (Quiet Valley) has sustained him in the trenches, and he returns there 'to be made whole again'.[109] The healing is also associated with a woman, Flora, the daughter of Tŷ-Mawr, who embodies the quiet, unsullied beauty of the valley she inhabits. Vaughan emphasizes Welsh otherness; it is as if the deracinated, urbane London artist, Mark, needs to re-establish his connection with the world of nature and tradition, now available only in Wales. There is a gesture of appropriation, certainly, with Mark insisting upon his place in a Cwm Tawel which is not too friendly towards strangers, but there is no doubt that the novel legitimizes this metaphorical planting of the Union flag in Welsh territory. The consummation of the relationship between Wales and England is delayed – through a somewhat melodramatic but nonetheless fascinating plot – until the Second World War. Here, the scene of the action shifts to London, where Britons, both Welsh and English, are united in the terrors and suffering of the Blitz, so lately over when Vaughan published the novel. Mark and Flora are reunited, and the final vision is one of stoic survival; as Mark observes: 'You've come through . . . we both have.'[110] Nevertheless, the most powerful writing in this novel comes when Vaughan is exploring the psychological scars of war on the individual; as Mark observes, 'It is over. But it hasn't done with us yet.'[111] Mark's sense of peace in 'Bro Tawel', explicitly associated with the still waters of the twenty-third Psalm, contrasts starkly with the desolation of his experience in the war, where he spent:

> Four springs in a countryside pitted with craters, like the dead landscape of the moon; four autumns of mire, clotted with human blood, in which no grain ripened. [112]

A contemporary of Vaughan, the Welsh-language writer Dilys Cadwaladr, is also concerned with war and gender, though her sympathies, as Kate Roberts observed, were with 'people of low status' ('pobl o radd isel')[113] struggling to make a living, unlike the more middle-class milieu of Vaughan's characters. Cadwaladr became a prominent figure in Welsh-language culture during the 1930s up until the 1950s. She was the first, and one of the few women ever to win the Crown at the National Eisteddfod, with her 1953 poem 'Y Llen' (The Veil). A Caernarfonshire woman, like her contemporary Kate Roberts, Cadwaladr followed a similar path in studying at the University College of North Wales in Bangor and becoming a teacher. Unlike Roberts, however, she spent a number of years in London and south-east England and was primarily a poet, though she enjoyed some success with her essays and short stories, in both Welsh and English. However, several critics have suggested that Cadwaladr did not achieve the acclaim that she deserved from Eisteddfod judges and others, partly because of her gender; for example, Rhiannon Davies Jones is quoted as saying 'She was someone from the margins and like one or two other literary women of her time she came under the whip of a clique of critics' ('Un o bobl yr ymylon oedd hi ac fel un neu ddwy arall o ferched llengar ei chyfnod daeth o dan lach carfan o feirniaid').[114] Cadwaladr's own writing sometimes expresses a sense of duality in her consciousness of herself as a woman and as a poet:

> Mae dwy fenyw yn trigo yn ein tŷ ni. Maent yn gwisgo'r un dillad, yn bwyta'r un bwyd ac yn hawlio'r un gadair freichiau pan ddel yr awr hamdden anfynych i'w rhan. Yn wir, mae'r ddwy'n gwisgo'r un cnawd a'r un calon sydd yn curo iddynt. Myfi yw'r ddwy. Ond nid wyf wedi penderfynu pa un o'r ddwy yw myfi . . . Nid ydynt wedi dygymod a'i gilydd erioed. Ond mae un yn fwy bodlon ar ei chydymaith na'r llall. I'w diffinio'n fras dywedwn mai Bardd yw Hon a gwraig tŷ yw hon . . . Dyma fi ar faes yr Eisteddfod. Merch yn dod i gwrdd â mi ac er fy mod yn gwybod ei bod hithau'n fardd ni chefais ferch arall erioed i gydnabod Hon ynof i. Sgwrs i'r cyfeiriad yn dilyn – 'Ydi'r gŵr efo chi? O, rydw i'n leicio'ch het chi.' Minnau'n ei gadael i lusgo i gwr arall o'r maes. Un o ŵyr yr Awen yn dod i gwrdd a mi. 'Helo, Dilys fach, sut mae'r ysbryd? Oes tipyn o arddeliad yr Awen yn ddiweddar? Welais i fawr o'th waith ers tro.' Minnau'n teimlo fel dweud fy nghwyn yn erbyn yr hon arall – ei mynd tragwyddol; ei hen gydwybod bach anniddig; ei thrwsio a'i thacluso; ei bysedd prysur yn lladrata pob eiliad werthfawr.[115]

> [There are two women living in our house. They wear the same clothes, eat the same food and claim the same armchair when the rare moment of leisure presents itself. Indeed, the two wear the same flesh and the same heart beats within them. I am both of them. But I haven't decided which of the two is me . . . They have never become reconciled with each other. But one is more content with her companion than the other is. To define them broadly I'd say that She is a Poet and she is a

housewife . . . Here am I on the Eisteddfod field. A woman comes to meet me and though I know that she's a poet I never had another woman acknowledge Her in me. A chat in this direction follows: 'Is your husband with you? Oh, I do like your hat.' I leave her and drag my way over to another corner of the field. One of the men of the Muse comes to meet me. 'Hello, Dilys darling, how are your spirits? Has the Muse claimed you recently? I haven't seen much of your work for a while.' I feel like complaining about the other her – her constant activity; her uncomfortable little conscience; her mending and tidying; her busy fingers stealing every valuable second.]

Such an anguished expression of duality in the roles of poet and woman is comparable to the themes of duality already seen in the works of Welsh women writers such as Moelona and, somewhat differently, in Allen Raine. Although these women wrote in two distinct languages, their experience of being a 'woman of letters' in a Welsh context appears to be similar, and similarly problematic.

Despite the difficulties and apparent prejudice faced by Cadwaladr, she undoubtedly did enjoy some success, especially in National Eisteddfod competitions. Her powerful 1945 ode 'Bara' (Bread), written for the National Eisteddfod, deals in a majestic and epic fashion with the suffering and aftermath of the Second World War. 'Bara' emphasizes physical want and suffering, and is set in a landscape of post-war devastation:

Mae'r cnawd yn pydru ar sgerbydau'r plant,
   A bronnau'r gwragedd fel orennau gwyw.
Pa gellwair oerllyd yw murmuron sant?
   Heb fara, ar beth y byddwn byw?
[. . .]

Yr hwn a rydd im faeth a gaiff y galon
   Sy'n llusgo yn y llaid pan gerddwyf i;
A chaiff ei thalu'n llog i'r Temtiwr rhadlon
   Sy'n gwneud anialwch o'n credoau ni[116]

[The flesh is rotting on the children's bones,
The women's withered breasts, like fruit, are dead.
There's a grim joke in what the saint intones,
For what are we to live on, without bread?
[. . .]

He who gives me food will receive my heart
That's dragging in the dust and craves relief;
The heart that yields to the kind Tempter's art
Who makes a barren waste of our belief.]

Dilys Cadwaladr was primarily a poet, but she did publish one volume of short stories and a number of autobiographical writings. *Storïau* (1936) is, as its early reviewer, Kate Roberts, pointed out, an uneven collection. Some stories are rather cloyingly pious, while another, 'Yr Hen Oruchwyliaeth'[117] (The Old Stewardship), contains a disquieting caricature of a 'greasy', exploitative Jew, echoing some of the pervasive anti-Semitism of the period, powerfully challenged by the work of the Welsh-Jewish writer Lily Tobias, discussed below. Other stories, however, show a fine talent for satire, which is slightly reminiscent of the tone of Dorothy Edwards, when she allows a first-person speaker unwittingly to mock himself. Such is the case in Cadwaladr's 'Y Pagan', whose first-person speaker is one of a progressive community of artist types who have taken over the Welsh village of Abereira and have 'cleansed' it of its native Welsh population in order to do so.[118] Another memorable story in quite a different register is 'Y Peswch' (The Cough), in which a young girl listens, horrified, to the persistent coughing of her mother in the room next door.[119] The cough itself acquires a nightmarish life of its own until the inevitable end, when the mother dies and the child is bereft in the sudden silence. Cadwaladr stated that the story was directly autobiographical – she lost her mother, after a long illness, at the age of eleven.[120] Madness is the subject of the story entitled, ironically, 'Dyn Call' (A Sane Man). From the point of view of the child narrator, Uncle Huw is perfectly sane and sensible: he does things children understand, such as playing around and believing in fairies. However, the narrator is sent away to be a maidservant miles away, and by the time she returns, two years later, she finds that Uncle Huw has been sent to Denbigh asylum ('gwallgofdy Dinbych').[121] Two other strong stories are 'Y Forwyn Ffôl'[122] (The Foolish Maid) and 'Y Gwesteion'[123] (The Guests), both of which have central female protagonists but from opposite ends of the social spectrum. The 'foolish maid' is Miss Pugh, a newly retired headmistress who has kept herself under a tight rein of discipline all her life. She has sacrificed love and now that it manifests itself again, it is too late. Ann in 'Y Gwesteion' is 'the poorest person in the parish' ('y dlotaf yn y plwyf')[124] and the story concerns her sacrifice to buy jam and cheese for the schoolteacher who promises to visit. However, the teacher forgets her promise and the old woman dies in disappointment, the mice creeping out to eat the cheese. Clearly there are echoes here of Caradoc Evans's notorious story, 'Be This Her Memorial',[125] but Cadwaladr's story is full of empathy for the penniless old woman, in contrast with the cold savagery of Evans's satire.

A contemporary of Cadwaladr, the English-language Welsh poet Lynette Roberts, was just as ambitious and even more iconoclastic in her poetic output. She attempted the epic mode in some of her most notable poetry of the Second World War, an unusual, authoritative voice for a female poet to adopt. As we have seen so far, with the exception of Dilys Cadwaladr and her late nineteenth-century forerunner, Cranogwen, Welsh women poets tended to adopt shorter, lyrical forms. Although the grand sweep of epic verse has often, if erroneously, been regarded as beyond the scope of the female poet, it is clear that a number of women poets of this period felt that the experience of war called for epic expression. Roberts is a bold and experimental war poet, whose major work is the book-length 'heroic poem', 'Gods with Stainless Ears'.[126] Although this was not published until 1951, it is a poem which chronicles, albeit in a fictionalized, surrealist and often hallucinatory style, some of Lynette Roberts's own experiences during 1941–3 as a woman left alone by war in a small village in rural Carmarthenshire, Llanybri. Roberts's editor, Patrick McGuinness, has expressed the tone of her work very aptly in stating that 'her poems reflect the drudgery, fretfulness and inertia of one woman's life in wartime'.[127] The poem is an extraordinary mixture of humdrum domestic detail and epic grandiloquence. She has been described as a 'naive modernist', whose work is challenging and innovative but lacks the characteristic irony of the better-known modernists, like T.S. Eliot (who was her editor at Faber in the 1940s and 50s). Roberts's work has a distinctive verbal texture; as Tony Conran puts it, she 'throw[s] her language at you like a bombardment':[128]

> Overseas battles in circles of lust:
> Spirit put to no better purpose than
> Grain of sand. Overwhich. Backwards and
> Forwards soldiers ran. Such battles of mule
> Stubbornness; or retreat from vast stone walls,
>
> Brought non-existence of past, present and
> Future 1, 2, 1, 2, 1, 2, left, right, left, right,
> Accumulating into a monotonous pattern
> Of dereliction and gloom. When battles should be
> Fought at Home: as trencher-companions. *He at my side.*[129]

In this section the female speaker laments and longs for her absent lover who, as a soldier, is engaged in fruitless, circular, barren battles abroad. The description contrasts with repeated positive evocations of 'Saint Cadoc's estuary', a bird-loud sanctuary whose ferryman, John Roberts, is a benign Charon and whose fertile soil, in 'striped tidy plot[s] aproned women work, / Spading clay and coal dust into "pele" jet'.[130] The juxtaposition is clear: the soldiers' circular marching in foreign fields is pointless, while the women who stay behind, suffering from *hiraeth* for their men, are engaged in productive work, such as making coal bricks for the domestic hearth. However, Roberts's domesticity is not cosy; she emphasizes, too, women's suffering – the loss of a baby in Part IV, which the woman bears alone, 'no near doctor for six days'.[131] By the last part of the poem, the woman is reunited with her soldier lover and there is a cinematic science-fiction fantasy of escape, but eventually they are forced to return, to a bay which has been frozen and tarnished by mechanized war:

> . . . Down, gunner and black
> Madonna with heart of tin . . .
> . . . To the bay known before,
> The warm and stagnant air raising wellshafts
> Of putrid flesh sunk deep in desert sands. Stepped out onto
> Blue blaze of snow. Barbed wire. No man of bone.
> A placard to the right which concerned us:
>
> *Mental Home for Poets*. He alone on this
> Isotonic plain: against a jingle of Generals
> And Cabinet Directors determined
> a stand. Declared a Faith. Entered 'Foreign
> Field' like a Plantagenet King: his spirit
>
> Gorsefierce: hands like perfect quatrains . . .
> . . . Catoptric on waterice he of deep love
> Frees dragon from the glacier glade
> Sights death fading into chilblain ears.[132]

It is difficult to determine the tone of the ending; on the one hand, there is a suggestion of defiant, even nationalistic, rebellion in the image of 'freeing the dragon' from the ice which entraps it, and the suggestion of death receding into silence perhaps looks towards a tenuous survival, yet the chillingly modernist, technological landscape which has overwhelmed the formerly knowable, communal and natural bay leaves a bitter aftertaste. The narrative of the poem, despite being explained in a prose 'argument' preceding each section, is actually less coherent and less convincing than the poem's overall impressionistic evocation of a west Wales enclave becoming a wasteland, all the more striking for the strange vocabulary drawn from chemistry, botany, and geology which is used to create this unnerving, cinematic picture. Nevertheless, Roberts's modernist techniques are no more puzzling or disorientating than those of T. S. Eliot himself in 'The Waste Land'. It might even be that Eliot championed Roberts's work because he saw in it a Second World War version of his own anguished, truncated epic of the First World War and its aftermath. Unfortunately, 'Gods with Stainless Ears' – perhaps partly because of the poet's gender and nationality – has suffered critical neglect until very recently.

Another writer of the period who has suffered complete neglect until recently is the Jewish-Welsh novelist Lily Tobias, who offers an interesting and distinctive view of Wales in her work. The implicit identification between the Welsh and the Jews in a range of early twentieth-century Welsh women's writing becomes in the work of Tobias both explicit and problematic. Just as we observed Moelona's feminist and nationalist allegiances coming into conflict in her novel *Ffynnonloyw*, so Tobias repeatedly dramatizes the potential and actual conflicts between Welsh and Jewish identities. Tobias, born and raised in Ystalyfera, like the later novelist Menna Gallie, was sympathetic towards both the Welsh language and Welsh nationalist aspirations, although her political allegiance was emphatically socialist. Her early works explore parallels between Welsh and Jewish cultures and aspirations, as indicated by the cover of her first published work, *The Nationalists and other Goluth Studies* (1921), which shows a Star of David and a Welsh dragon intertwined.[133] In the later novel *Eunice Fleet* (1933), as Jasmine Donahaye has pointed out, Tobias deliberately downplays both Welsh and Jewish cultural difference 'in order to make her overriding pacifist message more palatable to an English audience'.[134] Nevertheless, the construction of the conscientious objector as the hero of the text, together with its call for 'radical political change',[135] can be seen as arising directly out of a distinctively south Welsh pacifist and socialist tradition.

During the period 1921–45, then, the effects of the First World War and the Depression may be seen on the ways in which Welsh women writers respond to and represent Wales. Many, understandably, lose faith in Wales as a soteriological landscape or 'land of the white gloves', and their writings construct an Other Wales of lost sons and brothers, growing political activism, labour unrest, unemployment, rural depopulation and poverty. In the work of authors such as Kate Roberts and Elena Puw-Morgan, labouring-class women's experience is foregrounded in a new way, placing the penniless maidservant and the struggling mother at the centre of consciousness. Writers from a different class background (such as Eiluned Lewis) nostalgically evoke a Welsh rural idyll, while acknowledging the encroaching proximity of the industrialized South. The effects of the First World War are felt by the Welsh women at home in many of these writings, most movingly in Roberts's *Traed mewn Cyffion*. At the end of the period, the Second World War is also addressed as a contemporary catastrophe by writers such as Lynette Roberts, Hilda Vaughan, Dilys Cadwaladr and Kate Bosse-Griffiths. In these writings the mechanized destruction of the war comes terrifyingly closer than in representations of the First World War, threatening literally to tear through Wales. Hilda Vaughan juxtaposes the bombing of London with the peace of rural Wales in *Pardon and Peace*, but reveals clearly that Wales is itself not a timeless Eden immune from destructive forces; it, too, is ravaged. Vaughan's prolific output also dramatizes the un-idyllic aspects of life in rural mid Wales, focusing particularly on issues of women's inheritance and land-ownership, also a prominent concern in Welsh-language women's writing, such as that of Elena Puw-Morgan. One of the continuing tropes of Welsh women's writing of this era, as in the first two decades of the century, is that of dispossession and eviction; arguably, the women of Wales had been cheated of the 'sacred place' promised by the 1904–5 Revival and have been left instead with a fallen land, literally scarred, and bereft of many of its young people.

3 Awakening Place: 1946–1977

Deirdre Beddoe has argued that during this period Welsh women were subjected to contradictory pressures, pushed back towards traditional domestic roles and femininity on the one hand, 'after their wartime sortie into the world of paid work', and on the other, impelled forward to greater liberation by economic and technological advances, as well as by their own ambitions.[1] Of course, Welsh women writers themselves frequently had direct experience of wartime service in both World Wars: Hilda Vaughan, for instance, 'served for two years in a Red Cross hospital and subsequently for three years as organizing secretary of the Women's Land Army in Breconshire and Radnorshire, a job which she did well'.[2] Others, like Kate Bosse-Griffiths, were staunch pacifists. In the Second World War, Judith Maro, born and raised in Jerusalem and trained in handling arms and self-defence, served in the ATS, tasting her first, strange experience of anti-Semitism from the British army chaplain she worked alongside.[3] Myfanwy Haycock worked both in a munitions factory and a barrage balloon factory, though neither of those experiences colour the nostalgic, Georgian lyricism of her verse.[4]

After the period of austerity and rationing which followed the end of the war, political developments began to change the face of Wales in the 1950s and 60s. In 1947 the coal industry was nationalized, bringing a marked shift in working practices and experiences for industrial workers, a shift reflected, for example, in Menna Gallie's 1962 novel, *The Small Mine*. During the later 1950s Plaid Cymru gained in popular support and its first MP, Gwynfor Evans, was elected in 1966. Saunders Lewis's radio speech, 'Tynged yr Iaith' (The Fate of the Language) of 1962 had direct political consequences in the founding of *Cymdeithas yr Iaith Gymraeg*, which grew in strength and efficacy during the 1960s and 70s. The physical landscape of Wales was itself being transformed, with the flooding of valleys to construct dams, the planting of huge areas of coniferous forests by the Forestry Commission, and the depopulation of the Welsh hill-country, so movingly lamented in R. S. Thomas's poetry of the 1950s. In the 1970s Wales began to experience the new wave of feminism that was changing women's lives and expectations in the western world, helped along by technological and medical advances, such as the invention of the contraceptive pill. All these changes find their expression either directly or implicitly in the literary production of Welsh women of the period.

Many works of the late 1940s, not unnaturally, are set just before or during the Second World War period and consider the ways in which the experiences of those years changed Wales and its people. Jane Ann Jones's 1949 novel *Y Bryniau Pell* (The Far Hills) displays a marked shift in tone from the comic satire of her *Storïau Hen Ferch* (1937). The text is in three parts, each of which has a topographical subtitle: 'Haul ar Fryn' (Sunshine on a Hill), 'Yr Anial Dir' (The Wasteland) and 'Y Bryniau Pell' (The Far Hills). The setting is Flintshire during the period 1926–46. Kate Morris is the central consciousness of the novel, an intelligent, sensible and liberal woman married to John, a railway signalman and ardent socialist. The Morris family, with their two children, Nan and Alun, are juxtaposed with the family of the *Mans*, the Revd Isaac Jones and his wife Miriam, their adopted daughter Lina and son Ifor John. Initially, the politicized topography is hopeful ('haul ar fryn'), with Kate working diligently for peace in the 'Cynghrair y Cenhedloedd'[5] (League of Nations) and John believing in the coming socialist revolution. The Jones family, conversely, seems to represent a moribund, apolitical Wales, where chapel and propriety take the place of ideals. Three of the children 'escape' Wales in early adulthood to gain jobs in England, while the fourth, Nan, leaves Wales in the final pages of the book to go and join her Australian serviceman husband in his country. Despite this exodus, the characters are sporadically self-conscious of their Welshness. When Nan first meets Lyn, the Australian who will become her husband, she is deeply offended when he assumes that she is English. With a touch of her old humour, Jane Ann Jones remarks: 'Suddenly, Nan was more of a Welshwoman than any of the hot-headed members of the

[Welsh] Nationalist Party' ('Ar unwaith, yr oedd Nan yn fwy o Gymraes na'r un o aelodau chwilboeth y Blaid Gendlaethol').[6]

The Dinbych (Denbigh) Eisteddfod in 1939 proves a watershed for all the characters – in what they realize are the last days of freedom, they enjoy being safely Welsh on the eisteddfod field, spotting famous names such as Caradog Prichard and Kate Roberts. Meanwhile, John has vivid memories of his own experiences of war in France in 1914–18 – the whole horror of it comes back to him. His worst fears are realized when their son, Alun, is killed in action and Lyn is taken prisoner in Germany. The womenfolk take some comfort from hymns, especially the verse, 'I gaze across the far hills / Seeking you constantly, / Come, my Love, it's getting late / And my sun's almost setting' ('Rwy'n edrych dros y bryniau pell / Amdanat pob yn awr, / Tyrd, fy Anwylyd, mae'n hwyrhau / A'm haul bron mynd i lawr').[7] As this quotation from the Williams Pantycelyn hymn indicates, the 'far hills' which give the novel its title are not simply descriptions of the distant lands to which the young soldiers and airmen must travel in the war, or even references to the remote Clwydian hills behind the little village of Llan Morfa, the novel's setting; rather, they are landscapes of the imagination, indicative of desire, whether that be hope of a Christian afterlife or for consummation of passions in this life. Nan imagines the Blue Mountains of south-west Australia not simply as a geographical destination, but as a symbolic promised land. Yet the Australian, Lyn, is continually taken aback by Welsh people's patriotism – he observes that they think of themselves as a 'chosen people', '[c]enedl etholedig'.[8] The end of the novel is not triumphant in tone at all; it is suffused with the sadness of loss and separation. Wales is a different and despoiled place from what it had been at the beginning of the novel, though Kate, the mother figure, is left to struggle on alone in the 'hen wlad' (old land) because she cannot bring herself to abandon it.

The year 1949, the date of publication of *Y Bryniau Pell*, saw the beginning of the second phase of Kate Roberts's writing career, one which would be even more productive than the period 1925–37, when she published six volumes of fiction. A number of critics have noted that both her writing periods seemed to have been precipitated by an experience of personal loss, namely the loss of her brother in the First World War and the sudden death of her husband, Morris T. Williams, in 1946. Her first publication after this bereavement was *Stryd y Glep* (Gossip Row, 1949). This is described on the frontispiece as a 'stori fer hir' (a long short story) and is set in one of the years immediately preceding the Second World War.

Stryd y Glep is the diary of Ffebi, a woman in late middle age who has been confined to bed for the past three years, as a result of an accident which has damaged her spine. Thus, the confines of her world have shrunk to the four walls of her sickroom, and this constricted space is used by Kate Roberts as an image of the withering and narrowing of Ffebi's soul. Once a week, on a Sunday evening, her room becomes the centre where all the inhabitants of the street come together after chapel for an intensive session of gossip: 'This house is worse than chapel house on a Sunday for gossiping' ('Mae'r tŷ yma yn waeth na thŷcapel ar nos Sul am hel straeon').[9] Despite Ffebi's disability, or possibly partly because of it, she is an enthusiastic and unpitying purveyor of gossip. In a way, she behaves like the queen of the street, holding court and being pernickety about who is included in her magic circle and who is excluded. Her diary is written in an extremely lively, colloquial style and appears to offer an unmediated reflection of Ffebi's innermost thoughts. This reflection is not particularly edifying. Roberts is experimenting with placing a thoroughly unheroic character at the centre of her fictional world; the experiment is successful, and unexpectedly ends with the reader feeling some degree of sympathy with Ffebi, despite her machinations.

Roberts employs irony at the expense of her principal character, since the reader can see from an early stage in the narrative that Ffebi is in love with a neighbour and old friend, the widower, Dan, but Ffebi herself seems quite unaware of her own feelings. Her unacknowledged love makes her behave cruelly towards another woman who has her eye on Dan, Miss Jones. Gradually, though, Ffebi becomes more self-reflective and begins to realize what motivates her own, often underhand, actions. She begins to perceive that this little community which gathers around her is pointless and inconsequential:

meddwl y byddaf i am bob Stryd y Glep yn y byd yma, a phob sgwrs, a'r holl filiynau o bobl ym mhob gwlad yn y byd, a phob un yn dweud neu wneud rhywbeth ar nos Sul . . . Felly, pa bwysigrwydd a oedd yn heno i ni? Dim, ond un noson arall a'i siarad gwag wedi mynd i lawr efo'r afon i'r môr.[10]

[I think about every Gossip Row in this world, and every conversation, and all the millions of people in every country in the world, and every single one of them saying or doing something on a Sunday evening . . . So, what importance did tonight have for us? None at all, it was just one more evening with its empty talk gone down the river to the sea.]

'Gossip Row', then, is seen as a microcosm, not merely of the 'milltir sgwâr' (square mile) or even of Wales, but of the whole world. Nevertheless, Ffebi's emphasis on the activities of the Sunday, and her confederates' weekly dissection of the minister's usually unsatisfactory sermon, makes this particular construction of 'Gossip Row' unmistakably Welsh. Despite this less than flattering picture of Nonconformist Wales, it is the minister himself, the sincere Mr Jones, who eventually helps Ffebi see that 'this narrow old street is having an effect on you' ('hen stryd gul yma'n effeithio arnoch chi').[11] By the end of the diary, Ffebi resolves to change her life, but there is no real closure to her story; Roberts deliberately leaves open whether that resolution will be acted upon or whether 'stryd y glep' will carry on with its gossip much as before. Roberts's literary representation of pre-war Wales, then, is negative: an introverted, incestuous place where women's lives, particularly, are restricted and unfulfilling. Ffebi's paralysis can be interpreted symbolically as an image of the way traditional Nonconformist Wales hobbles women's desires and aspirations.

The diary format with which Kate Roberts experimented in *Stryd y Glep* is used again in some passages of her next novel, *Y Byw Sy'n Cysgu* (The Living Sleep, 1956), which is also a deeply pessimistic novel, concerning a woman, Lora Ffennig, who has been abandoned by her husband. Technically, it is an experimental novel which takes Kate Roberts away from her usual realist mode into lengthy passages of dream and interior monologue. It is possible to see the novel as an exploration of Roberts's own feelings after her bereavement, when she was also 'left' by her husband; at any rate, the penetration into Lora's inner world is deep and convincing. She begins to depend on the journal that she writes, looking forward to pouring out her feelings into her book, rather like the character Ann Goodman in Margiad Evans's 1932 novella, *Country Dance*. Lora sees this therapeutic act of writing as an effort at self-knowledge: 'going to meet her own self' ('mynd i gyfarfod a hi ei hun').[12] For Lora is deeply repressed by her upbringing and her moral values; she knows that she would take her husband back if he were to return, not because she loves him but in order to appear respectable.

Another man, Aleth Meurig, wishes to marry Lora, but she refuses
to seek a divorce through the courts; as Meurig reflects,

> Pobl o'r wlad oeddynt o hyd, a Chymry at hynny, ac yr oedd pobl
> Cymru yn methu mwynhau eu pleserau am fod arnynt ofn peidio â
> bod yn dduwiol, ac yn methu mwynhau eu duwioldeb am fod arnynt
> eisiau dilyn eu chwantau.[13]

> [They were still country people, and Welsh people to boot, and the
> people of Wales were unable to enjoy their pleasures because they were
> afraid of not being pious, and they were unable to enjoy their piety
> because they wanted to pursue their desires.]

Not much is resolved in the workings of the plot: Iolo does not
return, Lora does not marry again, but there is a sense in which
Lora has found an awakening at last from her 'living sleep'.[14] At the
same time that this is a novel which engages specifically with Welsh
society and gender politics, it may also be seen as reflecting some of
the British literary Zeitgeist. The year of the publication of *Y Byw
sy'n Cysgu*, 1956, was also the year in which John Osborne's *Look
Back in Anger* premiered on the London stage. The notion of the
'living sleep' is addressed in Osborne's play by Jimmy Porter, who
challenges his audience with the suggestion: 'I've an idea. Why don't
we have a little game? Let's pretend that we're human beings, and
that we're actually alive. Just for a while. What do you say? Let's
pretend we're human.'[15]

There are some similarities between *Y Byw Sy'n Cysgu* and
another Welsh novel, published in the following year, Kate Bosse-
Griffiths's second novel, *Mae'r Galon wrth y Llyw* ('The Heart is at
the Tiller' 1957). This work juxtaposes two women, one, Siân, who
espouses traditional gender expectations and the other, Doris, who is
more forthright and feminist. (Siân is very similar to Lora Ffenig, in
Roberts's novel, in her situation as a 'wronged' wife and in her
concern for appearances and respectability.) Bosse-Griffiths goes
further than Kate Roberts, however, in addressing topics which were
still widely held to be taboo in Welsh writing, especially by women,
including adultery, attempted suicide and abortion. In common with
her earlier stories, however, this is primarily a novel of ideas, in which
characters debate moral issues and conundrums with one another.
Bosse-Griffiths is, in some ways, an intellectual novelist not dissimilar to Raymond Williams, who published his first novel, *Border*

111

Country, three years later. Unlike the allegorical setting of Bosse-Griffiths's earlier story, 'Fy Chwaer Efa', however, this novel has a recognizably Welsh setting, alternating between a small town in rural west Wales and a university city (like Swansea) on the south coast during the 1930s. The novel has a satirical edge when it discusses small-town mores; for the inhabitants of Bryn Coed, *parchusrwydd* (respectability) is everything. Scattered throughout the text are unattributed gossiping voices – the communal opinion of Bryn Coed, not unlike the inveterate gossipers of Roberts's *Stryd y Glep* – commenting on the behaviour of their neighbours.

The main character, Doris, a trainee nurse, clashes with her academic father continually; she starts to learn Greek and he asks her why she doesn't learn something practical, like shorthand, betraying his own limited views of gender roles.[16] Despite Doris's ambitions and strength of personality, she is morally strict, even dogmatic, believing implicitly in the 'Profiad Mawr' (Great Experience) which awaits her once she meets the right man. Unfortunately, when she does meet Arthur, the 'Profiad Mawr' is denied her because he is already engaged and soon to be married to Siân. The description of Doris's resultant unhappiness uses an interesting and specifically south Welsh spatial simile: 'A wall had risen up around her and she could not escape from it, like a collier closed off from the world by a fall of stones, and who beats against the wall that traps him' ('Yr oedd mur yn tyfu o'i hamgylch a hithau'n methu ei osgoi, fel glöwr sy'n cael ei gau i ffwrdd oddi wrth y byd gan gwymp o gerrig, ac sy'n curo yn erbyn y mur a ffurfiodd o'i gwmpas').[17] Doris eventually marries another man, John, and Arthur fulfils his promise to Siân; there is a convincing exploration of the two unhappy marriages, which on the surface appear 'perfect'. Arthur's description of his home is apt: 'We have a house in a quiet little town. It's like an enchanted castle. Whoever comes in is turned into a wooden doll' ('Mae gennym ni dŷ mewn tref fach dawel. Mae'n debyg i gastell hud. Pwy bynnag ddaw i mewn, fe gaiff ei droi yn ddol bren').[18] After the death of one of her children, Doris makes a decision, rejects *parchusrwydd* and contacts Arthur – an adulterous affair begins, for Doris realizes that she is not the kind of woman who can sacrifice herself indefinitely. Ultimately, the affair is discovered and Doris dies from the after-effects of trying to induce in herself an abortion. Near the end of the novel Siân vindictively burns a satin dress bought by Doris for her daughter, Eluned, a scene which appears to be a deliberate echo of the closing description of Elena Puw-Morgan's *Y Wisg Sidan*. Since Bosse-Griffiths is such an overtly feminist writer, it may not be too far-fetched to suggest that the burning of that emblem of femininity when the character is a small girl, rather than when she is an old woman, as in the earlier novel, is suggestive of some of the advances made in feminism in the intervening period. Nevertheless, on the whole, the novel presents a bleak picture of a Wales where contraception and abortion are unavailable, and women are still expected to uphold flawless reputations and perform traditional roles. Bosse-Griffiths is particularly astute in revealing the hypocrisy and sheer spite which simmer under the surface of apparently idyllic small Welsh towns. What she is not so successful in doing is creating believable characters; they all tend to be embodiments of ideas and intellectual positions.

Generically, *Mae'r Galon wrth y Llyw* masquerades as a romance; both the title and the original dustjacket, featuring a fashionable-looking young woman, give this impression. Nevertheless, it is unmistakably a novel of ideas and, in this regard, can be regarded as representative of a slight generic shift in Welsh women's writing. The novelists of the early decades of the century used the romance form as a matter of course, even if they made attempts to subvert it in some ways, but from the late 1950s onwards women writers often abandon the romance and experiment with less formulaic fictional forms. Alternatively, if romance occurs, it is anatomized and questioned, instead of being taken for granted as a desired and inevitable 'happy ending'.

Margiad Evans's work as a novelist has been discussed earlier, but in this period she also produced a volume of poems, *A Candle Ahead* (1956). Published just two years before her death, it consists of a series of mystical, intense first-person lyrics, which engage with the natural world, memory and disappointed love. Only 'To My Sister Siân' refers specifically to Wales and, in tone, it is not dissimilar to Eiluned Lewis's *Dew on the Grass*, conjuring up an idyllic childhood and an inseparable sibling relationship. Evans evokes a lost landscape of 'candles of daffodils', 'the haunted graveyard', 'the jay woods . . . mushroom mountains . . . the old cider orchards'.[19] The sisters in childhood are seen as completely self-sufficient and self-absorbed: 'All the places were us, we were all the places / . . . we were our country.'[20] The implicit suggestion here is that such total introspection and lack of other allegiances and relationships is impossible in adulthood; like Lucy at the end of *Dew in the Grass*, the child begins to perceive the reality of countries other than those of her own imagination, countries which may demand loyalty and even sacrifice.

Eigra Lewis Roberts's early novels, beginning with *Brynhyfryd* in 1959, are often seen as representing the 'generation gap' which came into being after the end of the Second World War, and which is already hinted at in the contrast between parents and children in a novel such as Jane Ann Jones's *Y Bryniau Pell* (1949). *Brynhyfryd* (Pleasant Hill, 1959) is, as the title indicates, a novel about a place. Brynhyfryd is a row of houses near a village in north Wales; the novel concerns the lives of the characters who live here, their interconnections and intrigues and, above all, their varying attitudes towards the place. The descriptive opening sets the scene – a foggy, sleepy Monday evening, with nothing much happening. In the opening paragraphs, no people appear; instead, the narrator refers to Brynhyfryd as if it were itself a person, in possession of everything and everyone in its vicinity: 'Brynhyfryd's lights . . . Brynhyfryd's people . . . Brynhyfryd's doors . . .' ('goleuadau Brynhyfryd . . . pobl Brynhyfryd . . . drysau Brynhyfryd . . .').[21] An atmosphere of quiet monotony is established. Marian, a lonely and repressed woman in her late twenties, takes pride in her immaculate house in Brynhyfryd, which has taken the place of the lover who abandoned her eight years before. For her, Brynhyfryd is her life; next door to her, though, is Gwenan, who regards Brynhyfryd as a 'a hole of a place . . . a hell of a hole' ('twll o le . . . cythral o dwll'),[22] and longs for escape, in contrast to her mother, who revels in 'the heaven of her back-kitchen with its stove which was her god' ('nefoedd ei chegin fach a'i stôf yn dduw iddi').[23] Another family, the Thomases, appear contented in Brynhyfryd, but Elin, the mother, secretly longs for a lost past life of freedom with her first husband, Chris, an artist. Widowed and remarried, she is on the surface a perfect Welsh Mam, a little old-fashioned in her dedication to housework. She enjoys her washing day on Tuesdays because it gives her time on her own to dream and think about the past; she refuses her eldest daughter's suggestion that they buy one of the new washing machines: 'life would be just a naked farce if she had to stand there, her hands folded, watching some square machine robbing her of her Tuesday mornings' ('ni fyddai bywyd ond ffars noeth petai hi'n gorfod sefyll yno, â'i dwylo ymhleth, i wylio rhyw beiriant sgwâr yn ei rheibio hi o'i bore Mawrth').[24]

Times are changing and youth culture is beginning to creep even as far as Brynhyfryd: Gwenan and her friend, Pari, go to the Club to hear 'the skiffle band from Gors' ('bois sgiffl y Gors').[25] Gwenan longs for a new world of freedom away from the oppressive respectability of Brynhyfryd, whereas her brother Robin, though he enjoys going to the cinema to see Marilyn Monroe, wants to stay in Brynhyfryd forever. Gwenan remembers a verse she learned at school, about 'The land beyond the mountain, its hedges always green, / The land of fairies and giants, and a myriad wonders' ('Y wlad tu hwnt i'r mynydd, a'i llwyni byth yn wyrdd, / Bro'r tylwyth teg a'r cewri, a rhyfeddodau myrdd'), a dream landscape for which she unrealistically craves.[26] Alun Thomas, meanwhile, initially feels oppressed by Brynhyfryd and then gradually comes to recognize it as part of his growing commitment to Welsh Nationalism. In the eisteddfod, Alun defends Wales against a fellow student who argues that the country has no future, and suddenly comes to the realization 'how much Wales meant to him. Wales, and Brynhyfryd. Brynhyfryd was Wales to him' ('gymaint yr oedd Cymru yn ei olygu iddo. Cymru, a Brynhyfryd. Brynhyfryd oedd Cymru iddo ef').[27] This is a very overt description of the way in which the 'milltir sgwâr' can become a microcosm for Wales as a whole. Gwenan, though, cuts the ties, balks at attending chapel and moves to Penmor, a seaside town, where she gains her independence. Eigra Lewis Roberts was only nineteen when she won the National Eisteddfod Prose Medal for *Brynhyfryd*; her youth may be partly responsible for the authenticity of her rendition of the younger generation's rebellion against their elders.

Her 1966 novel, *Tŷ ar y Graig* (House on the Rock), also revolves around a sense of place and belonging. The central character, Enid, is someone who has never felt at home anywhere, especially not in the north Welsh slate-quarrying town where she was born. Her father, a quarryman all his adult life, had moved there from the countryside, and Enid feels obscurely cheated of a rural homeland that she idealizes and longs for but can never have. She explains:

> pan es i oddi cartra' yn gynta' . . . es i'r wlad, i Sir Gaernarfon. Ac mi welis ffynnon a rhedyn. Mi ddalias amal i flewyn o wair rhwng fy nannadd. Yr oedd o i gyd gen i. Ond theimlais i ddim. R' o'n i'n ddiarth er imi aros yno ddwy flynadd . . . A diarth yr ydw i wedi bod, byth ers hynny. Lle bynnag yr awn i, ni a chi oedd hi.[28]

[when I first left home ... I went to the countryside, to Caernarfonshire. And I saw a spring rising amid ferns. I held a few blades of grass between my teeth. I had it all. But I felt nothing. I was a stranger although I stayed there two years ... And I've been a stranger ever since. Wherever I went, it would be me and them.]

Enid's 'strangeness', her inability to belong, has made her into an embittered and vindictive, as well as a lonely woman. She now lives in London and seems to relish its anonymity. The novel chronicles a rare visit to her north Wales home at Christmas, when she determines to spoil what she sees as the deadly respectability of her sister, Mari, and their mother by revealing the secret of Mari's having had an illegitimate child years before. For Enid, the family house, 'Bron Graig' (Heart of the Rock), and the slate tip behind it are ugly reminders of her unhappiness and isolation. The title reference to the 'house on the rock' is both a literal description of the family home and a biblical allusion, which is used against her sister by Mari when they quarrel. Mari remembers her grandmother's advice to 'build her house upon a rock', a concept which Enid dismisses with scorn. She resolves never to return to her mother's house again: 'If mother wants to see me, she'll have to meet me on my own territory.' 'And where's that? [asks Mari] Are you going to graze on someone else's land forever?' ('Os ydi mam am fy ngweld i, mi geith fy nghyfarfod i ar fy nhir fy hun.' 'A lle mae hwnnw? [gofynna Mari] Wyt ti am bori ar dir rhywun arall am byth?')[29] Mari's taunt about 'grazing on someone else's land' is apter than she knows, since the only relationship the lonely Enid has in London is with a married man, Peter. While Mari and her mother are at the heart of a traditional Welsh community, Enid is an outsider who secretly mocks their conventionality; of her mother, she thinks: 'You've got your chapel and your WI. And above all else you've got your respectability' ('Mae ganddoch chi'ch capal a'r WI. Ac mae ganddoch chi'ch parch yn fwy na dim').[30]

Both of Eigra Lewis Roberts's novels of this period deal centrally with the relationship of the individual and the native place. Her work represents a traditional Welsh culture and society clashing with new ways of life and expectations, especially for women. She shows how migration from the country to the town, from farming to industry, from Wales to England, has transformed Welsh society, which is constantly in the process of remaking itself, and yet at the same time the 'old ways' are, for some communities, remarkably resilient. She is particularly adept at revealing how place and a sense of belonging can be restrictive and enchaining (and it is this, above all, perhaps, which has led many critics to compare her work with that of Kate Roberts), but at the same time she also presents, in the character of Enid, a dispiriting portrait of a life without any roots.

Kate Roberts's *Y Lôn Wen* (The White Lane, 1960) is subtitled *'Darn o Hunangofiant'* (A Fragment of Autobiography), and it takes the form of a series of 'pictures' of different aspects of Roberts's early life. The text is less a personal memoir than a portrayal of a family and a whole community, as indicated by the titles of some of the chapters: 'Diwylliant a'r Capel' (Culture and the Chapel) and 'Fy Mam' (My Mother). In fact, for an autobiographer, Roberts is noticeably reticent to say much about herself.

The first chapter, entitled 'Darluniau' (Pictures) is couched in the present tense and offers a series of vivid, chronological snapshots of the author's early childhood. When she visits her grandmother's house, the child's gaze takes in every detail of the interior and the garden:

> Mae dyrnau pres y dresel yn fy wynebu fel rhes o lygaid gloywon. Oddi ar y mur mae dau ewythr yn edrych arnaf o dan aeliau trymion . . . Mae cwrlid coch ar y bwrdd a Beibl mawr yn agored arno, sbectol ar y Beibl a'i breichiau wedi croesi fel coesau pry' . . . [Tu allan] mae cychod gwenyn ar un ochr fel nifer o dai bychain twt, ond nid wyf i fod i fynd yn agos atynt . . . Nid oes ardd debyg i hon yn unlle. Mae fel llyfr wedi ei gau efo chlesbin.[31]

> [The brass knobs of the dresser face me like a row of glistening eyes. From the wall two uncles look at me from beneath their heavy brows . . . There's a red cloth on the table and a big Bible is open on it, a pair of spectacles on the Bible with its arms crossed like the legs of an insect . . . [Outside] there are beehives along one side like a line of neat little houses, but I'm not supposed to go near them . . . There's no garden like this one anywhere else. It's like a book with a clasp to close it.]

Despite her enjoyment of her grandmother's house, the old woman is strict and makes Kate feel inadequate; she reminds her that at her age (ten) her mother had been sent away as a maidservant. Other memories in these fragmented pictures are of the dead body of a quarryman being carried past on a cart; a cold evening in the *seiat* with people 'speaking their experience' ('dweud eu profiadau'); the community coming together for haymaking and choir practices; the death of a calf, at which her mother cries. The 'white lane' of the title leads towards the highest mountains:

Yr ydym yn dringo ac yn dringo nes cyrraedd Pen 'Rallt Fawr. Yr ydym yn gweld reit at Bont y Borth, ond yn gweld peth arall na fedrwn byth ei weld o'n tŷ ni – y Lôn Wen, sy'n mynd dros Foel Smatho i'r Waun-fawr ac i'r Nefoedd.[32]

[We climb and climb until we reach Pen 'Rallt Fawr. We can see as far as Borth Bridge, but we can also see something else that we can't see at all from our house – the White Lane, which goes over Moel Smatho to Waun-fawr and to the Heavens.]

Roberts adopts a very different, adult, academic tone in the narrative of 'Fy Ardal' (My Region), drawing on historical research about the founding of the villages of Rhosgadfan and Rhostryfan, near Caernarfon. The text becomes almost a social history of the area, animated by detailed personal recollections. The interpenetration of literary and real landscapes is suggested by Roberts's remark that when she first read *Wuthering Heights* she immediately thought of her own native region.[33] Interestingly, she also mentions the fiction read in her household at the turn of the century – she remembers particularly enjoying the works of Winnie Parry and Fanny Edwards in *Cymru'r Plant* (Children's Wales), though she did not find Gwyneth Vaughan much to her taste.[34]

In *Y Lôn Wen*, we can see Kate Roberts responding to the impulse to chronicle a disappearing world, much like her predecessor Eluned Morgan, and also in an autobiographical mode, though Roberts is much less revealing of her own feelings than her Romantic predecessor. The last chapter of *Y Lôn Wen*, entitled 'Y Darlun Olaf', is particularly poignant in its shift from the meticulously documented past to the impoverished and regretful present. She reflects:

Pan fûm yn ysgrifennu'r pethau hyn fe gododd y meirw o'u beddau am ysbaid i siarad efo mi. Fe ânt yn ôl i gysgu eto. Ysgrifennais am fy nheulu a'i alw'n hunangofiant, ond yr wyf yn iawn. Fy hanes i fy hun yw hanes fy nheulu . . . Digwyddasai popeth pwysig i mi cyn 1917, popeth dwfn ei argraff.[35]

[As I wrote these things the dead arose from their graves for a while to talk to me. They will go to sleep again. I have written about my family and called it an autobiography but that description is correct. My own history is the history of my family . . . Everything important happened to me before 1917, everything which had a lasting impression.]

In this moving final chapter, Roberts converses with the dead who obligingly rise from their graves, but, in a deeper sense, the memoir is about childhood. The child that Kate Roberts was before 1917, the year in which she lost her brother in the First World War, is the child who comes to life in the early 'pictures' of *Y Lôn Wen*. And that child is still vividly alive in Kate Roberts the elderly woman, still asking questions on the last page of the book.

Roberts's skill at adopting the child's point of view and in bringing alive the immediacy of a child's perceptions is also very much in evidence in one of her most popular works, published just a year before *Y Lôn Wen*, in 1959: the volume of interlinked stories entitled *Te yn y Grug* (Tea in the Heather). This text has enjoyed popularity in its English translation as well and can be regarded as another of those works, quite numerous in modern Welsh women's writing, which are generically hybrid, being simultaneously both juvenile and adult fiction. Like *Y Lôn Wen*, too, there are elements of autobiography in *Te yn y Grug*, which perhaps accounts for the sense of authenticity that the text seems to exude. Its popularity may also be due to its humorous tone, a distinct change from Roberts's characteristic note of sadness. This is largely owing to the comic creation of the irrepressible character Winni Finni Hadog.

The title story of the collection has Begw, the eight-year-old protagonist and, one suspects, a fictional projection of the author herself in her life 'before 1917', going for a picnic on the mountain-side with her friend, Mair. Roberts conveys Begw's intense sensual excitement and anticipation over the wonderful new invention that her mother has prepared for her to eat on the picnic: a bright, quivering, red jelly in a long-stemmed glass. Mair's mother, the minister's wife, is dubious about letting the girls go alone to the mountain, since she is worried that they might be accosted by tramps. But the girls manage to escape and they are indeed accosted, by Winni Finni Hadog, a personage considerably more alarming for them than any tramp. Winni, who swears like a trooper and is dressed in rags, most unlike the two 'proper' little girls, orders them to sit down on a patch of grass in the middle of the heather and proceeds to shock them with her talk. She reveals that she will go into service when she leaves school the following year and plans to go far away, perhaps to London. Her attitude towards her parents is disdainful and she has a defiant look on her face; for Begw, Winni becomes 'a kind of prophet ... looking just like the picture of Daniel in the lions' den' ('fel rhyw fath o broffwyd . . .yn edrych yr un fath â'r llun o Daniel yn ffau'r llewod').[36] Winni confesses to being a dreamer who often has her 'arse whipped before going to bed' ('yn cael chwip din cyn mynd i 'ngwely').[37] Her audience of two are agog and horrified by the extremity of her language, but Winni carries on obliviously, talking always of escape from her violent home. Her dream of freedom consists of becoming a maid-servant to Queen Victoria herself:

> A mi ga'i wisgo cap startsh gwyn ar ben fy shinón, a barclod gwyn, a llinynna hir 'dat odra fy sgert yn i glymu. A mi ga'i ffrog sidan i fynd allan gyda'r nos a breslet aur, a wats aur ar fy mrest yn sownd wrth froitsh aur cwlwm dolan a giard aur fawr yn ddau dro am fy ngwddw fi. A mi ga'i gariad del efo gwallt crychlyd, nid un 'r un fath â'r hen hogia coman sy ffor' ma. A ffarwel i Twm Ffinni Hadog a'i wraig am byth bythoedd.[38]

> [I'll have a white starched cap on my chignon, and a white apron, and long strings down to the hem of my skirt to tie it. And I'll have a silk frock for going out at night and a gold bracelet, and a gold watch on my breast fastened to a bow-knot brooch and a great gold chain in two twists around my neck. And I'll have a handsome sweetheart with curly hair, not one like these common old boys around here. And farewell to Twm Finni Hadog and his wife forever.]

Winni's narrative is received very differently by the entranced little girls and by the adult reader. We can see the poignancy of Winni's dreams and the sadness of her circumstances, yet for Mair and Begw she is a creature of almost boundless power, like the prophet Daniel. Winni makes herself a crown from some tendrils of fern and dances around, calling herself the 'Queen of Sheba'. The painfully proper Begw cannot help but notice, as Winni twirls around, that she is wearing no knickers under her rags. Her desire for a 'ffrog sidan' (satin dress) echoes that of Mali Meredur in Elena Puw-Morgan's earlier novel; in both writers' work there is an unbridgeable chasm between the girl's desire and what she achieves. Suddenly, though, Winni stops her dance, grabs Begw's picnic and eats the lot, including the longed-for jelly. 'And now,' she announces, 'I mean to thrash you' ('A rŵan,' meddai . . .'r ydw i am ych chwipio chi').[39] After her thrashing, Begw escapes over the mountain and lies down on a soft bed of moss, where she begins to recuperate from her fright and disappointment:

> mor braf oedd bod ar wahân, yn lle bod ymysg pobl . . . Yr oedd y distawrwydd yma yn braf. Pob sŵn, sŵn o bell oedd o, sŵn cerrig yn mynd i lawr dros domen y chwarel, sŵn saethu Llanberis, bref dafad

unig ymhell yn rhywle, a'r cwbl yn gwneud iddi feddwl am ochenaid y babi wrth gysgu yn ei grud gartref.⁴⁰

[how nice it was to be apart, instead of being among people. . . This silence was nice. Every sound, it was a sound from far away, the sound of stones going down over a quarry tip, the sound of shot-firing from Llanberis, the bleat of a lonely sheep far off somewhere, with all of it making her think of the baby's sigh as he slept in his cradle at home.]

Despite the thrashing, a relationship is established between Begw and Winni, whom she still admires; in later stories, though, when Winni does go into service, she returns a very different, tamed person: 'She isn't the same Winni' ('Nid yr un Winni ydy hi'), thinks Begw.⁴¹ The anarchic dreamer has been transformed into someone who wears knickers and tidy clothes and goes to chapel on Sundays.

If *Stryd y Glep* presents a negative picture of a contemporary Wales, and *Y Lôn Wen* a regretful reconstruction of a vanished past Wales, *Te yn y Grug*, true to its generic hybridity, offers the reader a more balanced view of a child's Wales, which is full of poverty and injustice, and yet animated by a strong perception of the landscape's austere beauty and the close ties of an integrated community.

Such a landscape and community are also represented in Brenda Chamberlain's *Tide-Race* (1962), an autobiographical account of the author's fourteen-year stay on Bardsey Island (*Ynys Enlli*) off the coast of the Llŷn peninsula in north Wales. Chamberlain was a native of Bangor and had trained as a visual artist in London before returning to Wales in the mid 1930s. She was both a painter and a writer – of prose and verse – and some of her books are an interesting combination of the two art forms. *Tide-Race* itself is a case in point, being illustrated throughout with Chamberlain's distinctive drawings.

It is tempting to compare *Tide-Race* with *Y Lôn Wen*, since ostensibly they have many similarities: both are autobiographical prose accounts published in the early 1960s by north Welsh women, and are texts which pay close attention to the land and people of the 'square mile' evoked. However, they are markedly different in tone, and in their conception of that 'square mile' and their place in it. As we have seen, *Y Lôn Wen* is more of a social and cultural history than a personal memoir; *Tide-Race*, conversely, is an idiosyncratic personal memoir which expresses an artist's often aesthetic and imaginative response to the landscape. Tony Conran has aptly observed of Brenda Chamberlain that her 'great act of fiction was herself, steering her imagination between the real islands of a real outside'.[42] While Roberts describes a society from the viewpoint of someone deeply enmeshed within its complex network of relations, Chamberlain pays curious attention to the complexities of relationships among the islanders, but she does so largely from the point of view of a footloose outsider. Whereas Roberts emphasizes the specific, Welsh-language culture of the Rhosgadfan of her childhood, there is in Chamberlain a sense of an elemental, almost mythical landscape, which exceeds Welsh cultural specificity. Indeed, it could be argued that the fact that Bardsey is an island is far more important to Chamberlain than the fact that it is a *Welsh* island. Later on, Chamberlain went to live on the Greek island of Ydra and wrote a book, *A Rope of Vines* (1965), conjuring up her life there. Finally, if Roberts chronicles the way of life of a people rooted in the land for several generations, Chamberlain describes an artist who self-consciously 'returns to the land' in an effort to find a more authentic and elemental way of living. Yet both writers conjure up memorable images and scenes which they have themselves witnessed and cherished in their artists' minds, paying great attention to the minutiae which might escape the notice of less observant witnesses. Moreover, both Welsh women writers are fascinated by the voices of the past: Roberts figures what she has achieved in her autobiography, as we have seen, as a conversation with the temporarily resurrected dead, while Brenda Chamberlain hears, as she states in a poem in the later *Poems with Drawings* (1969): 'the dead whisper with the dead / the living gossip with the dead.'[43]

Although *Tide-Race*, in its poetic, almost mystical preoccupation with the sea and its voices, is frequently seen as a unique portrait of a singular place and individual, there are quite unexpected echoes of earlier works by Welsh women. Allen Raine's obsession with the power of the sea, for instance, is frequently expressed in quasi-mystical terms, while Chamberlain's fascination with the cave finds an echo also in the novels of Raine. Moreover, Chamberlain's belief that by returning to this 'primitive' and holy island in the Irish Sea she was approaching her own family's Celtic (Manx) roots finds an echo in later Welsh women's writing, such as the poetry of Hilary Llewellyn-Williams, which resurrects old Celtic mythology in order to reinvent a Wales in which women can feel at home. For Chamberlain, though, this mysterious island of voices is not simply an idyll; on the contrary, it contains palpable danger and an uncanny ability to set the individual on the path of existential quests. As Tony Brown remarks, '[l]and and sea writhe with expressive (and often threatening) life in Chamberlain's work'.[44] Brown has also suggested that *Tide-Race* can be seen as a kind of unresolved dramatization of Chamberlain's search for selfhood as a woman, as a work which is redolent of the questions beginning to open up in the 1960s about femininity and masculinity.[45]

One scene in *Tide-Race* which might be seen to illustrate this search for selfhood is the narrator's encounter with the female seal in 'The Cave of Seals' chapter of the volume:

> Below us, a seal cow lay on her back in the bottle-green gloom of the cavern. With head out of water and flippers waving us to come down, down, to the depths of the sea, her brown eyes besought: Come to me, come to me . . . I leaned far over into darkening air; and her mild eyes spoke of human feelings. She took me down to my deepest roots nurtured on legend and fantasy. She told me that once I was a lonely woman living on a desert beach, without husband, without children; and if in the spring I was crowned it was with the sea-tangle of my own wreathing.[46]

In this chapter, the narrator returns again and again to the image of the seal, dreaming of being transformed into one, of living life as a selkie, both woman and seal, of stealing a seal's baby and being pursued by her. The image also recurs in Chamberlain's poems, such as 'Seal cave':

> Mother seal, seal cow,
> Your eyes almost compel me to a salt death.
> Your eyes are so full of knowledge,
> It would be no surprise
> To find you had understanding
> Of how it is I am a lonely woman
> Living on a lonely strand.[47]

As the above quotations indicate, there is no strong differentiation between Chamberlain's poems and prose; not only do the same concerns recur in both genres, but often the same images and phrases. Somewhat like Margiad Evans in her late autobiographical works, Chamberlain tends to ignore generic boundaries; the two are also similar in that both were accomplished visual artists, too, and added to their generic transgressions by introducing visual art into their literary works.

Evans and Chamberlain also share a quasi-mystical vision of the natural world. In *Tide-Race*, for example, just as the seal is viewed in human terms, so the island itself is figured as a human body:

> At this northern end are black sea caverns. Above the caves the rock is white and worked over in raised veins, polished and fine as ivory. Some of these rock-veins were thin as spider web, others were thick as human arteries. The stone would seem to be composed of petrified tissues, skin, muscle, delicate bones ... Falling to our knees, we touched the remains of our ancestors ... their ivory-bright bird-bone perfection, the metamorphosed flesh.[48]

This extraordinary description is both a reference to the history of Bardsey Island as a holy site, where reputedly twenty thousand saints are buried, and a rhapsodic personal expression of belonging to the land itself. The 'rock' here is very different from the *graig* (rock) described by the contemporary female novelists of the slate-quarrying areas (notably Jane Edwards and Eigra Lewis Roberts), and yet the strange identification between the human body and the rock is not dissimilar. While the quarrymen's veins run with the dust of the grey rock that sustains them, the white rock of Bardsey appears to be dissolved in the veins of the woman artist who settles there.

At first glance the work of Brenda Chamberlain could not be further removed tonally, politically or geographically, from the work of her somewhat younger contemporary, Menna Gallie. Gallie's novels *Strike for a Kingdom* (1959) and *The Small Mine* (1962) are important and rare examples of Welsh industrial novels by a female writer. The scarcity of such works is explicable by historical and social circumstance. Although the paid industrial work of the first half of the century – and the terrible dangers attached to that work – was overwhelmingly male-dominated, it was the womenfolk who had to labour constantly to sustain their families and the community as a whole. The evidence provided by Dot Jones's research on Rhondda women's lives strongly supports the suggestion that women had to shoulder an even heavier burden than their menfolk in these societies.[49] Life expectancy was shorter for women than for men and, before the advent of pit-head baths, much of women's daily lives would be concerned with the constant struggle to maintain cleanliness, in impossible circumstances. In *The Small Mine*, set in the early 1960s, Flossie, the mother figure, recalls that earlier experience: 'It's like old times, Joe, to see a collier looking like a collier . . . you're more of a man in your dirt, like.'[50] Gallie, born and raised in Ystalyfera, was in a position both to speak with authenticity of the industrial experience and to view that experience through the prism of a university education and a later life lived largely outside the communities of which she writes. Her lifelong socialism and her fluency in Welsh also meant that she was uniquely well placed to give voice to the industrial experience which had hitherto largely been represented through a male perspective.

Perhaps surprisingly, given the subject-matter of these novels – a murder, a strike and a death underground – Gallie is primarily a comic writer. She manipulates language to create a racy, hybrid, recognizably south Welsh speech, full of wit and grotesquerie. She is an irreverent novelist who does not shy away from satirizing some of the foundational institutions of Welsh society, such as the chapel. In *Strike for a Kingdom*, for example, one of the workers complains that his wife has become obsessed with religion: 'she goes down that chapel they have in Clydach and comes home with diarrhoea and messages'.[51] Similarly, she mocks those with social pretensions who affect being unable to speak Welsh, such as Evans the police inspector, who 'spoke Welsh but preferred not to let it be known that he suffered from this disability'.[52] Gender roles are also explored in a largely comic mode, with male pretensions being deflated and middle-class women's notions of propriety being openly mocked: at the funeral of Mr Nixon, the mine manager, a sister-in-law of the deceased is described like this: 'So corseted was she and firm that she felt to the touch like a dead crusader on his tomb.'[53]

The plot of *Strike for a Kingdom* is set against the background of the miners' lock-out which took place after the 1926 General Strike. Interwoven with the men's labour disputes is a personal drama involving surreptitious love affairs and exploitation of women by the odious Mr Nixon, the mine manager, who is found murdered. The investigation of his murder constitutes the plot, but Gallie's novel is hardly a conventional whodunnit. On the contrary, the text – her first published work – is much more concerned with the vivid evocation of a place, a time and a community. The initial description of Cilhendre, a fictionalized version of Ystalyfera, is significantly seen from the perspective of 'the top of the tips', from where it is 'a little huddle of pigeon-coloured houses following the curves of the river Tawe, which plaited its way among them, with the road and railway for company'.[54] The description connotes the cosiness of nesting birds and is suggestive of a close-knit community, echoing

Eluned Morgan's use of the same image to evoke the Welsh settlements in Patagonia; the landscape itself is anthropomorphized, with the river needing 'company', like the people who live on its banks. Immediately, Gallie populates her landscape: the next paragraph presents us with the tips crawling with 'clusters of people, with bags and sacks, picking bits of coal', a scene suggestive of poverty and want, but the sadness is dispelled by their vivacity: 'they shouted and teased, strikers on holiday'.[55] This convergence of potentially tragic subject-matter with a robust comic style is highly characteristic of Gallie's work and contributes to making her novels slightly uneasy reading – there can be a modulation from the humorous to the heart-rending within the space of one paragraph.

The novel comes to an end, as it began, with a view of the Cilhendre landscape. This time it is a night scene, with the miners tracking Gerwin, who has been revealed as the murderer, towards the Big Rock at the top of the hill:

> The path they followed grew steep and the going hard. It was a sheep track and the grass was springy and slippery. Tufty hummocks of coarse grass grew on either side and on the right was a patch of burnt gorse skeletons . . . it was a picture of desolation.[56]

Yet the desolation is really a projection of the feelings of the band of reluctant miners, who count Gerwin as one of themselves and form an extremely reluctant posse; when Gerwin blows himself and the Big Rock up with dynamite stolen from the closed mine, in a sense the community of Cilhendre is healed again.

Gallie's 1962 novel, *The Small Mine*, is set some decades later, after the Second World War and the nationalization of the coal mines. Gallie's main concern here is with social change in the valley community, though again this is animated by a kind of detective plot. Structurally, the novel is daring, in that the character whom we might identify as the 'hero', Joe, is killed halfway through the text. As in the earlier novel, the landscape is strongly present in the work, often connected with a focus on the human body and physical, sensory experience. And this is where an unexpected parallel with Brenda Chamberlain emerges, for both she and Menna Gallie identify the human body and the rock with which it interacts. From the opening pages of *The Small Mine* there is an emphasis on Joe's strong, vital body, which proves ironic, given that he dies in an explosion in the 'small mine' where he works and it proves impossible to reassemble the fragments of his body properly to look like his living self. The link between the worker's body and the pit is a trope used by many industrial novelists, from Zola's *Germinal* to Welsh fictions such as 'Twenty Tons of Coal' by B. L. Coombes. It is also strongly present in the writing of the north Wales quarrying districts, such as in the works of T. Rowland Hughes and Kate Roberts. This identification is interesting because it presents a contrast to the tendency in rural-based writing, as we have seen, to identify the land with the *female* body. It is as if, in these industrialised landscapes, men have colonized the hills, while women are often seen in confined indoor spaces, such as the kitchen or chapel.

Social change is represented in this novel with the emblematic closure of the 'small mine', a throwback to earlier industrial practices which have been superseded by the highly mechanized new coal industry run by the National Coal Board. Another emblematic scene of social change is the burning of the old bardic chair on the Guy Fawkes bonfire. Joe is surreptitiously a poet, but he has to conceal this because it conflicts with his image both as a macho male and as a modern young man who wears stylish Italian shirts and shoes. On his own, though, as he walks up the mountain towards his death, he tries to compose a poem in his head. He sees a fox and is reminded of a poem on the subject – although it is not named, it is clear that this is R. Williams Parry's well-known Welsh-language poem, 'Y Llwynog' (The Fox). In the free indirect discourse of the text, Joe thinks:

> it's a fox all right – well, I'll be damned, just like that poem. That was on a Sunday too, the bells of the church calling us to service and the something something calling to the mountain. There he goes, he's seen me, yes, that's right too, that's how he went, like the poem; it happened, finished, like a falling star. Wouldn't mind if I'd written that myself.[57]

This allusion to Welsh-language literature is just one among many indications in the text of the characters' closeness to and familiarity with Welsh-language culture. Frequently, indeed, there is a suggestion that the direct speech of the characters is translated from the Welsh. One character, for instance, observes 'He may be one of those angels by the road and the devil by the hob for all we know', a direct translation of a well-known Welsh proverb.[58] In a sense, Gallie's work indicates that linguistic divisions in Wales are not as absolute as is often suggested; certainly, in terms of the literary tradition, Gallie is a writer who shows a clear debt to Welsh-language as well as English-language writing. The fictional world that Gallie carefully builds up in her south Welsh novels is an 'ethnoscape', defined, not by language, but by a common historical, cultural and social heritage.

Both of Gallie's Wales-set novels engage with gender issues in a Welsh cultural context. In *The Small Mine*, Flossie Jenkins is of the older generation of women who willingly perform their domestic roles and whose role in the novel is defined as that of the Welsh Mam. Once her son, Joe, is killed, she loses her role and her voice in the novel. Up until the accident, though, she is a formidable presence, ruling her household with energetic glee. She adheres to a rigid domestic system of labour which is analogous to the shift system operated in the coal mines; all through the working day she wears curlers in her hair as an emblem of being 'on duty', and only takes them out last thing at night when her work is done: 'combing out her sausage curls was Flossie's clocking-off signal'.[59] If Gallie uses terms usually associated with the male world of work in describing Flossie's working day, she reverses the process in her description of Dai Dialectic and Jim Kremlin's labour in the mine: 'They were both good colliers, taking pride in their roofing and in the proper organization of their stall, as a housewife is proud of a well-organized, uncluttered kitchen.'[60] The effect of these unexpected transpositions is to assign equal weight and importance to the work of both genders. Gallie may have been reluctant to accept the label 'feminist',[61] but her literary practice certainly suggests a belief in gender equality.

Returning again to Kate Roberts, another writer reluctant to describe herself as feminist and yet seeming to express unmistakably feminist concerns, her next published work after *Y Lôn Wen* was the novella *Tywyll Heno* (Dark Tonight, 1962) which centres on Bet, a woman patient in a mental hospital, who is suffering from severe depression. Roberts carried out research at the local, very large mental hospital in Denbigh (Dinbych – which is also mentioned by several other Welsh women writers) in order to write this text. As Deirdre Beddoe points out, Denbigh was one of a handful of large asylums built in Wales during Victorian times, whose 'very names . . . struck a chill in people's bones'.[62] What is immediately striking about Roberts's narrative is that it is couched in the first person – rarely are texts about madness written in the voice of the 'madwoman' herself. Bet, a writer, observes the other patients in their various attitudes of despair or indifference and then she begins to analyse why she herself is there:

Edrychwn ar y peth fel rhyw ystafell Cynddylan ar ganol cae ar fin goedwig, a minnau'n mynd o amgylch yr adfeilion tylluanog, yn edrych i mewn i'r gwacter di-dân, di-wely . . . Yn araf y daeth ac ni wn sut, heblaw bod y gair 'syrffed' yn fy mhen o hyd. Ysgrifennwn ef ar ddarn o bapur weithiau a cheisio gwneud cynghanedd ohono efo'r gair 'seirff' a methu.[63]

[The way I looked at it, it was like some 'Cynddylan's Hall' in the middle of a field on the edge of a forest, with me going about the owl-haunted ruins, looking in at the fireless, bedless void within . . . It came on slowly and I don't know how, except that the word 'surfeit' was in my head all the time. I would write it down on a piece of paper and try to make a line of *cynghanedd* with it and the word 'serpents' but I always failed.]

Bet figures her madness here in spatial and literary terms, alluding to the anonymous ninth-century poem about Heledd, mourning her brother Cynddylan's death and going mad with grief. The poem, 'Stafell Cynddylan', presents a heart-rending picture of the ruined home and the dead bodies scattered over the field of battle, being pecked at by eagles. Roberts's use of the trope is powerfully suggestive of Bet's extreme sense of loss and dispossession. The word 'surfeit', with which Bet is obsessed, indicates that she can take no more of her oppressively respectable life as a Nonconformist minister's wife. Again, as so often, Kate Roberts is effortlessly daring in her anatomizing of Welsh Nonconformist notions of respectability and in her stark revelation of the deadeningly oppressive gender role expected from the wife of the 'Manse'. While Bet is an ambitious and free-thinking writer, what is required of her is an endless round of tea-making and food preparation. Significantly, the phrase 'I ran to prepare food for them' ('rhedais i baratoi bwyd iddynt') echoes throughout the text.[64] By the end of the narrative, Bet has managed to initiate her own recovery, largely through a talking cure with her doctor; she emerges finally, feeling

yr un fath ag y byddwn yn y breuddwydion hynny a gawn, fy mod wedi mynd allan yn noethlymun ac yn methu dyfod o hyd i'm coban . . . Nid oedd arnaf eisiau dim yr eiliad honno ond mynd yn neb ac yn ddim, fel poeri'r gog yn diflannu oddi ar laswellt.[65]

[like I did in those dreams I used to have, that I'd gone outside naked and couldn't find my nightdress . . . I wanted nothing at that moment except to become nobody and nothing, like cuckoo-spit disappearing from the blades of grass.]

129

Again, like the tonally very different *Stryd y Glep*, this novella ends with the female protagonist on the point of remaking, of reinventing herself. Bet imagines a completely new start, from a position of nothingness, figured memorably in the simile of the cuckoo-spit dissolving on the grass.

While Kate Roberts's *Tywyll Heno* is a contemporary-set novella, which can be seen to engage with issues of female selfhood and notions of belonging very specific to the transitional period of the 1960s, some other Welsh women writers were turning from the contemporary to the historical. Marion Eames's first two historical novels, *Y Stafell Ddirgel* (The Secret Room, 1969) and *Y Rhandir Mwyn* (Fair Wilderness, 1972), deal with the migration of Quakers under Rowland Ellis from Merioneth to Pennsylvania in the seventeenth century. These novels offer an interesting comparison to the writings of Eluned Morgan, some fifty years earlier, which also represent the experience of Welsh migrants to the new world. Eames herself was a migrant, in that she was born in Birkenhead on Merseyside, a setting which crops up fairly frequently in twentieth-century Welsh writing, no doubt because of the number of Welsh people who lived there. Later, Eames moved with her family to Dolgellau, the place from where Rowland Ellis had set off on his journey to the New World three centuries before. Eames returns to the subject of migration in her 1978 novel, *I Hela Cnau* (The Golden Road).

Eames punctiliously chronicles the persecution of the Quakers in seventeenth-century Merioneth, and succeeds in breathing life into the history with vividly imagined characters, a mixture of historical personages and invented figures. *Y Stafell Ddirgel* ends with the migrants sailing to the New World and on a note of sadness; Marged, who stays behind, laments 'The virtue of our land is on board that ship. The loss . . . Oh! The loss . . .' ('Mae rhin ein bro ni ar fwrdd y llong yna. Y golled . . . O! Y golled . . .').[66] In *Y Rhandir Mwyn*, the efforts of the migrants to establish their colony and to maintain their Welsh identity are chronicled; initially, they are precariously perched in caves burrowed out of the Schuylkill river-bank. Gradually, through sheer hard work, they establish their community, but are always under threat, on the defensive. Like Eluned Morgan's Welsh Patagonians, the migrants go in search of a 'better world' but fail to find it. The second novel ends despairingly with an allusion to the story of Heledd (described above, in Kate

Roberts's use of the poem in *Tywyll Heno*) and the two characters, John and Dorti, poised but unable to make the return journey to Wales:

Camgymeriad oedd ein dod yma. Rhith oedd ein breuddwydion am y Gymru newydd, lanach. Rydan ni wedi troi'n cefnau ar ein mam. Gwag ydy'r castell heno, murddun yw'r gobeithion. Awn yn ôl, yn ôl i grombil y mynyddoedd . . .

Rhy hwyr . . . rhy hwyr . . . ni ddychwel y brodor. Estron yw yng ngwlad ei dadau. Rydan ni yma'n diwreiddyn yn y wlad hon am byth . . .[67]

[It was a mistake for us to come here. Our dreams of the new, purer Wales were just a mirage. We have turned our backs on our mother. The castle is empty tonight, the hopes are in ruins. We'll go back, back to the heart of the mountains . . .

Too late . . . too late . . . the native doesn't return. He is a stranger in his fathers' land. We are here rootless in this country forever . . .]

Although Eames's novels are temporally and spatially distanced from twentieth-century Wales, they are clearly capable of being interpreted as having a modern relevance. Certainly, the concern with 'roots', with defending a threatened notion of Welsh identity, is one which was of urgent concern to other writers of this period, though they frequently expressed those concerns in a contemporary setting and idiom.

One such novel is *Dechrau Gofidiau* (The Onset of Sorrows, 1962) by Jane Edwards, which can be seen as representative of the work of the younger generation of Welsh women writers who started to publish in the 1960s. In comparison with Eigra Lewis Roberts's *Brynhyfryd*, published only three years previously, in 1959, Edwards's novel seems much more bold and daring in its subject-matter, appropriately signalling the shift from the 1950s to the 1960s, although the novel is set in the previous decade. The novel opens with the revelation that the unmarried Bronwen Parry is pregnant and that she does not know which of her various lovers is the father of the unborn child. Bronwen's mother, Elin, has to break the news as best she can to her highly conventional, chapelgoing husband. More indicative of the taboo-breaking nature of this novel, even than the fact of Bronwen's pregnancy, is her attitude towards her 'transgression'; she does not feel ashamed and she is not ready to apologize to anyone. Similarly, Gwilym, a young man of a similar age to Bronwen, and one of the possible candidates for paternity of the child, revels in shocking his conventional parents: 'it was worth getting drunk if only to see his mother getting annoyed about it' ('roedd yn werth meddwi pe na bai ond er mwyn gweld ei fam yn cael ei chorddi').[68] The centre of consciousness of the novel, however, is Ceri, Bronwen's younger sister, who has to suffer the familial shame of her sister's condition in the narrow-minded and vindictive quarry-town of Llanhelyg.

Dafydd Parry, the novel's patriarch, is a pious quarryman who has very strict ideas about female chastity; when Bronwen's 'shame' is discovered, he repudiates her, she leaves their house and he pretends that she no longer exists. Again, as in the works of Kate Roberts and Eigra Lewis Roberts, a connection is made between the austere morality of people like Dafydd and the rocks on which they live and work. When Ceri begins to rebel against the tight reins placed upon her by her parents, she exclaims: 'Tell me what the hell you are willing for me to do apart from studying and going to chapel? . . . You're as lifeless and hard as the rock that Dad splits in the quarry', to which her mother retorts 'To a quarryman life is in the rock' ('Deudwch i mi be' gebyst ydach chi'n fodlon imi 'i 'neud heblaw stydio a mynd i'r capal? . . .' Rydach chi mor ddifywyd a chaled â'r graig ma' Tada yn ei hollti yn y chwaral,' . . . [a'i mam yn ateb] 'Yn y graig ma' bywyd i chwarelwr').[69] Dafydd's tyranny even extends as far as using a telescope to spy on Ceri, to make sure that she is not getting into trouble. Despite his surveillance and his obsession with his daughter's keeping the 'silver thread' ('llinyn arian')[70] unbroken, Ceri, like her sister, becomes embroiled in sexual experience, which is described in unwontedly explicit detail. The presentation of Dafydd is an overt deconstruction of the revered image of the *gwerinwr*, described by Gwyn Alf Williams as 'Welsh-speaking, Nonconformist, imbued with the more social virtues of Dissent, bred on the Bible and good practice, . . . open to the more spiritual forms of the wider culture and . . . dedicated to spiritual self-improvement'.[71] From the feminist point of view of Edwards's novel, this idealized image is nothing more than a sham; the patriarch is revealed as a self-centred, narrow-minded tyrant.

The convolutions of the plot of this first novel are certainly melodramatic, but Edwards's work is an important example of female awakening in the Welsh novel. Interestingly, Ceri's favourite place in the landscape is a large hollow called the *Bowlen* (Bowl) where she sits to do her homework, read and dream; the topo-graphical shift from the hilltop to the curving hollow may perhaps be taken as indicative of a shift in emphasis in women's writing of this period. It is notable that Michael, 'mab y Plas' (son of the Great House), who will inherit the quarry from his father, is pictured as standing on the hilltop surveying the world, proud of his possession of the land: 'ymfalchïodd yn ei eiddo'.[72] These two places – hill and hollow – are very clearly associated with female and male, and yet the denouement of the plot suggests that both Michael and Dafydd may be ousted from their rocky, patriarchal perches.

Although Edwards's novel is very culturally specific to Wales, offering an analysis of the particular ways in which patriarchal structures operate here, *Dechrau Gofidiau* is also in some ways a novel characteristic of women's writing in the early 1960s. It has many parallels, for example, with Edna O'Brien's *Country Girls* trilogy (1960–4),[73] which also portrays female protagonists, Kate and Baba, rebelling against a traditional, rural Irish Catholic patri-archy and gaining their first sexual experiences, which are figured as liberating. O'Brien's novels were banned in Ireland for a number of years, partly because of their explicit treatment of sex; although Jane Edwards's work was not censored, it was regarded by many in the Welsh critical establishment of the time as quite shocking.

Moira Dearnley's *That Watery Glass* (1973) bears some similari-ties to the work of her contemporary, Jane Edwards, in terms of its subject-matter, an illicit sexual liaison, and in its overt focus on female desire. Stephen Knight sees this novel as an example of the increasing convergence of Welsh-language and English-language culture in later twentieth-century Wales.[74] The novel concerns Gwendoline Vyvyan's obsessive desire for Sinclair, a first-year stu-dent in one of her university classes. Her feelings conflict strongly with her Welsh Nonconformist upbringing, but the feelings she has for the odious Sinclair appear to bring her a new and superior sense of 'emancipation, even salvation'.[75] Jane Aaron has analysed Dearnley's only novel, comparing it fruitfully with several contem-porary novels in Welsh, including Jane Edwards's *Byd o Gysgodion* (World of Shadows, 1964), which also deals with an illicit teacher-pupil sexual relationship.[76] These women novelists are beginning to explore the complex interrelationships between the different identi-ties required of women in the modern world, including sexual, national, professional, familial and gender identities. Often, as the tortured protagonists of Dearnley and Edwards reveal, these diverse identities pull the individual in quite contrary directions. The plots tend to lead to the discovery of a 'new' identity, not always a pleasant one; as Gwendoline in *That Watery Glass* reflects at the end of the novel: 'My attitude to him [Sinclair] had been hypocritical: I had merely made use of him during the fascinating process of discovering my nasty new self.'[77]

But it is not only the young who feature in women's writing of this period. Kate Roberts's *Hyn o Fyd* (A World like This, 1964) contains five short stories, largely concerning old age. 'Cathod mewn Ocsiwn' (Cats in an Auction) deals with the sale of the deceased Mrs Hughes's worldly possessions; Elen goes there to buy the 'cwpwrdd cornel' (corner cupboard), but returns home having failed in her mission. Elen is alone and ageing; she regards her meticulously polished and cared-for furniture as her children. Her experience at the auction, where the dead woman is denigrated and mocked by her erstwhile friends, dismays her and makes her aware of her own mortality. 'Everyone was selfish at an auction' ('Hunanol oedd pawb mewn ocsiwn'),[78] reflects Elen, but the bleak suggestion is that people are selfish and cruel everywhere, not just in an auction, especially if you are a single old woman, with no power, wealth or influence.

Increasingly, in the stories of the later period, Kate Roberts focuses on the lives and experiences of old people, especially women. Such characters are represented as being neglected and overlooked by society; it is as if they have lived on beyond their heyday into an alien age, in which their language, culture and values no longer have any relevance. The tone of these stories is poignant in the extreme; there seems to be no remedy for these characters' suffering except in the temporary escape of dreams and memories. This is the case in the story 'Dychwelyd' (Returning) in her 1972 collection *Gobaith a Storïau Eraill* (Hope and Other Stories). Here an old woman, Annie, sets out contentedly for the shops, but on her journey she is mocked and sworn at by a group of schoolboys. She becomes downcast, reflecting 'that she was good for nothing by now, just some old creature who was the object of scorn for schoolboy louts' ('nad oedd hi'n da i ddim erbyn hyn, dim ond rhyw hen greadur oedd yn destun gwawd i labystiaid o hogiau ysgol').[79] The story then returns us in flashback to Annie's childhood and shows us her intimate relationship with this landscape – the cottage with one window, 'like a one-eyed man looking out on the vast moorland' ('fel dyn unllygeidiog yn edrych ar y rhosdir maith'),[80] the lapwings, the heather, the ferns growing in the rocky sides of the quarry. Back in the present, Annie becomes confused and sets out on a journey to see her parents at their old house. The journey she undertakes (though she cannot find a path, all the sheep having left the mountain) is a journey into memory, into her own past, in an attempt to assert the selfhood that has been unhinged by the attack of the thoughtless schoolboys. The landscape, though, has changed. The one-eyed cottage now has two 'eyes' and is inhabited by an Englishwoman who cannot understand what Annie is saying. Most of the scattered farms are gone and a large factory has been set in the middle of the valley. She is regretful: 'she remembered how her teacher in school would tell the story of Math and Gwydion . . . how they would transform things with their magic wand. If only they could be there now to change the mountain back to what it was like years ago' ('cofiodd fel y byddai'r athro yn yr ysgol yn dweud hanes Math a Gwydion . . . fel y byddent yn newid pethau efo'u hudlath. Gresyn na fyddent yno rŵan i newid y mynydd i'r fel yr oedd ers talwm').[81] This rare allusion to Welsh mythology in Roberts indicates the unrealistic nature of Annie's anguished desire. She looks into the river and sees a solitary trout swimming there, at which sight she weeps. It is as if both trout and woman are the sole creatures of their kind left in an alien world. Ultimately, Annie finds her way to her old home, though it is now surrounded by new houses. The boundary between reality and dream is deliberately blurred here, so that she actually seems to enter the kitchen and sits down to a meal with her long-dead parents. As her mother remarks: 'There's only memory left now' ('Dim ond cofio sydd rŵan').[82] The story figures Annie's death, but it does so in a dreamlike way which suggests that the three of them – mother, father, child – go to sleep together. It is a masterly story, showing how Roberts had lost none of her technique in old age (she was eighty-three when this volume of stories was published, and she would live on for another thirteen years). It is tempting, of course, to suggest that the old women in Roberts's late stories are projections of the author herself and her own perception that she had survived from a wholly Welsh Wales into a country which seemed increasingly alien. Indeed, Saunders Lewis, her contemporary and friend, suggested as much in a review of *Hyn o Fyd* some years earlier, where he describes her in this way:

> She . . . lives alone in her mid-seventies, remembering a rich monoglot society that spoke a language aglow with idiom and a traditional

vocabulary; she is scornful of the impoverished vocabulary of this televisionary Wales; she demands no sympathy from it and writes a prose it cannot match.[83]

Not all of Roberts's later stories deal with old age, however. In the story 'Y Daith' (The Journey) from the 1969 volume, *Prynu Dol* (Buying a Doll), she returns to the year 1912 and traces the journey of young Dafydd Huws, who leaves his home in the quarrying community of north Wales for a better life in the 'Sowth'. His parents are sad to see him leave, but at the same time they are aware of their good fortune that at least he is still alive, unlike their neighbour Lias Roberts's son of the same age, who was killed the year before in a quarry accident. Dafydd's impressions as his train approaches its destination are expressed with great immediacy:

Rhedai'r trên yn gyflym, ac yn sydyn daeth o noethni'r wlad i ganol miloedd o dai; rhesi ar ôl rhesi; tomenydd tywyll, simneiau uchel; sŵn tramiau'n cloncian yn drwsgl . . . Rhedai'r trên heibio i gefnau tai a goleuni llachar yn eu ffenestri: câi gip weithiau ar wraig yn smwddio wrth y ffenestr, neu blentyn wrth fwrdd yn gwneud ei dasg ysgol. Goleuid yr awyr yn y pellter gan dân ffwrneisi; yr oedd popeth yn fyw; yn ddigon byw i roi rhyw deimlad o beidio â malio dim yn neb ynddo; teimlad o hyder ac antur.[84]

[The train travelled quickly, and suddenly emerged from the emptiness of the country into the middle of thousands of houses; row upon row; dark tips, high chimneys; the sound of trams clanking clumsily . . . The train went past the backs of houses with bright lights in their windows: he had the occasional glimpse of a woman ironing by the window, or a child doing his homework at a table. The sky in the distance was lit up by the furnace fires; everything was alive; alive enough to give him a feeling inside of not caring about anyone; it was a feeling of confidence and adventure.]

There is something both atmospheric and poignant in this description of arrival in the industrial town. Dafydd is nervous, but rising above his anxiety and his sense of the strangeness of the place is an irrepressible feeling of joy in being alive, having escaped from the quarry and the ineluctable sadness of his parents' lives. The glimpses of families living normal lives in their terraced houses reassures him, but at the same time he is aware of having flown the net of his own family responsibilities. He has a postcard ready to send his mother to announce his safe arrival, but he finds that immediately he has failed to perform his familial duty, since he has missed the last post. Dafydd's parents regard the 'Sowth' as an alien and unimaginably faraway place; they are left alone in a place seen as slowly dying, while the fires of the South burn bright. The story is suffused with sadness, therefore, but it is also animated by Dafydd's youth and optimism; the story leaves him in that moment of energy and purpose.

Juxtaposed with Dafydd's youthful enthusiasm is the regretful middle age of another character in the collection, the unnamed woman in the title story, 'Prynu Dol' (Buying a Doll).[85] She has some doll's clothes, hand-sewn by herself some fifty years previously, and she finally decides to buy a doll to dress in the clothes and to place as an ornament in her house. The clothes she made are now, of course, extremely old-fashioned, and are therefore like decorative antiques. The principal appeal of this story is linguistic: Roberts spends a page and a half giving a very detailed description of the doll's clothes, using a rich vocabulary of almost archaic words, which are lovely mirrors of the clothing itself. The intricacy of the stitching and the decoration is emphasized, implicitly contrasting with the mass-produced and sloppily made manufactured products of the modern age. There is also an implicit parallel drawn between the needlework of the past and the language of the past: both are precise, beautiful and almost redundant. The protagonist even has to resort to talking to her dog, just to use words which she never hears any more: 'geiriau fel ffaligragwd, gyrbibion, ulw, straffaglio, newydd sbon danlli grai'.[86] When the doll is dressed in the clothing, she looks almost alive and, as the old woman gazes at her, she begins to see herself half a century before. For a moment, she feels frightened and is tempted to throw the doll out of the window, but she resists and, by morning, the doll is perfectly innocuous once more. Roberts's use of the doll's clothes image is another example of the way in which Welsh women writers often use clothing metaphorically to explore gender identity. Unlike the 'wisg sidan' in Elena Puw-Morgan's novel, which connotes female sexuality, the doll's clothing in Kate Roberts is associated with childhood innocence and with an almost vanished culture and way of life. The complicated needlework accomplished by the woman's younger self was very much a required part of a girl's feminine accomplishments in the early twentieth century, a requirement which has now disappeared, as indicated by the young girls in the toyshop's astonished exclamations over the doll's clothing.

Kate Roberts's concern with the loss of the Welsh language, expressed elegiacally in 'Prynu Dol', is echoed in the work of much younger contemporaries, who were frequently active in the campaigns of the Welsh Language Society (*Cymdeithas yr Iaith Gymraeg*). Meg Elis's 1975 novel *I'r Gad* (To Battle) is one of the earliest works to give fictional representation to the political activism of members of Cymdeithas yr Iaith, established in the early 1960s. This and her later novel *Carchar* (Prison, 1978) are clearly novels of nationalist commitment, not unlike some of the novels of Moelona in the early decades of the century. However, these autobiographical texts have a much rawer sense of immersion in a struggle happening here and now. Published by the radical Welsh publishing-house, Y Lolfa, in Talybont, Elis's novels are aimed at a youthful market and state explicitly their aim of persuading more young Welsh people to get involved in direct political action. Like a number of other Welsh women writers of her generation, Elis was imprisoned for her Welsh-language campaigning activities, and the later novel, *Carchar*, gives a vivid first-person account of that experience. The courtroom in *I'r Gad* and the prison cell in *Carchar* are certainly new spaces in Welsh women's fiction; Elis presents them as places where a life-or-death battle is taking place, with the fate of the Welsh language in the balance.[87]

Women activists were prominent from the start of the campaigns of Cymdeithas yr Iaith. An increasing consciousness of Welsh difference manifested itself in a number of ways during the 1960s, including the founding of more violent groups, such as the Free Wales Army and *Mudiad Amddiffyn Cymru* (Wales Defence Movement). The Investiture of the Prince of Wales at Caernarfon Castle in 1969 crystallized much of the nationalist feeling, although attitudes towards the Investiture in Wales were extremely mixed. There is a dualism discernible in the literary production of this time, since young women writers of this period were simultaneously dismantling the traditional structures of Welsh cultural life, such as the chapel, patriarchal rule and double sexual standards, and upholding and defending the Welsh language and some of the cultural values connected with it. In a sense, Welsh women writers can be seen as trying to reinvent Wales as a place able to accommodate a new generation with different values and aspirations, and in which women played a central, rather than a helpmeet, role. Understandably, the overt political commitment is more pronounced in some Welsh-language writing, but the sense of Welsh difference and a new awareness of having suffered a type of colonization is also evident in some English-language writing of the time.[88]

What is striking about this generation of language activists is that they write directly and often polemically of their political convictions in their literary works; this stands in direct contrast with Kate Roberts, an exceptionally active political campaigner throughout her life, but one who never wrote overtly propagandistic stories or novels. And yet, as the poet and critic Bobi Jones has remarked, in a century when the Welsh language experienced a drastic and potentially terminal decline, 'to use a Welsh word is still a revolutionary action'.[89]

In this sense, the poetry of Nesta Wyn Jones is 'revolutionary'. All the poems in her first volume, *Cannwyll yn Olau* (Bright Candle, 1969), are spoken in the first-person voice. The effect is of a gentle, reflective voice meditating on the natural world, on history and on belonging. 'Cysgodion' (Shadows) has a first-person plural voice which speaks for the post-war generation, considering all the suffering and destruction experienced by those who lived through two World Wars. In contrast, 'we' are seen as 'Etifeddion yr oes feddal / A'n byd yn . . . weddol wyn' ('Inheritors of the soft age/And our world. . . reasonably white').[90] Haunted by images from the past wars, the new generation hears

> . . . eco rhyw sgrech
> Fel yr 'hedai yr hen eryr barus tua'r gorwel,
> A chysgod ei aden oer
> Yn ein fferu ninnau, am eiliad,
> Cyn ymadael.[91]

> [the echo of some scream
> As the old greedy eagle flew towards the horizon,
> And the shadow of its cold wing
> Made us freeze for an instant,
> Before it flew away.]

Yet another allusion to the poem 'Stafell Cynddylan', which offers a heart-rending description of the eagle of Pengwern tearing the flesh of Heledd's beloved brother on the battlefield, goes hand in hand with a contemporary consciousness of the possibility of a third World War. Jones is a poet who is adept at combining the traditional with a modern, often political consciousness. Technically and tonally, however, she excels at simple, lyrical pieces, such as 'Tegeirian' ('Orchid'),[92] descriptive of the everyday miracle of a wild orchid or the extremely well-achieved imitations of the 'hen benillion' (folk verse).[93] One of the few poems in the volume which refer specifically to a location in Wales is 'Cilmeri',[94] which is the place where Llywelyn Ein Llyw Olaf (Llywelyn ap Gruffudd) died in 1282. A potent *'lieu de memoire'*, Cilmeri is used by Jones here not just as a reminder of the past, but as inspiration for the future. The longest and most resonant poem in the volume, however, is 'Etifeddiaeth' (Inheritance).[95] Here, the first-person speaker meditates – typically, on a walk up the mountainside – on her memories of the past and her consciousness of the demise of the traditional culture which she has inherited:

> Ond daeth machlud haul i euro'r hen gwm
> A thrist ydwyf heno, heb yr hen fodlonrwydd . . .
> Ofn y crino a'r breuo yng nghymalau fy ngwreiddiau,
> A'r llyngyr sy'n rhemp ym mhridd fy mhridd,
> Ofn y diffodd rhydlyd ar lanterni'r gorffennol,
> Ofn ymddatod diwethaf cancr pob cadwyn
> Pan ddaw'r nos ddiymadferth.
> Fe lithrodd ein cyfoeth
> Yn geiniogau rhuddwawr
> Ar gerrig ein bro,
> Byth i'w casglu drachefn.
> Lled-syllaf yn syn
> Ar lwch y cen cerrig hyd fy nwylo chwith,
> Llwch llwyd ein hetifeddiaeth.[96]

> [But sunset came to gild the old valley
> And tonight I am sad, bereft of contentment . . .
> I fear the withering and brittleness in the joints of my roots,
> And the disease that's spreading in the earth of my earth,
> I fear the rusty extinction of the lamps of the past,
> And the final unravelling of the cancer in every chain
> When the helpless night comes.
> Our wealth slipped
> Like dawn-red pennies
> On to the stones of our land,
> Never to be gathered again.
> I peer curiously
> At the lichen dust on my sad hands
> The grey dust of our inheritance.]

The note of elegy is strong and poignant in this poem, expressed through images of sunset, withering, disease, extinction and unravelling. The image of the rusty lamps of the past being extinguished is particularly frightening, suggesting as it does the loss of enlightenment, religion, the knowledge of the way ahead. Nevertheless, this despairing poem is juxtaposed in the collection with a continuing joy in the natural world and a steadfast allegiance to the places which speak eloquently of the heroism of the past.

Nesta Wyn Jones's second book, *Ffenest Ddu* (Black Window, 1973), is a more confident collection than the earlier volume, containing poems about the actions of Cymdeithas yr Iaith and references to social and geographical changes, such as afforestation and immigration. Interestingly, despite the anxieties expressed about Anglicization in a poem such as 'Estroniaid',[97] (Strangers), Jones reveals a strong sense of sympathy and identification with Shirley Bassey, in a poem of the same name.[98] 'Pluo gwyddau'[99] (Plucking geese) is an intensely atmospheric poem which savours strongly of the poet's own farming background, but the most substantial poem in the volume is the title poem, 'Ffenest Ddu'[100] (Black Window). Highly symbolic, it juxtaposes the brightness of five windows illuminated by the sun with a perpetually dark window, which lies behind the speaker. This window appears to be the boundary between this world and the next, and it is a thin barrier at which the speaker listens and questions, wondering what lies on the other side. As a meditation on mortality, the poem works well because it is rooted in the concrete: the image of the dark window is both simple and multifaceted. The speaker's attitude towards it vacillates between resentment and longing:

> Hen ffenest ddu
> Na ddengys imi liwiau glöyn byw
> Na datgan imi diwn aderyn bach
> Mewn diwrnod;
> Y ffenest ddu
> Sy'n mynnu cadw rhagof i
> Gyfrinach hen ei gallu . . .
> er im roddi'm clust i wrando,
> Mi ni chlywais ddim
> O'r ochr draw,
> Dim ond hen ddrymio araf, swrth
> Fy nghalon fy hun.[101]

> [Old black window
> Which does not show me butterfly colours
> Nor declares to me the tune of a little bird
> In a day;
> The black window
> Insists on keeping from me
> The old secret of her craft . . .

though I cock my ear to listen,
I heard nothing
From the other side,
Only the drowsy, slow old drumming
Of my own heart.]

Nesta Wyn Jones is a modern poet who shows an acute consciousness of the contemporary world but at the same time is drawn
towards the metaphysical questions which have always troubled
poets, including the poets and hymn-writers of the Welsh literary
tradition. It is interesting, though, that she chooses to figure her
meditations on religious questions in domestic imagery, such as the
windows of the home. Perhaps this is an indication of the female
voice which speaks, though not overtly, in her works.

However, Jones should not be regarded as primarily a religious
poet, for many of her poems do engage directly with the political
realities of her time and, in that regard, are comparable to the more
outspoken works of writers such as Meg Elis and, slightly later,
Angharad Tomos and Menna Elfyn. One example is the poem
'Capel Celyn', which concerns the drowning of Tryweryn in the
early 1960s. The proposed flooding of the valley in Merioneth in
order to provide water for the city of Liverpool had been a
contentious issue throughout the 1950s; when it actually happened,
it was widely regarded as a symbolic event denoting Welsh subjuga-
tion to the government at Westminster. Nesta Wyn Jones's poem is a
lyrical elegy for Capel Celyn, the village drowned under the waters
of the dam. She juxtaposes 'now', when the calm waters of the lake
are bland and inscrutable, with 'then', when the children played in
'Cae Fadog' and eavesdropped on the conversation of farmers and
neighbours in 'Dodo Nel's front room. The poem ends with the
anguished lines:

> Fe aeth dydd o haf ar ddifancoll,
> A chwmwl isel sy'n sgubo'r dyfroedd.
> Does yma ond cŵyn y don
> Yn torri
> Ar draethell anadferadwy.[102]

> [A summer's day disappeared into oblivion,
> And a low cloud sweeps over the waters.
> Here, there is only the moan of a wave
> Breaking
> On an irrecoverable shore.]

The 'irrecoverable shore' mourned here by Nesta Wyn Jones is, in a sense, the old, traditional, monoglot Welsh life also mourned by Kate Roberts in her later works. Nevertheless, the root of the word *anadferadwy* (irrecoverable) is the word *adfer* (recovery or recuperation), which was precisely what a number of contemporary women writers were doing, both in their political campaigning and in their literary production. In a sense, the poem 'Capel Celyn' *does* recover the lost place for the reader, bringing it powerfully, if only fleetingly to life again. Moreover, English-language poets would soon be engaged in a similar process, as Gillian Clarke's poem 'Clywedog', also about the drowning of a Welsh valley in the construction of a dam, indicates. Clarke's poem ends on a very similar note of sadness to Nesta Wyn Jones's:

> . . . the mountains, in a head-collar
> Of flood, observe a desolation
> They'd grown used to before the coming
> Of the wall-makers. Language
> Crumbles to wind and bird-call.[103]

A contemporary of Nesta Wyn Jones, who was also educated at Bangor, though she later migrated to south Wales, is Sally Roberts Jones, whose second volume of poetry, *The Forgotten Country* (1977), is an apt text with which to end consideration of this period of Welsh women's writing. As the title suggests, it focuses attention squarely on Wales – Welsh history and topography, and what it means to dwell here – and at the same time it looks forward to the renaissance of Welsh women's poetry which was to occur in the following decades with the work of Gillian Clarke and Menna Elfyn, among others. Roberts Jones begins the collection with a note explaining that the poems had been written since 1967, 'when I came to live in Port Talbot . . . that often forgotten part of Wales which is neither rural nor wholly industrial, which uses both languages . . . a community to which one can be proud to belong, whether by birth or adoption'.[104] Like Menna Gallie, she is one of the relatively few women who write directly out of industrialized south Wales and, as the tenor of her note suggests, her work celebrates that neglected, mixed landscape. Roberts Jones's poems invite comparison with those of her Welsh-language contemporary, Nesta Wyn Jones; although using different languages, they both express a distinctively Welsh experience of the 'milltir sgwâr', and use that experience to reflect more widely on Wales as a whole and on existential issues, though of the Joneses, Nesta Wyn is a more metaphysical poet than Sally Roberts. Neither shows particular interest in gender, though the perspective in both is often recognizably female. The similarities in their work is another instance of what Jane Aaron has argued convincingly elsewhere: that the sharing of an ethnic identity is more important than the division suggested by linguistic differences.[105]

That Roberts Jones is conscious of belonging to a Welsh tradition is indicated by the volume's frequent references, not only to Welsh places, but also to mythology, history and poets of the past. A particularly striking example is the poem entitled 'Ann Griffiths', on the late eighteenth-century hymn-writer, which again indicates a sense of identification between the English-language Welsh poet and the female Welsh-language tradition. 'Ann Griffiths' is written in the first person, as if Ann Griffiths herself were speaking, and there are implicit allusions to the vocabulary and images of Griffiths's own work:

> My songs as light as ash are spent;
> My hope's elsewhere, a long descent
> In flesh and land – and yet the air
> Stirs with fresh music, calls me where
> Intricate webs of words begin.
>
> Lord, let me not be silent till
> All earth is grinding in Your mill![106]

Roberts Jones is not elsewhere a religious poet, so this poem expresses a remarkable sense of identification with Ann Griffiths, an identification which is also expressed by a whole, disparate range of Welsh women writers across the twentieth century, from 'Buddug' to Rhiannon Davies Jones and Eigra Lewis Roberts, the latter of whom wrote an award-winning play, *Byd o Amser* (1976), based on Griffiths's life.[107]

Elsewhere in the volume, Roberts Jones addresses, not the literary and religious traditions of Wales, but its history and social networks. 'Community', for example, presents a south Welsh community's response to a bereavement. The voice adopted by the poet here is, tellingly, the first person plural. Although she is, by her own admission, an 'incomer', she feels an overwhelming sense of belonging to this distinctively Welsh community:

No blood ties, it's true; our bonds
Are accent and place – and desire
For much the same ends . . .

We adapt. To the chimneys, the concrete,
The furnace, the smoke, the dead trees.
Our fields are the names of roadways,
Our flocks and our language are gone:
But we hold our diminished city in face of the sun.[108]

Paradoxically, the poem, which appears to be about death and bereavement, turns out to be a celebration of survival, despite the odds. Elsewhere, the voice is less hopeful – in 'New World', for instance, 'The legends are all tucked up / In the old folks' Home',[109] but there is still a determination to survive: the voice in 'Caretaker, Blarney Castle', inspired by an Irishman's knowledge of his country's past, will 'learn my heritage / So that our son will never know that lack'.[110]

This period saw the transformation of women's lives in Wales in many senses. Older women writers looked back on a vanishing past and compared it with the flux and uncertainties of the present. Yet the tone is by no means predominantly one of loss and regret; on the contrary, there is a palpable resurgence of nationalist feeling in the literary production of women in both languages. There is also a new awareness of the international feminist movement, which was beginning to demand changes in gender roles and expectations. As we have seen, these women writers' representations of Wales often differ starkly from one another, but there is, nevertheless, a strong sense of Wales awakening into a modern world of divided allegiances and political actions, in which women's traditional roles are beginning to dissolve and metamorphose into different forms.

4 Feminist Place: 1978–1996

The political awakening which we have explored in Welsh women's writing of the mid 1970s may appear to have reached an impasse with the 1979 Referendum, in which devolution was rejected, although this result had, arguably, been predetermined by a Labour government which mounted a strong 'No' campaign, led by Neil Kinnock. Oddly, though, this event did not appear to attenuate Welsh women writers' sense of Wales as a separate entity; on the contrary, the writers of the late 1970s and early 80s tended to speak up for Wales against Thatcherism, the Falklands War, the closure of the mines and the proliferation of nuclear weapons. But the period is not simply notable for a vigorous political vision; it is also distinguished for the sheer volume of new writers who began to publish at this time, including individual authors now recognized as among the most accomplished and influential of the century. In a sense, the women's movement, which began in the previous decade, can be said to have borne abundant fruit in the outpouring of literary work in both languages by women in this period. The political landscape is also tempered by a new lyricism in the diverse works of poets such as Menna Elfyn and Hilary Llewellyn-Williams, novelists such as Angharad Tomos and Siân James, and playwrights such as Lucinda Coxon.

The publication of *The Sundial* (1978) by Gillian Clarke marked the beginning of the career of arguably the most dominant and distinctive voice of Welsh women's writing in the last two decades of the twentieth century. The fact that Clarke is a poet, too, is indicative of the beginning of a renaissance in women's poetry in this period. Although Clarke had published a pamphlet in the early 1970s, *The Sundial* was her first 'slim volume', and what is remarkable is the assurance of the poetic voice from the start. Moreover,

Clarke is a poet with a topographical imagination; concerned with Wales and female identity, she expresses these central concerns through an exploration of the Welsh landscape. The cover of the volume has dark trees silhouetted against an orange sky and white hills, an intense sun shining brightly through the branches. Within, Clarke describes specific places in Wales, such as Pisgah, Mynachlog, Penarth, Ystrad Fflur, evoking them powerfully with her strong tactile and visual sense. At the same time, there is a tender regard for the animals in that landscape and a sense of identification with female animals. Watching a calf being born in a field, for example, the speaker:

> . . . could feel the soft sucking
> Of the new-born, the tugging pleasure
> Of bruised reordering, the signal
> Of milk's incoming tide, and satisfaction
> Fall like a clean sheet around us.[1]

Poems like 'Birth', 'Curlew' and, especially, the later poems 'Seals' and 'Swimming with Seals' inevitably recall Brenda Chamberlain's identification with animal life, and yet Clarke's creatures are much more rooted in a real, physical world, rather than in the realms of dream or mythology. The voice of the poems, here, is frequently that of a mother, who responds emotionally and physically to her children and to the natural world. In 1978 this was a new voice in poetry; the Welsh Mam may have played an important symbolic role in Welsh ideology for more than a century, but this was the first time she could be heard to speak, eloquently, tenderly, quietly, for herself. But this Mam is also a poet, who responds to the literary echoes of the Welsh landscape, too, as in 'At Ystrad Fflur' and 'Dyddgu Replies to Dafydd I', both of which engage with the poems of the medieval Welsh poet, Dafydd ap Gwilym: the poet fearlessly places herself in the same poetic tradition and gently provides a female vocal counterpoint to Dafydd's beguiling tenor.

As it develops during the following decades, Clarke's poetry begins not only to present glimpses of a Welsh rural landscape but to build up a map of Wales as a whole, to which the voice of the poems asserts a sense of belonging and allegiance. Poem sequences such as 'Letter from a Far Country' (1982) and 'Cofiant' (1989) trace a communal family history, in which the woman of today, living in rural Cardiganshire, traces her roots back to places like 'Crugan' and 'Ceryg-yr-Wyn', scattered all over the face of Wales.

'Hearthstone' symbolically installs a slate slab which evokes the 'quarryman, / in the glittering slip of rain / on million-faceted blue Blaenau, / the purples of Penrhyn' in the fireplace of Blaen Cwrt, in Ceredigion.[2]

Clarke is a poet not of confrontation but of reconciliation, which is not to say that her poetry is unchallenging. On the contrary, the emphatically female voice of her poems stakes a claim to Wales in a way which has not been heard before in Welsh women's poetry. In this regard, 'Letter from a Far Country' is the turning point in Clarke's poetry. A specifically feminist work of recuperation, Clarke attempts no less than a woman's history of Wales – a work which would not be attempted by an historian until almost twenty years later, as Clarke herself foresees:

> my
> letter home from the future,
> my bottle in the sea which might
> take a generation to arrive.[3]

Clarke's Welsh woman's history is, characteristically envisioned in spatial terms: 'First see a landscape. Hill country, / essentially feminine', and then she begins to populate it with all the unrecorded women, living in

> Bryn Isaf
> down there in the crook of the hill
> under Calfaria's single eye.
> My grandmother might have lived there.
> Any farm. Any chapel.
> Father and minister, on guard,
> close the white gates to hold her.[4]

The voice of the poem fluctuates between 'I' and 'we', speaking for the unrecorded ones, the Welsh women of the past, chronicling the domestic duties of their lives, interweaving personal memory with social and economic detail:

> In the black book of the parish
> a hundred years ago . . . the unsupported
> woman had 'pauper' against her name.[5]

In the present, '[t]he women are leaving', despite the call of the 'dead grandmothers, / Mamgu from Ceredigion, / Nain from the

North . . .'.[6] The letter to the 'husbands, fathers, forefathers' temporarily remains unposted; the exodus stayed for now, and the poem ends with a lyrical series of unanswered questions: '*Who will do the loving while we're away?*'[7] The poem hesitates in uncertainty at the end; animated as it is by a sense of injustice, it nevertheless does not enact the feminist revolution because the woman is, in fact, rooted in this landscape.

In the later work 'The King of Britain's Daughter' (1993) Clarke skilfully interweaves the mythology of Wales – specifically, the story of Branwen from the medieval mythic cycle of the *Mabinogi* – with her own personal history, in another poetic gesture of inclusivity and possession. Just as 'Letter from a Far Country' disinters the lost mothers, 'The King of Britain's Daughter' is a tribute to the father. It is a complex elegy for Clarke's father, which consists of an interweaving of memories of a wartime childhood and the mythological story of Branwen, who was exiled, rescued and eventually died of grief. The brief Section 6 exemplifies how skilfully the dual narratives are interwoven and how the news of war is first received and understood by a female child in a west Wales kitchen:

> When the world wobbled
> We heard it on a radio chained
> By its fraying plait of wires
> To the kitchen window-sill
> Between a sheaf of letters,
> Bills and things needing to be done,
> And a jar of marigolds.
> And over its Bakelite crown
> The sea, level as milk.
> The news came out of the sky,
> A mist off the sea,
> An incoming shadow
> Of rain or wings.[8]

The radio brings distant wars uncomfortably into the midst of an ordinary domesticity. The portentous news fixes everyone's attention on the physical object of the old-fashioned wireless, and the perspective of a child is suggested by the use of the word 'wobbled'. Despite the childlike register, the word is apt, evocative of a world of stability suddenly slipping off its axis, echoed also by the suggestion of the sea as a vessel of milk, which it is vital to keep level to avoid spillage. There is a hint of a pun on spilt milk lurking in the text; the suggestion of childhood transgressions, clumsiness, tears.

The miscellaneous objects grouped around the radio speak of a life of work and duty, lightened by the beauty of the natural world. The brittle Bakelite brings a message which will displace and transform this life. The final lines of the passage introduce the echo of the Branwen story: like Branwen's starling bringing the news of her incarceration over the Irish Sea, the mysterious waves of sound have brought this message of war; the future is unclear, but the shadows suggest impending sorrow and grief.

Place and history converge in Clarke's poems to present a Wales full of echoes and whispers of the past. In Blaen Cwrt, the old Ceredigion farmhouse evoked several times in her work, the poet is haunted by the ghost of Marged, a previous occupant of this house. In 'Beudy' (Cowhouse) the poet sits in the room which used to be the cowshed and imagines the ghostly other woman in this same place 'lean[ing] her cheek against the old cow's flank, / stiff hands warmed at the udder, / the milk singing'.[9] Over and over in these affirmative poems, the speaker *identifies*; using a first-person voice sometimes denigrated by critics as characteristic of the limitations of female poets' 'confessional' poems, Clarke effortlessly dispels the charge of solipsism by 'becoming' Others.

One other important aspect of Clarke's work is her emphasis on and use of the Welsh language. A Cardiff-born poet whose native language was English, but who learned Welsh in adulthood, Clarke is a poet who self-consciously asserts her belonging to a Welsh-language culture and history. Her poems are peppered with Welsh words and she frequently expresses her delight in the language, especially when it creeps into English unexpectedly, as it does in the well-known poem 'Llŷr', where the ten-year-old speaker, at her first Stratford play, is entranced by '[t]he river and the king with their Welsh names'.[10] Elsewhere, in 'Border', the speaker laments the loss of the Welsh language in the border country; when she speaks Welsh, she is met with incomprehension. She sees this loss as a loss of identity: the border is 'where the land forgets its name / and I'm foreign in my own country . . . History forgets itself'.[11] Clarke's role as a translator of many of Menna Elfyn's poems from Welsh to English is a further indication of the position she appears to hold as a willing bridge between the two languages of Wales. Nor is this role out of keeping with the overall tone of reconciliation and identification felt in her whole poetic oeuvre.

If Gillian Clarke is the dominant female voice in the English-language poetry of Wales in the last two decades of the twentieth century, undoubtedly her younger contemporary, Menna Elfyn, is the equivalent in Welsh-langauge poetry. Yet, from the start, Elfyn's poetry is more combative and forthright than Clarke's. Emerging from the same generation as other activist-writers, such as Meg Elis and Angharad Tomos, it is not surprising to find Elfyn's early poetry engaging provocatively with both language and gender politics. Both Elfyn and Clarke began publishing in the 1970s, and Elfyn's early volumes, such as *Mwyara* (Blackberrying, 1976), *Ystafelloedd Aros* (Waiting Rooms, 1978), *Tro'r Haul Arno* (Turn the Sun, 1982) and *Mynd Lawr i'r Nefoedd* (Going Down to the Heavens, 1985), like Clarke's, frequently reflect her life as a young mother and express both the tenderness and anxieties of that maternal role. Just as 'The Sundial' focuses on the absorbed playing of her infant son, Owain, several of Elfyn's early poems have as their starting point one of her children's thought-provoking sayings or actions. 'Tro'r Haul Arno' for example, reflects on a three-year-old's demand that the sun be switched on, which leads his mother to reflect:

> O! na fedrwn . . .
> Ond troi na thrin
> ni allaf,
>   na haul,
>   nac echel daear,
>   na chilwg pobloedd,
>   un osgedd bach.
>
> A rhwng diymadferthedd
>   fy llaw
> a dwylo'r drefn,
> mae bysedd direidus, ir
>   am roi o hygrededd ei haf
> haul difachlud
>   ar lwydni'r dydd.[12]
>
> [If only I could! . . .
> But I can't switch or change
>   either the sun,
> or the earth's axis,
>   or peoples' scowls,
>   one little bit.
>
> And between the helplessness
>   of my hand
> and the system's hands,

mischievous, fresh fingers
    want to turn from the integrity of its summer
an unsetting sun
    on the greyness of the day.]

Although the child's naive remark awakens a sense of helplessness in the mother and an obscure sense of oppression by an anonymous 'system', the poem ends characteristically on an optimistic note, suggesting that the infant may one day succeed in changing that system for the better. This poem is typical of Elfyn's early poems, in the sense that they present a new combination of domestic and familial detail with political idealism and a desire to change the *drefn* (system).

Again, the voice of the Mam speaks in these poems, and in a series of poems in *Stafelloedd Aros* (1978) Elfyn speaks movingly of the experience of miscarriage. At the time, this was very much a new voice speaking of hitherto unexpressed female experiences in Welsh poetry. By the early 1980s, Elfyn's poetry becomes more explicitly feminist in tone and, like Clarke, she is interested in disinterring a lost Welsh woman's history, as she does for example in 'Anhysbys – An sy'n hysbys' (Anonymous – Ann is known – an untranslatable pun – 1982). The voice of the poem revolts against the male critical establishment, which simply assumes that 'Anon', the author of so many poems in Welsh, was inevitably a man; she takes issue with them:

Hy! – haws ydy credu
mai gwraig
yw'r anhysbys
yn . . .
tynnu geiriau
o dan lawes profiad . . .

Amheuwch am unwaith,
chwi hyddysg rai . . .

Mae An yn hysbys
a'i distadledd
sy'n drallwysiedig
drwy feinwe defn
ein benyweidd-dra hen.[13]

[Huh! – it's easier to believe
that anonymous was
a woman

pulling words out
from the sleeve of experience . . .

Be sceptical for once
all you academics . . .
Ann is known
and her insignificance is poured
through the woven tissue
of our old femininity.]

Other poems such as 'Byw, benywod, byw' (Live, women, live, 1982) and the satirical 'Wnaiff y gwragedd aros ar ôl?' (Will the ladies stay behind?, 1986) bring a radical wave of feminism into traditional Welsh society. The latter is particularly effective because it is set in a chapel context: the women always 'stay behind' to prepare food and serve the menfolk, who hold the important offices in the chapel – '*Diaconydd. Trysorydd.* / Pillars of their society' (Deacon. Treasurer . . .), as Gillian Clarke puts it.[14] The voice of Elfyn's poem rebels:

Ar ôl
ar ôl y buom,
yn dal i aros,
a gweini,
a gwenu a bod yn fud,
boed hi'n ddwy fil o flynyddoedd
neu boed hi'n ddoe . . .

'Gwrandewch chi, feistri bach,
tase Crist yn dod 'nôl heddi

byse fe'n bendant yn gwneud ei de ei hun.'[15]

[Behind
yes, behind we have been
always waiting
and serving
and smiling and keeping silence,
whether it's two thousand years ago
or yesterday

'Listen here, little masters,
if Christ came back today
he would definitely be making his own tea.']

Hand-in-hand with this feminist polemic is a political commitment to the Welsh language. There are poems specifically discussing the campaigns of Cymdeithas yr Iaith and the speaker's personal involvement, such as 'Abertawe 5 Leeds 1 'A' Wing 0' (1982) and 'Wedi'r achos' (After the trial, 1982). Moreover, there are some poems which explicitly combine Welsh, feminist and pacifist politics, such as 'Cadwn y bwystfil rhag y mur' (Let's keep the beast from the wall, 1986) and 'Sul y Mamau yn Greenham, 1984' (Mothering Sunday in Greenham, 1984, published in 1986).

In addition to publishing her own poetry of commitment in the 1980s, Elfyn edited the pioneering anthology of Welsh women's poetry, *Hel Dail Gwyrdd* (Collecting Green Leaves, 1985). She was not only the editor but the inspirational force behind that anthology and a succeeding one, *O'r Iawn Ryw* (Of the Right Sex, 1991). Her introduction to the 1985 volume makes clear the celebratory and recuperative nature of the venture:

> Cyfrol sy'n ceisio gwneud iawn am ddiffygion y gorffennol, ynghyd â nawsio dyheadau ac awyddfrydau merched heddiw, yw ffrwyth y Flodeugerdd hon, ac un sydd yn rhan o'r profiad mawr cyffrous o fod yn ferched, yn Gymry Cymraeg, ac yn feirdd. Cip yn unig fydd y gyfrol ar y byd ymryddhaol a chaethiwus honno. (Nodyn: benywaidd yw byd, am y tro).[16]

> [The harvest of this anthology is a volume which attempts to make amends for the failures of the past, as well as to give a flavour of the desires and aspirations of women today, and it is also a part of that big, exciting experience of being women, Welsh-speakers, and poets. This book gives just a glimpse of that liberating and constricting world. (Note: Menna Elfyn makes the gender of the noun *byd* [world], feminine, as she says, for the present.)]

It is necessary to acknowledge, however, that not all Welsh women poets were as ready as Menna Elfyn, or, indeed, Gillian Clarke, to be labelled as 'feminist'. Both Welsh-language and English-language poets who published in this period were sometimes reluctant to be placed, as they saw it, in a ghetto of 'woman poets'. Poets such as Einir Jones, Sheenagh Pugh, Ruth Bidgood and Nesta Wyn Jones have expressed such anxieties publicly, some refusing to allow their work to appear in women-only anthologies.

It may be that the reluctance of some English-language women poets to embrace a specifically female public identity is connected with the fact that 'Anglo-Welsh' literary culture generally tended to suffer from an inferiority complex. As Gillian Clarke has noted, so-called 'Anglo-Welsh' literature was for many years regarded 'as not good enough or too local' for inclusion on exam-board syllabuses.[17] Others, like Christine Evans, are uncomfortable with the anger which appeared to them to be a dominant tone in much modern women's poetry. While Evans acknowledges that women's lived experience inevitably affects the rhythms and the poetic sensibilities of their writing, she is reluctant to accept that 'imagination is subject to the limitations of gender'.[18]

Notwithstanding this understandable reluctance to be pigeon-holed, Christine Evans's poetic practice, as demonstrated for example in her collections *Looking Inland* (1983), *Cometary Phases* (1989) and *Island of Dark Horses* (1995), tends to foreground women's subjectivity and female experience, often in conjunction with an acute perception of time and place. *Cometary Phases* begins with a poem entitled 'Thunder above Llanberis' which is a palpably atmospheric poem, conjuring up the tension before the storm and the preternaturally acute senses of the 'we' of the poem, as they climb the mountain away from the tourists on the little train, sheltering in a quarry from the downpour. Like Chamberlain, Clarke and other women writers, Jones expresses an intensely felt awareness of the land, seen in corporeal terms, the rocks of the quarry forming 'not . . . walls / but wounds'.[19] In poems like 'Tree Wife' and the 'Cometary Phases' sequence, the voice does become explicitly female; in the latter, birth is figured as a fraught sea-journey:

> Twelve years ago tonight
> caught up in a swirl
> stronger than the moving tides
> of sea or air, mere hundred-fathom-stirrers
> we brought each other
> to an unknown shore.
> I was the boat, the frail-hulled rocking craft
> my blood the tide
> but you were the pilot
> you gauged the moment, steered
> both of us home
>
> on the rim of the last stretched wave
> where the journey begins.[20]

To say that Evans's poetry of this period is reminiscent of Gillian Clarke's (as is that of a number of other strong poets of the time, such as Hilary Llewellyn-Williams and Kathy Day) is not to suggest that Evans's poetry is derivative. On the contrary, Evans has a distinctive voice and a powerful north Welsh allegiance, but the subjects she addresses and the way in which she evokes an animated and gendered landscape appear now to be the fruit of this feminist period in Welsh women's writing. Similarly, like Clarke, as an English-language writer Evans is acutely sensitive to and sympathetic with the Welsh language and culture amid which she lives, as expressed in her well-known poem, 'Second Language', dedicated to her pupils 'Carys P., Carys T., Elena, Manon, Nia and Teyrnon':

> Five girls and a boy riding a name out of myth
> whose language fills the mouth like fruit
> who have grown in the delicate light
> of an old walled garden that was once the world . . .
>
> In their calm faces I can find no clues
> that they are still at ease in their own skins
> that dredging for this voice has drowned no other
> and my teaching has not made them strangers.[21]

Working as an English teacher, Evans felt anxiety about the danger of loosening the ties of Welsh speakers to their language. Indeed, in a poem such as this, the teacher seems almost in thrall to her pupils, in awe of their connection to a mythologized land which she, too, clearly desires. In later poems there is a shift; the voice of the poems becomes more securely that of a native, not an incomer. The identification with the land becomes more intense but never sentimental, because the speaker farms the land and depends on it and the sea for survival. *Island of Dark Horses* (1995), a detailed and loving evocation of Bardsey Island, where Evans lives and farms for part of the year, invites comparison with Brenda Chamberlain's representation of the same place. For both artists, Enlli has a dual being, as a place of mystery and of the mythological imagination and history on the one hand, and as a place of practical living, where people struggle with the forces of the sea and weather to scrape a living, on the other. Morover, Evans sees Enlli and the Llŷn peninsula very much as part of Wales (arguably, unlike

Chamberlain, for whom a sense of national identity seems irrelevant). In the poem 'Llŷn', for instance, she describes the view to seaward from the tip of the peninsula:

> The sea we look out over is a navel
> the wrinkled belly-button
> of an older world: after dark
> like busy star-systems, the lights
> of Harlech, Aberystwyth, Abergwaun
> wink and beckon. The sun's gone down
> red as a wound behind Wicklow. A creaking of sail away
> Cernyw and Llydaw wait.
> Once, here was where what mattered
> happened. A small place
> at the foot of cliffs of falling light;
> horizons that look empty.
> If we let ourselves believe it,
> fringes.[22]

The use of the Welsh words for Cornwall (*Cernyw*) and Brittany (*Llydaw*) here indicate not only a sense of an historicized landscape, from where the ships set sail a century before, but also a successful integration into the Welsh-language culture that the speaker could only envy in the earlier poem, 'Second Language'. Moreover, the use of the first-person plural 'we' in the penultimate line suggests a sense of shared and defiant national identity, a refusal to be written off as marginal or peripheral. Certainly, in Evans's writing, as in Elfyn's and Clarke's, Wales is the central place of consciousness, the old 'wrinkled belly-button' described in Evans's 'Llŷn', with its inevitable connotations of maternity and origin.

Hilary Llewellyn-Williams, too, offers us an engaging, sometimes surreal 'shape of Wales'. Landscape and the world of nature are as central to her poems as they are to those of Christine Evans or Gillian Clarke. In her poem 'Capel Mair' (Mary's Chapel), from the 1997 volume *animaculture*, for example, she appears to turn away from the more mythologically inflected poems of her earlier volumes, *The Tree Calendar* (1987) and *Book of Shadows* (1990), to a representation of contemporary Wales. The ruined chapel on the hill is glimpsed from the motorway and it becomes the subject of a historical meditation on its meanings:

> Why was the chapel built here
> so high, such a weary climb
> from the valley, such a trial

for old joints, for the mothers
of toddlers . . .?

    . . . the chapel stands alone
on the hill, to the Mother of sun
and snow whose place this is . . .
        . . . Old, old,
older than church or Celtic battlements

her shape in the land, river and tree and stone.[23]

Although the poem begins with mundane modern reality – the motorway and the nearby steelworks – it ends with a return to the vision established in Llewellyn-Williams's earlier works: the land of Wales as spiritually animated by a mother goddess, that being glimpsed also in many of Gillian Clarke's poems. 'Capel Mair' captures well the austerity of the Welsh landscape – the ruined chapel looking down on the industrialized lands below – but beyond that contemporary consciousness there is a more elemental one, which is glimpsed by a number of the writers of this generation and affords a different configuration of feminism from the more politically active one of, say, Menna Elfyn or Meg Elis.

While Hilary Llewellyn-Williams finds the elemental Mother in the landscape itself, Catherine Fisher attempts to connect with her own 'Great-grandmother' in the poem of that name. A Newport-born poet, Fisher's ancestors came from Ireland, and in the 1988 volume, *Immrama* (Sea Voyages), she engages in voyages of the imagination back and forth across the Irish sea. In 'Great-grandmother' the voice of the poem addresses the long-dead woman directly, revivifying her through the unpromising 'dusty trail of documents', which nevertheless is represented as a walk through the forest of genealogy.[24] She finds on one document her great-grandmother's cross, in lieu of a signature: 'only two snapped twigs show where you passed'.[25] She brings 'Hannah O'Connor' back to life, imagining her 'work-worn' fingers, figuring herself as a hawk swooping on its prey. The meeting at 'our crossroads' is momentary, but the illiterate Hannah is acknowledged and paid tribute to as 'the begetter of history'. The history of Ireland lurks like a shadow behind her – 'all my Dark Ages'. Although Fisher is in several ways very different from many of her overtly feminist contemporaries, this is a poem which shows the coalescence of the personal and cultural memory, embodied in the almost forgotten female ancestor. That the explanation 'Hannah O'Connor – her mark' written underneath her fragile cross, described as 'slightly disapproving', is in a male hand remains unspecified, but the poem does suggest, without effort, the gendered nature of Hannah's insignificance. The poem raises her from this lowly status and, by implication, puts her on a par with the ancient kings and queens of Tara.[26] What is striking about this excursion into family history is that the temporal is figured in terms of the spatial, and is contained within unprepossessing physical objects, such as the tremulous cross inscribed on the page. A similar melding of the historical and topographical takes place in Ruth Bidgood's fine poem, 'Kindred', where the speaker walks through an austere moorland landscape, 'hear[ing] the stony flow of the stream / as speech' and coming at last to a ruined cottage where:

> [s]omething calls, with a voice
> seeming at first as alien
> as the stream's, yet inescapable
> and after a while more like
> the calling of kindred. [27]

Angharad Tomos's 1991 novel *Si Hei Lwli* (Hush-a-Bye-Baby) is another text which goes in search of the dead grandmother. Eleni takes her cantankerous great-aunt Bigw on a car journey to visit the grave of Eleni's grandmother. Tomos's Prose Medal-winning novel is a kind of Welsh female 'on the road', which takes on an allegorical dimension when it becomes clear that the physical journey is also a journey backwards in time. The novel contrasts starkly with Tomos's earlier *Yma o Hyd* (Still Here, 1985), which, rather than the freedom of the road, has as its setting a prison cell, where the protagonist, the symbolically named Blodeuwedd, has been incarcerated as a result of her civil disobedience in the Welsh-language campaign. At one point in the novel, Blodeuwedd is summoned to the governor's office, but as she waits outside she hears news of the nuclear missiles arriving in Greenham and she becomes angry:

> Be gebyst dwi'n i wneud mewn carchar Sais yn aros yn amyneddgar am gerydd? . . . Dwi'n troi'n sombi. Dwi run fath ag oen bach yn disgwyl tu allan i'r lladd-dŷ. Dyna sut betha ydan ni'r Cymry bellach . . . Mam bach, dwi'n rhedag! . . . A rhedag i ffwrdd wnes i – ffwl sbîd i lawr y corridor . . . rhedag . . . rhedag . . . rhedag . . . achos tra dwi'n rhedag dwi'n rhyddrhyddrhyddrhydd . . .[28]

[What the hell am I doing in an English jail waiting patiently for my punishment? . . . I'm turning into a zombie. I'm like a little lamb waiting outside the slaughter-house. That's what we Welsh are by now . . . Holy Mother, I'm off! . . . And I ran away – full speed down the corridor . . . running . . . running . . . running . . . because while I'm running I'm freefreefreefree . . .]

All of Tomos's novels have female narrators and firmly place the woman at the centre of a strong conception of Wales and a continuing, if beleaguered, Welsh identity. Tomos's work is committed both politically and in a religious sense, as becomes more evident in her later work, such as *Wele'n Gwawrio* (Behold the Dawn, 1997). Her most unusual novel is *Titrwm*, published in 1994, a poetic text narrated by Awen, a young pregnant women who is unable to hear or speak but communicates with her unborn child, Titrwm. This novel stands out among Tomos's oeuvre, not only for its distinctive, experimental style but also because it has no overt political 'message'. Nevertheless, it is a celebration of the Welsh language in all its poetic richness; published by the always combative press, Y Lolfa, it has the following note on its final page: 'This is a mysterious book written in the Welsh language to an unborn child. A catalogue record for this book is not available from the British Library.'[29] Clearly, the book is capable of an allegorical reading; like Menna Elfyn's 'Cân y di-lais i British Telecom / Song of a voiceless person to British Telecom'[30] the isolated, silenced state of Awen (whose name means 'Muse') may be seen as a symbol of the condition of the Welsh-speaker in the British state. In Elfyn's poem, Welsh-speakers are like refugees, 'possessors of nothing but their dispossession, / mufflers over their mouths' ('yn heidio'n ddieiddo; / cadachau dros eu cegau').[31]

Such dispossession, as we have seen, is a recurring theme in Welsh women's writing, and can be found also in English-language work of this period. Glenda Beagan's short story 'Scream, Scream', published in her first published volume of short stories, *The Medlar Tree* (1992), is a striking example. The initially quiet, atmospheric setting, a female psychiatric hospital ward, is invaded by an ear-splitting, un-ignorable scream. The scream appears to have a terrifying life of its own, above and beyond the tiny body of its producer, Mrs Jenkins, 'the last of the Jenkinses of Sgubor Fawr'.[32] Gradually, Mrs Jenkins's scream begins to express the anguish of all the various kinds of women, 'mad' and sane, within the ward. In an extraordinary, poetic passage Beagan writes:

It's as if the scream slowly inhabits them all, slowly expresses them all. It's as if the terror slowly seeps out of it, while another nameless quality enters. What does it consist of, this blend of dark voices beyond Mrs Jenkins' own, far beyond, ungovernable, timeless voices without meaning or order, but shot through with a rhythm they recognize, a substance they have felt themselves, all of them . . . It is a medley of voices, the cry of aftermath, of battle and birth, of sap and sinew.[33]

Mrs Jenkins is a childless woman who is the last of her family to live in the remote Welsh farmhouse of Sgubor Fawr; her scream is the expression of a specifically Welsh sense of cultural dispossession, but at the same time it is also, as the above passage indicates, an expression of a specifically female anguish and despair. Strangely, however, when the scream stops, there is a sense of catharsis – the demons have been released and there is a suggestion of healing calm. Mrs Jenkins, unabashed, has a cup of tea and prepares stoically to return home.

As well as short stories, Beagan also published one volume of poetry, *Vixen* (1996). Many of the poems here are about Welsh mythological figures, such as Blodeuwedd, Arianrhod and Melangell, figures who in Beagan's imagined landscape still inhabit the hills of Wales. The first-person speaker is often sitting on hilltops, waiting, or on quests to be reunited with some elusive female spirit of the place or 'to find a speech, a tongue / to fit interstices / of this land worn close as a skin'.[34] Elsewhere, in poems such as 'Triskel', she adopts a first-person plural voice, speaking perhaps for the border people of the old Flintshire, where she herself has her roots:

And if we are the disinherited
assembling here the coiled myth
of our life, in a region budding
at the nodal point
of history's dichotomies . . .

you'll find we speak a brightly hybrid tongue
and watch with skill the blowing of the winds.[35]

Again, there is an acknowledgement of dispossession but, at the same time, an assertion of survival; like Angharad Tomos, Beagan is expressing the feeling of being 'yma o hyd' (still here).

Beagan is also one of several women authors at this time who use the mythical figure of Blodeuwedd in their writing. In the *Mabinogi* story Blodeuwedd is a woman constructed out of flowers by the male magicians, Gwydion and Math, but she refuses to obey her masters, following her own sexual desires; her punishment is metamorphosis into an owl. It is not surprising, then, that the feminist ethos of this period should have found Blodeuwedd such a promising subject: Blodeuwedd becomes, for many writers, a feminist heroine, who refuses the male order and gains her freedom, not an emblem of sexual immorality who is punished for her sins.

By the turn of the century, Blodeuwedd had herself become something of a stereotype in Welsh women's writing, but it was almost as if every female writer was obscurely called upon at this stage to interpret Blodeuwedd.[36] Beagan's version has the woman as owl speaking and celebrating her freedom: 'Out of the coppiced hazels I skim / into blue light . . . So how is this punishment?'[37]

Not all women poets took to the *Mabinogi* and the hills, however. A poet such as Jean Earle remained firmly rooted in the prosaic streets of south Wales, which she nevertheless views with an artist's transformative vision. Her poem 'Grandma's House' is another text which addresses the grandmother directly and effects a return journey to interrogate a personal, female history. The speaker returns in imagination to childhood and remembers walking down the tunnel to her grandmother's house: 'It is like being born, / Dark and dangerous'.[38] The contemplative voice of the poem muses on how 'memory makes us', the 'wooden plait' decorating the barometer on her wall recalling her grandmother's braided hair; when she taps the barometer, 'you are with me: sofa and hotter fire'.[39] Though the evocation of the domestic here is warm and enticing, the memory is not without fear, as the 'dark and dangerous' approach suggests; at the end of the poem, Mr Stokes, the grandmother's widower neighbour, is remembered, not seen but heard, always playing his violin. The impressions made on the child are indelible: 'Whenever I meet a violin, / Mr Stokes is remembered'.[40] Another poem about memory from the same collection is 'Quaker's Yard Junction, 1950', which conjures up a similar south Wales urban setting, redolent with the sights and sounds of a particular place at a particular time:

> Colliers bundling whippets
> To Pontypridd races.
> Schoolchildren, banging doors.

> . . . Trucks noisily travelling. Lewis-Merthyr,
> Powell Duffryn, Ebbw Vale, Cory's . . .
>
> Over the bridge, to fetch milk
> From the village. Waiting the signals' click
> Against sunset.
> Emerald and red
> Sequins the echoing bottles . . .
> Stars the long mind.[41]

Again, personal and national history coalesce in a vivid picture of place which, by the 1980s, was utterly transformed. The incantation of the names of the huge coal-mining companies echoes hollowly in a contemporary Wales where more than half the coal-mines had closed down in the wake of the bitter miners' strike of 1984–5. Yet the poem is by no means despairing; as Earle says in 'Grandma's House', 'memory makes us', and the 'long mind' of this poem stretches back in a gesture of inclusion and possession. The place is transformed, but the memory remains.

History, imagined spatially and pictorially, is also present in genres other than verse, notably the novel. Following in the footsteps of previous Welsh female historical novelists, such as Gwyneth Vaughan and Marion Eames, Gweneth Lilly set her 1984 novel, *Orpheus*, in Roman Britain during the fourth century AD. Despite the chronological distance which Lilly creates, the novel can be seen to engage with contemporary debates about colonialism and Welsh identity. The characters of Lilly's novel are Romanized Brythons, whose duality is indicated initially by the fact that they have two names, in Brythonic and Latin. The main protagonist, Trystan, for instance, is also called by the Romanized form of his name, Drustagnus, while his cousin Llywernawc is also, in Latin, Lovernacus. Clearly, the Brythonic names for a Welsh reader set up echoes of contemporary Welsh: 'Llywernawc', for instance, means 'fox', which is similar to one of the modern Welsh words for fox, *llwynog*. The attitudes of the Brythons towards the Roman colonizers vary considerably, from the cheerful collaboration of Trystan's mother, who affirms 'We're all Romans now' ('Rydan ni i gyd yn Rhufeiniaid bellach'),[42] to the bitter resentment of Llywernawc, who reluctantly sends his son to school to learn Latin because 'if he wants to stand his ground against the devils, he's got to learn their language' ('os ydi o am ddal ei dir yn erbyn y diawl'od, rhaid iddo ddysgu eu hiaith nhw').[43] The society represented is sustained by slave workers, and there are vast social divisions between the high-status Roman officials and the slaves who run their households, divisions which are significant for the romance plot in the novel, since Trystan, a free mosaic-artist from a respectable Romanized Brythonic family, falls in love with a slave girl, Serena.

However, Lilly confounds readerly expectations of a romantic plot for, when Trystan succeeds in buying Serena's freedom, she reveals that she is actually the lover of her master, Lucius Plautus, and runs back to the villa, where she is murdered by his jealous female relatives. Complicating the plot is the existence of a number of secret religious cults, including that of Orpheus and the new religion from the East, Christianity, though the Brythons still maintain their loyalty to the 'old gods'. In the end, Llywernawc tries to persuade Trystan to leave Corinium and return with him to farm the land: 'Haven't you noticed how the tide has turned? They're coming back to the land and to the hills and are building houses and farming the land as I do' ('Dwyt ti ddim wedi sylwi fel y mae'r llanw'n troi? Maen nhw'n dod yn ôl i'r wlad a'r bryniau, a chodi tai a thrin y tir fel finna').[44]

Like Dorothy Edwards's short story, 'The Conquered', which also draws implicit parallels between the British and the Roman Empires, and the relation of the Welsh to both, Lilly's novel *Orpheus* can be seen as a text which masquerades as an innocuous, carefully researched historical novel, but has an underlying and challenging post-colonial subtext. In *Orpheus*, the representatives of imperial rule are corrupt and conniving, but their house is divided against itself and appears to be collapsing from within. Trystan is the artist who stands in the middle, representing the society to itself in his mosaic floors, receptive to new ideas and cults but also sensitive to the call of the 'old gods'. He develops a new understanding of the ways in which women are enslaved in his society and realizes that for him, as an artist, freedom means everything: 'without that, how could I be a craftsman worth his salt?' ('heb hynny, sut y galla' i fod yn grefftwr gwerth fy halen?')[45]

Another historical novel of this period, Siân James's *A Small Country* (1979), is set in rural west Wales just before and during the First World War. Rather than the male artist figure who is the protagonist of Lilly's *Orpheus*, James's main protagonist is Catrin, a young woman searching for a sense of identity and vocation. She longs vaguely to be an artist but resigns herself to training as a nurse; the advent of war strengthens her resolve:

> Now that the war had come, it seemed the appropriate time for putting aside personal vanities like love affairs and painting and drawing, and for making a serious commitment . . . The outbreak of war enabled her to forget herself and really think of herself as a nurse.[46]

Another woman, an ardent young English suffrage campaigner called Rose, also becomes a nurse, switching her energies to a patriotic and idealistic 'struggle to defend the civilization of the world'.[47] However, her first contact with real wounded soldiers and their terrible personal testimonies rids her of her illusions: 'Her ideas of warfare had been so remote; men on horseback looking rather fine . . . Stark, unhidden fear was something she had not considered.'[48]

Tom, Catrin's brother, joins up because he thinks it his duty; rather like his namesake, Twm, in Kate Roberts's *Feet in Chains*, he also believes 'it will all be over by Christmas'. Also like Roberts's characters, Twm is moved by the plight of Belgium, 'a peaceful little country, not much bigger than Wales'.[49] However, like Owen in the earlier novel, Tom's experiences in the war make him suddenly aware of his Welsh identity, one at which he has previously scoffed as an Oxford-educated, sophisticated young man. In a letter to his sister, Tom expresses his homesickness poignantly:

> I intend to come home. And when I do, I shall be like old Prosser, never venturing beyond Erw Fach Bridge . . . When I think of the civilization we're fighting for, I can only think about the patch I know best . . . It seemed so strange that in this place, with all hell's forces of destruction let loose about me, I should be concerned with things like the language and culture of our unimportant small country: I suppose we must all fix on something to keep us sane.[50]

Yet another attitude to the war is expressed by a old man who has never left his local 'patch':

> The bloody English . . . wanted me to fight once; against the Russians, I think, or the Turks. Not I. My family fight against the bloody English, not for them . . . My father burnt his ricks in the tithe war, ready to starve rather than pay the tithes . . . My grandfather was one of Becca's maidens in the hungry forties. They were fighters if you like . . .[51]

This construction of Welsh history is one of continual resistance, a willingness to fight but only on Welsh terms. The novel also reveals, through Tom's experience, how the 'square mile' functions as a microcosm of the whole nation, especially in times of crisis.

James's novel clearly positions itself in relation to a Welsh female tradition of writing about war, primarily with relation to Kate Roberts's *Feet in Chains*, which is constantly echoed and alluded to in the text. In some ways, though, James is rewriting Roberts's account of the family, gender and marriage from a later, explicitly feminist point of view. Where Roberts highlights the role of the suffering mother in war and emphasizes the cohesiveness of the family and its demand for propriety and duty, James's family is falling apart through adultery and Anglicization, her female characters challenging their traditional roles and taking the opportunities offered them by the war – ironically – to forge a vocation for themselves. Thus, despite the obvious disjunctures between *A Small Country* and *Orpheus*, it is striking that both authors have used the genre of the historical novel to explore contemporary ideas about national and gender identity.

Another of Siân James's novels, *Love and War* (1997), is set in a west Wales town during the Second World War. Rhian, a young schoolteacher, has a husband away at war and a lover, Gwynn, who insists on obeying his call-up papers, despite Rhian's impassioned pacifist and nationalist arguments against doing so. The focus in this novel is very much on the anxieties and trauma of those left behind in rural Wales; James's innovation here is that she mixes tragic material with a great deal of social comedy. Rhian's mother-in-law, for example, is outraged that their local minister is preaching Christianity:

> To hear him carrying on about the Germans being God's children, only led astray, is deeply offensive, don't you think so, Rhian? Gwilym Martin, Horeb, isn't such a milksop, I can tell you. No, Mr Martin gets to the point quick enough, praying for the forces of God to smash the legions of Satan, and no nonsense about forgiveness either. I'd switch to Horeb in a minute, only Bryn's afraid of losing custom in Tabernacle.[52]

Another young teacher at Rhian's school, Miss Mary Powell, Maths, has a fiancé fighting in Burma called Alun Brooke. However, bizarrely, this fiancé turns out to be an elaborate figment of Miss Powell's imagination, much to Rhian's disgust, since she has spent many hours empathizing with Miss Powell over the fate of this non-existent person. Indeed, 'Alun Brooke' has become more real to Rhian than her almost forgotten husband, Huw. Mary Powell, unhinged, commits suicide by drowning herself in a river. Despite this death, and that of Gwynn in the war, the final pages of the novel emphasize a sense of survival and endurance; a baby is born and Rhian finds herself, after all, 'glad to be alive'.[53] Rhian had earlier attempted to persuade Gwynn not to join up, partly on pacifist and partly on nationalist grounds; she sees his proposed action as 'joining the English army':

> He says my concept of Wales is over-romantic, that the Welsh way of life I talk about is no different from the way of life of any poor, radical, non-conformist section of society in any part of Britain.
>
> I say that our language and literature make us a separate nation so that we are set apart from any other section of society. We are a nation with a national culture and if that's an over-romantic idea, I admit to being over-romantic.[54]

But Siân James is not exclusively a historical novelist; a number of her novels and short stories have contemporary settings, including *Storm at Arberth* (1994). The novel has two central female protagonists, Marian, who is a level-headed widow, and her flamboyant friend, Sally. As the title suggests, the novel is set in Pembrokeshire, and the plot revolves around Sally's making a foolhardy expedition to one of the peaks of the Preseli mountains, in search of a lost female identity. Sally is experiencing a mid-life crisis in which she feels that she has lost her sexual power; the trip to the mountain is an attempt to regain that from the 'mother goddess' herself. What is invigorating in James's narratives is the way she maintains an ironic viewpoint, often mocking her characters' crackpot ideas but at the same time allowing us to empathize with and understand them. She also ironizes the romance genre that she habitually uses:

> Oh, don't be so maudlin, [Marian] told herself. People are forever sleeping with people these days without making a great song and dance about it . . . In Victorian times, people . . . thought that love conquered all and made the world go round, but now we know it's only a wholesome, health-giving experience like jogging and bran.[55]

The mountain-climbing episode in the novel is reverberant with literary echoes, a kind of pastiche of the literary landscape, as well as a reclaiming of it. Arberth is the site of Pwyll's court in the Mabinogi and the setting for several stories about Rhiannon, or Rigantona, the Brythonic horse goddess. The Pembrokeshire setting, thus, allows James to draw on an ancient Welsh world of myth and matriarchal power, but the undercutting humour is always present:

'Goddess,' Sally continued. 'It makes me angry that we only have words like Goddess and Priestess, words which indicate a diminution, a reduction. We should have something different and larger and essentially female.'

'Thank goodness for witch,' Marian said, 'and of course trollop. Will you have a scone, Mrs Dainton?'[56]

Another novel from this period which explores women's sexuality, bereavement and the Welsh landscape is Catherine Merriman's *State of Desire* (1996). Set in south-east Wales, the novel focuses on Jenny, a widow, still bereft after the death of her husband a year before; the plot concerns Jenny's 'reawakening', both into an ill-advised sexual passion with a younger man and into a new political consciousness, as she opposes the plan to establish an opencast mine on the hill close to her house. The novel draws parallels between the female body and the mountain which Jenny and her friend Sal attempt to 'save'. In one of her letters to her dead husband, Jenny elaborates these parallels:

Sal reckons she's sorted everything for me. In terms of opencasting, would you believe? You're the overburden. Clearly visible, looming barrow-like on the horizon, but half grassed over, you'll be glad to hear, and only a hazard when the wind's blowing. I'm down in the void, digging out the goodies. That's Mark, and Gareth too, I suppose. I said, no way, I'm trying to fill in black holes, not dig them out, but she said, what, with penises? and that it amounted to the same thing. It doesn't though, does it? I'm not digging anything out. Not acting out of rapaciousness, or greed. Nor out of malice or vindictiveness. If I'm forced to use the same metaphor, with you as overburden, then I'm the mountain, aren't I? The damaged, bereaved mountain. And all I'm trying to do, I'm sure, is restore myself.[57]

Merriman's novel is underpinned by both an ecological and a feminist ideology; interestingly, this also intersects with a new sense of belonging to Wales. Jenny is an English migrant who comes to Wales initially as an 'adventurer, not [a] settler . . . [she and Pete were] English dropouts, playing at self-sufficiency or self-enlightenment'.[58] But then she becomes pregnant and 'discovered the Welsh: midwives, health visitors, other pregnant young women' and begins to gain a sense of her patch of Wales, 'to feel a resident . . . consolidating. Digging in.'[59] The death of her Welsh husband temporarily sets Jenny adrift again, but the threat of the multinational company destroying 'her' mountain re-establishes her connection with Wales and with her own grieving body. There are a number of parallels between Merriman and Siân James as novelists; both focus on female desire and acknowledge that the sexual imperative frequently leads women into difficult situations, so that there is a shared interest in the intimately personal. But, at the same time, these personal and sexual quests are situated within a specifically Welsh cultural and political landscape; gender identity and national identity interweave in unexpected ways. Both James and Merriman show how the removal of the sexual taboo from the romance genre has allowed modern twentieth-century women novelists to explore the complexities of female identity in a way which was not possible for predecessors such as Allen Raine or Gwyneth Vaughan.

Both James and Merriman are accomplished short-story writers as well as novelists. Although James is concerned with gender and national identity, she is equally interested in class issues, and these are frequently explored in her short stories. Like a number of her foremothers in Welsh women's writing, she attempts to represent the experiences of female characters who have been rendered voiceless in society. A number of examples of this can be found in the short stories of her 1996 collection, *Not Singing Exactly*. 'Happy as Saturday Night' is a first-person, dialectal narrative in the voice of a girl from the tough Cardiff estate of 'St Beuno's'. Although St Beuno's is fictional, the story presents a bleakly realistic picture of life in such a place, made all the more poignant for the narrator's unquenchable optimism:

> I've got these good mates, see, and we has a great time on a Saturday. We works hard in the bleeding factory all week and it's all for Saturday night. Afternoons we might go to Goldees or Top Girl and try on some clothes and we like things that are sexy, real sexy I mean, we're not afraid of flaunting ourselves because we always sticks together, so we're always safe.[60]

Throughout the narrative the unnamed speaker repeats the pronoun 'we', emphasizing the solidarity of the five girls who go out together every Saturday night. Janice is the only one of the group who is married with a small child; the husband, Charlie, is regarded as 'some sort of a new man',[61] because he allows Janice out with her friends once a week. One night, though, the narrator returns with Janice to her flat after their night out, very late, because they haven't the fare for the taxi. While the narrator tries to sleep on the sofa, she hears a commotion:

> At first I think it's someone in the next flat but then I recognizes Janice's voice and she's crying and saying, 'I couldn't help it. It wasn't my fault' . . . and Charlie shouting, calling her a slag . . . And then there's another sort of noise and Janice shouting, 'No. Please. No, no, no.' And I pulls the blanket right over my head because I knows exactly what's going on but I'm too frightened to get up and help her. I just have to lay there and listen to it, the thud, thud, thud, thud, until it suddenly stops.[62]

The focus on domestic violence in this story is representative of an increasing willingness in women writers towards the end of the century to bear witness to this continuing oppression, which many women suffer. It appears, shockingly, in Clare Morgan's impressive short story, 'Losing', which presents a scene of domestic violence through the eyes of an uncomprehending young girl.[63] After glimpsing a neighbour, Mr Bristow, beating and kicking his sister, she is amazed to find the same man come out of the house as normal and give her a lift: 'He seemed the same. Quiet and tidy. You would never have thought there was any harm in him. His hair grew down in a brown wave in front of his ears. She didn't like that. But his hands were clean. He seemed neutral.' When she gives him a packet of fresh bantam's eggs, he 'took them not roughly . . . but gently, the effort of gentleness making his fingers quiver'.[64]

The unnamed girl is beginning to learn the nature of the patriarchy in which she lives, hidden under an innocuous and 'neutral' façade. On the day when she begins her first period – 'losing', as her mother calls it – she gets an insight into the adult world that she is about, tentatively, to enter. She has a moment of insight as she returns home: 'She felt for the first time a sense of herself in relation to everything else, as if she were part of a single system, a fragment of something hurrying towards its own special destiny', and at the very end of the narrative she approaches her own house, 'the door opened and her mother stood back, waiting for her to go in'.[65] This subtle story figures the trajectory of a woman's life in spatial terms: the young girl enters the domestic space over a threshold which is presided over by her mother. Yet inside the domestic space of the kitchen, the woman's domain is interrupted and chilled by the threatening masculine presence: 'not until nearly an hour later . . . could the kitchen rid itself of the cold blast his opening and closing of the door had let enter'.[66] This story presents a pessimistic view of Welsh women's position in society; it is almost as if the girl accepts that this is her position – she is on the 'losing' side, by virtue of her gender.

In both Siân James's and Clare Morgan's stories, the ill-treatment of women is complicated and exacerbated by economic dependence and class position. Sally Roberts Jones, whose early work has already been mentioned in the previous chapter, is a poet who sees class as a far more urgent limiting factor in the emergence of a poet than that of gender, noting that neglected women artists recovered by feminist scholars tend to be middle class, when 'potential working class artists in whatever medium rarely, if ever, had . . . [the] benefit of developing their artistic ability'.[67] Jones makes strong claims for the Welsh literary environment as unconstrained by the issue of class, and thus inclusive of women in ways not possible for mainstream English culture: 'In Wales things are different; social class has little or nothing to do with being a published poet . . . and, relative to their numbers, women are equally well represented in anthologies and publishers' lists, and equally well discussed by critics.'[68]

Roberts Jones's view of the critical establishment may be rather too positive but there is some truth in the view that Welsh women writers, reflecting Welsh society generally, have been less restricted to the middle class than have their English contemporaries. Nevertheless, as the stories of James and Morgan discussed above indicate, class is a determining force in Welsh writing and affects female characters' conception of themselves and their relation to the nation. In the 'underclass' characters portrayed by Siân James in 'Happy as Saturday Night' and in other stories by her, such as 'Not Singing Exactly', class position increases the characters' sense of helplessness and dispossession.

Although a number of the Welsh women writers of earlier periods, such as Kate Bosse-Griffiths in the 1940s and 50s and Jane Edwards in the 1960s, broke taboos regarding the expression of female sexuality in twentieth-century Welsh fiction, it was not until the 1990s, with the publication of Manon Rhys's novel, *Cysgodion* (Shadows), that sex was openly and daringly treated by a woman writer. Indeed, the subject of *Cysgodion* is, precisely, female sexuality and the various pleasures, dilemmas and problems that it brings to Welsh women in the modern age. Rhys's novel is also modern in its self-reflexivity, for the central character of the text, Lois Daniel, is

171

herself a novelist, writing a work called *Cysgodion* about the life of
the Welsh artist, Gwen John, and her relationship with the French
sculptor, Rodin. Lois Daniel's novel and Manon Rhys's interweave
cleverly on the page, while the story of Gwen John and Lois's own
rather lurid sexual life run in revealing parallel. Lois, in studying
Gwen John, is trying to understand the masochistic relationship with
the man she called 'Master', for ostensibly, at least, Lois herself is a
feminist, an independent and successful woman with no time for the
self-abnegation which traditional notions of femininity require.
However, Lois's story shows how a modern Welsh woman still
suffers from the duality that afflicted ambitious women in the past in
different ways – one is reminded, for instance, of Dilys Cadwaladr's
tortuous relationship with her 'other' self, mentioned in chapter 2. In
the case of Lois, it is not a duality between the housewife and the
artist, as experienced by Cadwaladr, but a duality between the
feminist and the sexual being who craves male attention, suffers
from insecurity and jealousy – even of her own daughter – and who
appears to be reliving the self-sacrifice of the woman artist about
whom she is writing. *Cysgodion* is a daring book, not only because of
the detailed description of sexual desire and sexual acts, but because
Lois herself is a deeply unappealing central character, referred to,
regrettably accurately, in the novel as a 'hen bitsh' (old bitch).
Cysgodion is a novel which engages with the 'shadows' of the past
and with the problems of being a woman artist; what the novel
suggests is that the patriarchal order of the past, despite the advent of
feminism, is by no means over yet, at least not in Wales. The novel
expresses an ambivalent attitude towards feminism, as do some of
the poets of this period, though all are in some way engaging with
gender identity to a hitherto unprecedented degree.

Manon Rhys's earlier volume of short stories, *Cwtsho* (1988), is
also taboo-breaking, in that it deals with the difficult subject of
child abuse in a Welsh context. The tacit assumption perhaps had
been, as Lois Daniel's daughter exclaims in *Cysgodion*, 'Dyw pobol
ddim yn neud pethe fel 'na'n Gymraeg!'[69] (People don't do those
kinds of things in Welsh.) Indeed, it is in the 1990s that a number of
texts beginning to engage directly with such abuse begin to appear.
Another example is Siân Evans's 1996 play, *Little Sister*, first
performed by the Made in Wales theatre company in Cardiff. This
play deals with the rape and corruption of a sixteen-year-old girl,
Lisa, who is thrown out by her religious father and finds
herself working in a 'hostess' club in the capital. The play is

really an anatomization of the patriarchal structures which continue to oppress women, whether they be shown in paedophilia or
in religious mania. Perhaps most disturbing is the way in which Lisa
and Helen, who also works in the club, begin to discuss other
women in the same terms as men discuss them:

LISA: 'The girls in this place in Newport were smart. But young. None
of them looked more than twenty.'

HELEN: 'And they were doing well?'

LISA: 'Packing them in.'

HELEN: 'Fresh meat.'

LISA: 'If that's what they want then that's what we have to give
them.'[70]

Siân Evans's play is also indicative of Welsh women writers' new
confidence and achievement in the dramatic genre in the last
decades of the century. Although there were some individual examples of plays written by Welsh women earlier in the century, such as
Jane Wogan by Mallt Williams, the co-written plays of Hilda
Vaughan, performed on the London stage, and a considerable body
of short plays written for amateur productions by writers even of
the calibre of Kate Roberts, it cannot be said that there was a *female*
theatrical tradition in Wales in either language until the latter years
of the century. One play which may be taken as representative of the
new and long-delayed breakthrough of Welsh women into professional playwriting is Lucinda Coxon's *Waiting at the Water's Edge*
(1995).
    Although Coxon was born in Derby, her play draws on her own
family history, returning to the experiences of her grandmother,
born in Rhydyfelin but forced to leave her homeland as a young girl
to go into service in England. *Waiting at the Water's Edge* is an
experimental play which explores class and gender relations, as well
as migration and displacement. In using her grandmother's experiences as a starting point, Coxon is identifying with the forgotten
Welsh past in a way which is reminiscent of Gillian Clarke's
resurrection of the grandmothers in 'Letter from a Far Country'. We
can also compare Coxon's play with Marion Eames's 1978 novel, *I
Hela Cnau* (The Golden Road), which deals with the experience of

female migration from Wales to Merseyside in the later nineteenth century. Like Coxon, Eames was born in England, owing to her own family's migration there; it is interesting to see how these two dissimilar writers, working in different languages, modes and genres, not only focus on the same historical experiences but also examine the same issues of identity and belonging, from a specifically female perspective.

I Hela Cnau echoes Elena Puw-Morgan's *Y Graith* (1943) at times, particularly in its narration of Rebecca Parry's early, humiliating experiences as a parlourmaid in Broom House, Birkenhead. Here, like Dori in the earlier novel, she is ill-used and taunted about her Welshness; in one key scene she is treated like 'anifail syrcas' (a circus animal) by being summoned upstairs and called upon to 'say soomthing in Welsh for uz'.[71] Soon, however, she becomes assimilated into English life, losing her Welsh accent, though still participating in the Welsh cultural life on Merseyside, particularly the chapel. Ruth McElroy has suggested that the novel's quite complex and ambivalent exploration of notions of Welsh identity, home and belonging, can be read as Eames's covert intervention in contemporary debates on those issues in the run-up to the 1979 Referendum.[72] Eames represents a range of different subject positions with regard to nation and gender in her group of interacting Welsh migrant characters on Merseyside. Rebecca's two suitors embody conflicting ideologies, for instance, since Dani is more interested in commercial success than in preserving his Welshness, whereas Simwn suffers from *hiraeth* for Wales and feels guilty for leaving his homeland at a time of political strife. When Simwn asks Rebecca towards the end of the novel whether she, too, misses her 'home' in Wales, she replies: 'to her, Wales was, above all else, her father, and since she felt completely alienated/exiled from him, she felt similarly alienated/exiled from Wales. Quite a willing exile at that' ([i]ddi hi, ei thad, yn anad dim, oedd Cymru, a chan iddi deimlo'n alltud hollol oddi wrtho, teimlai yr un modd mai alltud oedd hi o Gymru. Alltud digon bodlon hefyd').[73] Unwilling to accept her apparent indifference, Simwn persists, saying that one day they will have to choose between being Welsh people or Birkenhead people; Rebecca loses patience and plumps for Birkenhead: 'You could say that Birkenhead has saved me ... sometimes I wish I'd been born an Englishwoman' ('Mi elli di ddeud mai Byrcinhead sy wedi f'achub i ... ambell waith ... mi fasa'n dda gen i 'taswn i wedi fy ngeni'n Saesnes').[74] Despite the struggle of her early years, Rebecca has flourished in the new 'freedom' she finds in the English city; Simwn accepts this sadly: 'You know why, don't you? . . . You don't like being on the losing side' ('Mi wyddost pam, yn gwyddost?. . . Mae'n gas gen ti fod ar yr ochr sy'n colli').[75] Simwn's words are a very close echo of the words used by Dorothy Edwards in her 1926 story 'The Conquered', when the rich border-dweller, Gwyneth, is 'on the side of the conquerors'. Nevertheless, in the romance plot which underpins the novel, it is Simwn with whom Rebecca remains at the end, not Dani. The ambivalences of the text with regard to notions of belonging are not neatly resolved; as Ruth McElroy observes, '[h]ome, as both domestic place and figurally, as nation, exists . . . as a place of conflict, alienation and belonging'.[76] Possibly, that indeterminacy in Eames's novel reflected the mood of Wales itself in the year before the Referendum; the resulting 'No' vote in a sense echoes Rebecca's own inability to reassert a diminishing Welsh identity.

Lucinda Coxon's play, *Waiting at the Water's Edge*, is set in the 1920s and, like *I Hela Cnau*, involves two young girls, Violet and Susie, migrating from Wales to England as maidservants. The opening scene is set on a wind-blown Welsh beach, the setting connoting a place of transition. Vi and Su meet and both are poised to leave Wales; Vi is from Senghennydd and she talks of hearing the explosion in the mine which killed 439 men in 1913. Since then both she and her father 'went strange'.[77] Her father took to building boats, though they lived miles from the sea; spared by some sixth sense on the day of the explosion, he nevertheless dies later 'with his lungs'.[78] The play slowly veers away from naturalism as Vi becomes involved with her employer's son, Will Couth, accidentally kills him and then assumes his identity, travelling to Nova Scotia as the coal-owner's son to break a miners' strike. As she slowly learns to perform masculinity, Vi (now 'Will') realizes that 'we'll have to go in hard. It's the only way I'm safe.'[79] She is merciless in her efforts to break the miners. She realizes that Nova Scotia is 'just like bloody Wales';[80] it 'used to be a place to come to. Now it's a place to leave.'[81] Vi reflects at the end of the play, addressing Will's mother: 'you and I will not be judged by whether or not our people come home. We will be judged by the quality of our waiting.'[82] This is a play which deliberately blurs the boundaries between master and servant, between male and female, crossing class and gender divisions as well as migrating between countries of power and sites of exploitation. The emphasis on 'waiting' echoes Gillian Clarke's depiction of the woman's age-old role: 'the girl ... must keep. And wait. And pass time.'[83] In the past, the girl also 'stays'; however, both Coxon and Eames suggests that women's frustrations are not necessarily at an end with the 'freedom' to migrate. On the contrary, in Coxon's rather despairing play, economic pressures and psychological damage conspire to make real freedom impossible. In Eames's more positive view (admittedly set in the more prosperous late nineteenth century, rather than on the eve of the General Strike), the Welsh female migrant seizes control of the means of production and begins to forge a new identity for herself, according to her own choices, not those thrust upon her by notions of propriety and duty.

Turning now from the drama and the novel once again to poetry, Eluned Phillips's poem, 'Clymau' (Ties) is another text which engages with Welsh migration and national identity. However, in almost every other way, it differs from Lucinda Coxon's eclectic, hybrid, postmodern approach. It was the winning poem in the Crown competition of the 1983 National Eisteddfod, is based on the contemporary Falklands/Malvinas War and in two alternating verse-sequences parallels events of 1865, when Welsh migrants first sailed to Patagonia, and 1982, when Welsh soldiers again found themselves en route to South America, for very different reasons. In the opening sequence, Welsh people are evicted from their home, Pantglas (the period of evictions during which *I Hela Cnau* is set), and decide to sail from Liverpool to Argentina on the ship *Mimosa*; en route, a daughter dies and is buried at sea. Despite their grief, they throw themselves into work in their new land, recreating a new 'Pantglas'. They are seen in heroic terms, like Arthur's knights seeking for the Holy Grail:

> Ymchwil feunyddiol drwy'r oriau dyfal
> Fel marchog Arthur yn ceisio'r Greal,
> Nes darganfod ffrwd risial, a synnu
> Gweld dŵr yn saethu o lestr yr anial.[84]

> [Daily search through the eager hours
> Like an Arthurian knight questing for the Grail,
> Until a crystal stream is found, and he wonders
> To see water shooting from the barren dish.]

In 1982, a latter-day son of Pantglas joins the British army and is sent to fight in the Falklands. The voyage south of the *Sir Galahad* (with ironic echoes of the earlier pioneering Welsh knights) is compared with the earlier voyage of the *Mimosa*. The ship is hit and explodes, there is mourning for a dead soldier, explicitly likened to the warriors of Catraeth. In the hospital there is a strange meeting between a young man from Buenos Aires and the blinded son of Pantglas; they speak the same language, Welsh: 'they are two from the same family' ('dau o'r un tylwyth ŷnt').[85]

In a sense this is a television ode (just as 'Letter from a Far Country' is a radio poem), which works most vividly when it is describing scenes actually screened at the time of the Falklands War. The description of the *Sir Galahad* is both televisual and has echoes of the Old Testament and of the Twrch Trwyth in the Mabinogi:

> Mae Syr Galahad fel rhyw anghenfil,
> A'i cheg ar angor fel genau morfil.
> Sudda'r tanciau yn ufudd i'w chrombil,
> A'r gynnau swrth yn wrych ar ei gwegil.[86]

> [The *Sir Galahad* is like some great behemoth,
> Its mouth wide open like the jaws of a whale.
> The tanks sink obediently into its maw,
> And the sullen guns like a hedge on its back.]

Despite its attack on British imperialism, the poem has a conservative ideology which appears to hearken back to earlier periods of Welsh women's writing. 'Clymau' laments the Anglicization of Wales and the advent of English and European migrants to rural west Wales, representing such migrants in negative terms (whereas the Welsh migrants to Patagonia are unproblematically presented as heroic pioneers).

Phillips expresses a similar sense of loss in a sonnet set firmly on home territory, 'Y Pertni Coll' (The Lost Hedges). Here, she tenderly names the fields of her 'bro' (native place): 'Parc Iago, Parc yr Asyn a Pharc Main; /Parc Sticil, Parc y Gog a Pharc y Gelli'[87], lamenting the loss of their hedges, which concealed 'a riot of marvels',[88] (reiat o syndodau). Surrounded now by electric fences, the fields appear vulnerable, unsheltered. Phillips's moving perception of the vulnerability of her rural

177

world is characteristic of a new ecological consciousness in Welsh women's writing of this period.

Just as Phillips embraces the intimately local and faraway conflicts, so too does Menna Elfyn in 'Eucalyptus', the title poem of her 1995 collection of the same name. The source seems to have been a news report, rather than a visual image, of the first Gulf War in the early 1990s. A note explains that the poet had heard that the pungent scent of eucalyptus pervaded the streets of Baghdad at the time since, in the absence of electricity, the inhabitants of the city were using eucalyptus oil to cook with and to heat their homes. The poem then is full of images of taste and smell, conjured up by the word 'eucalyptus' and its personal memories. The eucalyptus lozenge which eased the speaker's throat and helped her to breathe in her childhood is now helping – literally – to keep families alive as the bombs burst all around them. The imagery employed is both domestic and sacramental – families gather together at the 'table of blessedness' ('bwrdd bendithiol').[89] The poem expresses a palpable sense of empathy with people suffering in a war not of their own making, asserting a sense of community across cultures, based on simple physical needs and family ties:

> Yr olew syml:
> Fu'n dal anadl cynhaliaeth
> Gan lathru goleuni
> Dros fywydau gloywddu.[90]

> [The simple oil
> that once kept me breathing,
> now over blackened lives
> shines like light.]

Elfyn's linking of the personal and domestic with the global and political might be seen as a similar impulse to that which impelled Lynette Roberts to create her peculiarly hybrid science-fiction Llanybri in 'Gods with Stainless Ears', though the poetic results for Elfyn are certainly more lucid. Nor is this yoking of the personal and the political unusual in Elfyn's poetry, as we have seen. Arguably, though, that insistence on the personal and the domestic in a time of war is characteristic of anti-war protest writing, which many Welsh women poets produced during this period. The focus on the personal and intimate challenges the tendency of the war machine to depersonalize and even dehumanize. Further examples are Joyce Herbert's 'When I Stood There Among Bullets', Gillian Clarke's 'No Hands', 'Olwen Takes Her First Steps on the Word Processor in Time of War',[91] and Section 6 of the poem sequence, 'The King of Britain's Daughter', discussed above.

While Welsh women poets of this period engage passionately with contemporary events, they also ruminate on the past, especially the past as inscribed on the landscape of today. One example of this tendency is Merryn Williams's 'Black Mountain Cairns', an ostensibly simple yet reverberant poem about self and landscape, the present and the past. The speaker describes the anonymous heaps of stones found, inscrutable, on the summits of the Black Mountains, surmising that they 'were raised to assure the lonely traveller/someone had come here before' and concluding 'each time I pass I add another stone.'[92] This, surely, is both an assertion of belonging and a reassuring gesture of continuity. As such, it is characteristic of women writers of this period who simultaneously uphold traditions and transgress gender boundaries.

In 1996 Menna Elfyn published a collection of poems which in its format set out to break down linguistic boundaries, the bilingual volume, *Cell Angel*. While she had already published in the previous year a *Selected Poems (Eucalyptus)* which had provided English translations of a range of her poetry, this was the first time that she – or indeed anyone – in Wales had published a completely bilingual new volume of original verse. Moreover, the English versions of Elfyn's original Welsh poems were not simply literal prose renditions but were poems in their own right, written by the established poets Gillian Clarke, Elin ap Hywel, Joseph Clancy and Tony Conran in collaboration with Elfyn. To underline the novelty of this publication, it came out under the imprint, not of a Welsh publisher, but of Newcastle upon Tyne-based poetry specialists Bloodaxe.

The 'cell' of the title refers to the prison cell where the poet was imprisoned for some time as a result of her language campaigning, but, as the curious conjunction of the title suggests, the cell becomes a place of spiritual contemplation. In 'Cwfaint/Nunnery', for example, the speaker asserts:

Lleianod cadwedig ydym yma. Wedi'r swpera
awn yn ôl i fyd ein myfyr. Yr un a wna rai'n sypynnau
heb gnawd. Yma, ni yw'r ysbrydol anwirfoddol,

yn dal y groes â'r troseddwyr rhwng ein gobennydd,
yn gyndyn mewn aberth, yn dyheu am adenydd.[93]

We are anchorites. After supper
we turn to contemplation. We make fleshless
bundles. Like it or not we're spiritual

bearing our little crosses under our pillows,
stubborn in sacrifice, waiting for wings.

In other poems, Elfyn explores cultures in faraway countries that she has visited, such as Vietnam, but experiences them and presents them through a distinctively Welsh lens. In a sequence of poems in memory of the Welsh historian Gwyn Alf Williams, who died in 1995, she includes one poem which looks back explicitly on the Referendum of 1979, the year of disappointment for many, which initiated this period of Welsh women's writing. She recalls Williams's railing against the result:

'Ai llwch yn y gwynt ydym?' llefaist
'Ai deunydd crai hanesion eraill,
Ai llwyth sy'n cycyllu mewn coedwig
Wrth weld adain hollt, gan filwg ambwl?'[94]

['Are we dust in the wind', you wailed?
are we raw material of other folk's histories?
are we a tribe blindfold in a wood?
are our wings chopped by a blunt billhook?']

Elfyn presents him, in his incensed passion, speaking for 'cenedl cnu un ddafad farw / a dead sheep's fleece of a nation', like a native American performing a ritual dance and then walking sadly back into the wilderness. However, the later poems in the sequence use Gwyn Williams's own words, 'The journey goes on', to suggest a hope for a different future, a hope that arguably would be realized, two years after his death, in the second Referendum, of 1997. This sequence commemorating the passionate Marxist and nationalist historian Gwyn Alf Williams, an English-speaking Welshman who learned Welsh and became,

through his books and television broadcasts, almost the conscience of a nation, shows how linguistic and gender divides are
increasingly breaking down in the writing of this period.

Despite the ostensibly separate growth of the two language
traditions in the literature of Wales, it is true to say that the
borders around the linguistic territories were never hermetically
sealed. If the influence of English literature and culture is
increasingly evident in Welsh-language writing in the course of
the twentieth century, what is as striking is the reciprocal
influence of Welsh on Anglophone writing in the same period.
Examples such as the poetry of Gillian Clarke or Christine
Evans and the novels of Siân James show that Welsh exists at
the heart of their works, not just as sprinklings of 'local colour',
as might be found in the earlier novels of Edith Nepean, but as
a central medium of the culture's expression. Increasingly, as
Menna Elfyn's publishing practice demonstrates, bilingualism is
becoming the norm, and literary texts are beginning to show the
interpenetration or interstitiality of the two languages in everyday Welsh life. Elaine Showalter has stated, with reference to
American literature, that:

> The languages of various groups are perpetually intersecting,
> translating each other; minority or post-colonial cultures appropriate
> and subvert the language of the dominant through the strategies of
> neologisms, syntactic fusion, interlanguages, substitutions, and
> allusion. Indeed, 'interlinguistic play' and binguality is one of the
> most striking features of minority literatures. Such writing is always
> double-voiced . . .[95]

The 'seepage'[96] between English and Welsh literature (in both
directions) has been profound and became more, not less, evident
towards the end of the century. Clearly, the attitude towards the
Welsh language is somewhat different in an author who writes in
Welsh from one who writes in English; nevertheless, both are
writing in the same context of encroachment upon and erosion of
that native tongue. Often, and perhaps unexpectedly, writers in
both languages during this period express a similar sense of commitment.

In later twentieth-century Welsh women's writing, we can see
that language politics, notions of nationality and belonging, and
the complexities of gender and sexuality all tend to intersect in
the literary exploration of Welsh women's subjectivity. Thus, for

example, Menna Elfyn's poetry is never simply about The Language; it is about the language, women's and men's lives, sexual relationships, motherhood, poetry, religious faith, war, issues of justice and freedom across the world, and the possibility of expressing this heterogeneous experience in two modern languages which are informed with a consciousness of a distinct literary tradition.

5 Hybrid Place: 1997–2005

The 'Yes' vote in the Devolution Referendum of 1997 and the subsequent creation of the Welsh Assembly have undoubtedly changed both the concept and the reality of 'Wales' as a political, and, arguably, a cultural and social place. Welsh women's literary production at the turn of this century shows a strong awareness of Wales as a land emerging from a history of colonization and beginning to assert and celebrate a hybrid culture, created by that experience of colonization, yet now asserting its difference from a cohesive 'British' identity. Recent criticism[1] has fruitfully explored the theory that modern Wales is post-colonial, though this approach has also incurred voluble opposition, mainly from some historians. Whereas many female voices in literary works from earlier in the twentieth century (in both languages) lamented the loss of a more or less unified Welsh culture of a golden age before Anglicization, migration and urbanization, recent voices are more likely to speak of a hybrid conception of Welshness. Hybridity is a term much used – though not without contentiousness – in post-colonial theory and, in the construction placed upon it by critics such as Homi Bhabha, it is a colonial inheritance which, paradoxically, can be a means of contesting oppressive imperial forces and an assertion of autonomous agency.

Sharon Morgan's *Magic Threads* (1997) is a play which takes the form of a monologue, a patchwork of song, poetry, memory and fairy-tale, hybrid both in form and content. It continues the emphasis already found in the work of the poets of the early 1990s on the rediscovery of the grandmother, a trait also found in Rachel Trezise's novel, *In and Out of the Goldfish Bowl* (discussed below). The shift from a concern with Mam (the mother) to a search for the grandmother in Welsh women's writing in recent times is interesting and may indicate a change in self-definition: possibly the mother may be seen as embodying an unacceptable feminine role, whereas the almost forgotten grandmother and great-grandmother may offer a more positive image.

Magic Threads presents the grandmother as strong and potentially dangerous: she is associated with the garden, needlework and food, but she is also employed in the tin-works and – fantastically – 'in the darkness of her pantry, in the depth of her saucepan she creates DYNAMITE'.[2] The 'magic threads' of the title are associated with the grandmother's rag mats and patchwork quilts: 'she's sewing her children's lives'.[3] Morgan's play contains echoes of the feminist reappropriation of needlework in the 1980s and 90s as an emblem of female creativity and cooperative work, most memorably expressed perhaps in Alice Walker's *The Color Purple* (1982). This celebratory reinvention is a far cry from needlework as an exhausting and demeaning chore, and an economic necessity, as it is represented, for instance, in the novels of Elena Puw-Morgan.

The grandmother is seen as 'Omniscient/omnipotent', her power 'pagan / It came out of the mountain earth / Mountain water ran in her veins'.[4] In the kaleidoscopic pictures presented in the monologue, a female history of Wales is suggested – religion, migration, work – but the narrative eschews chronology and the discourse of history, choosing instead the fairy-tale formula, 'once upon a time', to tell the multiple stories. Linguistically, the text is mixed, for the play is interspersed with 'hen benillion' and folk songs in Welsh; the play also exists in a Welsh-language version, *Ede Hud*. The use of the anonymous songs may suggest their unacknowledged female authorship (as indicated also in Menna Elfyn's poem, 'Anhysbys – An sy'n hysbys'), for the monologue goes on to question 'where are our mothers' talents?'[5] The voice figures these talents as curled-up blossoms 'cwtshing' deep down: 'They go from womb to womb, / Waiting, waiting, waiting . . . What if the flowers burst out?'[6] As Hazel Walford Davies points out, 'the monologue . . . breaks down barriers of form'.[7] A hybrid existing somewhere between the dramatic monologue, the theatrical soliloquy and the public speech, the form goes hand in hand with content in Sharon Morgan's work, which builds up a Welsh women's history through the voice and fragments of stories and images.

A similar 'patchwork' technique is used by Angharad Price in her narrative, *O! Tyn y Gorchudd* (Oh! Pull Back the Veil), which won the Prose Medal at the National Eisteddfod in 2002. Masquerading as an autobiography, its first-person speaker, Rebecca, is a relative of the writer, who actually died at the age of eleven in 1916; this book is a fictional account of the life she might have had. Reminiscent in structure of Kate Roberts's *Y Lôn Wen*, with its vivid fragments of memory and its attempt to delineate the life of a family and a community, not just an individual, it is, nevertheless, a more poetic and more experimental work than Roberts's. The representation of the *bro* (native area) is central to the work's conception, and it continues a tradition in Welsh women's writing of animating the landscape and of seeing it as a female entity. The description of the stream which flows through Rebecca's native valley exemplifies this:

Trawsffurfia'i hun ganwaith ar ei thaith trwy'r cwm ... Yn haul cyntaf mis Mawrth bydd yn llances, yn byrbwyll a heriol yn nhawdd y Gwanwyn, yn ddidrugaredd ar ei gwely. Yng nghynesrwydd mis Mehefin teimlo'n llai na hi ei hun y mae, yn sibrwd geiriau bach yn ddagreuol, yn llyfu ymylon dolennau. Yn nrycinoedd mis Hydref hen stormes wridog ydyw, yn hidio dim am orlifo'i glannau ei hun ...[8]

[She transforms herself a hundred times on her journey through the valley ... In the first sunshine of March she's a minx, reckless and defiant in the Spring thaw, merciless on her bed. In the heat of June she feels less than herself, whispering little words tearfully, licking the edges of her loops. In the tempests of October, a flushed she-storm, thinking nothing of overflowing her own banks ...]

Cwm Maesglasau is not simply animated, but historicized – it is a place still peopled by the ghosts of the monks and hymn-writers of its past. Price gives particular attention to the unrecorded labour of women, as well as to the painful realities of the deaths of children; after all, the narrator is herself a resurrected dead child. Rebecca is a seamstress, and her work provides the self-referential image at the end of the text: 'Creais yma gwilt clytwaith o atgofion i'm cadw'n gynnes drwy'r gaeaf olaf'[9] ('I created here a patchwork quilt of memories to keep me warm through the final winter'). The combination of fact and fiction, poetry and history, language and image in this highly innovative and beautiful work indicates that hybridity of form, as well as of content, is increasingly important in contemporary Welsh women's writing.

Compared with the early 1900s, the late 1990s and the early years of the new millennium have seen a great burgeoning of Welsh women's poetry in both languages. Mererid Hopwood was the first-ever female winner of the Chair in the National Eisteddfod in 2001, with her *awdl* (ode) 'Dadeni' (Rebirth), which deals with the death of a baby from the mother's point of view. Gillian Clarke and Menna Elfyn, who began publishing in the 1970s, have continued to be productive into the new millennium, with Clarke publishing *Five Fields* in 1998 and *Making the Beds for the Dead* in 2004, and Elfyn publishing another bilingual volume, *Cusan Dyn Dall/Blind Man's Kiss*, in 2001 and a new Welsh-language volume, *Perffaith Nam* (Perfect Flaw), in 2005. Meanwhile, in the 1990s a new and immediately acclaimed poet, Gwyneth Lewis, began to publish verse in both English and Welsh, beginning with the Welsh-language *Sonedau Redsa* (Redsa's Sonnets) in 1990 and the English-language volumes *Parables and Faxes* (1995) and *Zero Gravity* (1998). Her most recent collections are *Y Llofrudd Iaith* (The Language Murderer, 1999) and *Keeping Mum* (2003). Since the inauguration of the Welsh Assembly Government, Gwyneth Lewis has also had an official status as National Poet, while her words, in both Welsh and English, are to be seen in the design of the Wales Millennium Centre in Cardiff. If, early on in this study, it was clear that Welsh women writers had to battle against a patriarchal culture which sought to render them invisible, that appears to have changed completely in the Wales of the new millennium, even if many Welsh women writers still focus on the lost women's history of the past.

Gwyneth Lewis is an unusual poet in that she writes and publishes verse in both English and Welsh, which are not transla-tions of each other. As she says laconically in her preface to *Keeping Mum*, 'it's a difficult domestic arrangement, but it holds'.[10] In this sense, she may be representative of a new generation of poets who are truly bilingual. Her two earliest English collections, *Parables and Faxes* (1995) and *Zero Gravity* (1998), share a similar vision, which might be described as an inventive combination of the technological and the theological. Unlike her contemporaries, Menna Elfyn and Angharad Tomos, Lewis is not a committed language campaigner, though her love for, and fascination with, both her native tongues is always evident in her poetry. She differs from her peers in lacking an overt political commitment, either to language politics or to feminism; instead, her poetry impresses with the cold brilliance of its craftsmanship. Hers is a clever poetry, in the sense that the English Metaphysical poets were clever; like them, she yokes together apparently disparate worlds (as symbolized by the coupling of 'parables' and 'faxes' in the title of her first collection). She often deals specifically with the state of being bilingual, as in the poem 'Mother Tongue', where the speaker's gradually increasing, surreptitious use of English is described as a developing and familially disapproved drug addiction:

> I started to translate in seventy-three
> in the schoolyard. For a bit of fun
> to begin with – the occasional 'fuck'
> for the bite of another language's smoke
> at the back of my throat, its bitter chemicals.
> Soon I was hooked on whole sentences . . .
> . . . If only I'd kept
> myself much purer, with simpler tastes,
> the Welsh might be living . . .[11]

The Welsh language is, nevertheless, still very much living in the poetry of Gwyneth Lewis herself and of Menna Elfyn, whose 2005 volume, *Perffaith Nam*, does not reproduce poems from her two preceding bilingual volumes, but presents new poems written in the period since 1990. Dedicated to her mother, who died in 2003, this volume's main theme is, as the poet explains in her Preface, 'the desire to cast off the flaws that plague us through our lives . . . to join together that which is split within us' ('yr awydd i fwrw ymaith y brychau sy'n ein plagio trwy'n bywyd . . . cyfannu'r hyn sy'n hollt ynom').[12]

The paradoxical nature of the title, *Perffaith Nam*, or 'Perfect Flaw', is echoed repeatedly in the poems within. The nature of Elfyn's concern with paradox is philosophical and, occasionally, theological. Time and again one hears the voice of the poems wrestling with metaphysics and finding that the only way forward is through an embracing of the paradoxical. In 'Molawd i'r Lleuad (ar drothwy rhyfel)' (Praise-poem to the Moon (on the threshold of war)), for example, she writes:

> O fynd yn ddigon pell
> Y down o hyd i'r hyn sy'n agos,
> O ddringo'n uchel
> Down o hyd i ddyfnder
> A chael y galon newydd
> Ar y tu fas i ysgyfaint du'r nos.[13]
>
> [Through going far enough
> We come across what is near,

187

Through climbing high
We come across depths
And find the new heart
On the outside of the night's black lung.]

The phrase 'perffaith nam' itself is found in several poems, including 'Botwm i'r Botwm Bol' (A Button for the Belly-Button), where it is her daughter's pierced navel: 'A button the shape of the world / Everyday, perfect flaw' ('Botwm siap y byd yw, / Nam perffaith, beunyddiol').[14] It's also found in the long poem on Simone Weil entitled 'Y Forwyn Goch' (The Red Maid), where Weil's death is mourned in the lines:

Onid perffaith nam
Oedd dy gladdu mewn mynwent i'r tlodion? . . . Gwacáu dy hunan
    er mwyn bod yn ddim
A bod yn ddim iti oedd cyfandod.[15]

[Was it not a perfect flaw

That you were buried in a pauper's grave? . . . Emptying yourself in
    order to be nothing

And being nothing was wholeness for you.]

Weil is addressed in this important poem as a kindred spirit, a philosopher and revolutionary, a 'saintly fool', a red maid, who was born with 'a flaw on [her] soul, a birthmark on [her] heart' ('Nam ar enaid, man geni ar dy galon).[16]

Though Elfyn is sometimes a metaphysical poet, she is also frequently a humorous one, displaying a grotesque sense of humour and a penchant for puns to rival that of R. S. Thomas and, indeed, Gwyneth Lewis. In 'Bronnau Ffug',[17] (False Breasts), for instance, based on the story of a woman who found that her lover had stolen the money used to give her cosmetically enhanced breasts, Elfyn tells some outrageous jokes about half-empty cups and the word *bron*, meaning both 'breast' and 'near'. There is an undertone of feminist satire here, as elsewhere in the collection, despite the fact that in one poem a solemn, tongue-in-cheek litany is intoned above the grave of feminism ('Litani ar gychwyn claddfa' (Litany at the start of a burial)). Elfyn is also adept at catching the rhythms of ordinary speech, as in the humorous poem 'Ymwelydd' (Visitor), where a well-meaning Job's comforter visits a patient:

Glywoch chi be 'wedodd e?
Ddim yn clywed, chwel,
Cancer, medde'r doctor.
Ulcer? Oh, that's good.
A oedd y boi bach ifanc
ddim yn leico gweud yn ots.
Ie, iechyd, be wnelen ni hebddo?
Byddwch chi'n well 'to'n glou –
Er, ma' golwg golau leuad arnoch chi.[18]

[Did you hear what he said?
He didn't hear too well, see,
Cancer, said the doctor.
Ulcer? Oh, that's good.
And the young fellow
Didn't like to say different.
Yes indeed, health, what would we do without it?
You'll be better soon again before long –
Though you are looking pale as the moon.]

It is not surprising to find that these poems are more cosmopolitan than those of Elfyn's previous all-Welsh collection, *Aderyn Bach mewn Llaw*, but it is unexpected to find that they are more tightly constructed formally. The *vers libre* of the earlier work is largely abandoned in favour of more regular rhyme and complex alliteration. Even a villanelle makes an appearance ('Iâ Cymru',[19] (Wales's Ice)). Most of the poems are in the first person, but these are not generally confessional or personal poems in the same way that 'Y Gneuen Wag' (The Empty Nut) or 'Angladd' (Funeral) were, in Elfyn's work of the late 1970s. Rather, these poems tend to be questioning, probing, punning soundings, sent out from an individual point of view but asking questions relevant to all of us.

In the long sequence of poems entitled 'Melltith y Mamau' (The Mothers' Curse), the therapist Rhiannon states:

Mae rhywbeth o'i le
Ynom i gyd. Dynion, un X yn eisiau
A merched un X yn ormod.
Cris croesi, creu croesau
Yn glymau amdanom.[20]

[There's something out of place
In all of us. Men, one X missing
And women one X too many.
Criss crossing, creating crosses,
All tied up in knots.]

Though she sees the knots (*clymau*) that entrap us, Elfyn also acknowledges the bows (*dolennau*) which link us together. Elfyn is a poet of healing who, despite satirical impulses, is fundamentally both compassionate and celebratory. Although both Menna Elfyn and Gwyneth Lewis are capable of writing satirically and humorously, in their recent work they share an interest in theology and philosophy. These concerns, far from making the two poets' work abstruse, are tightly connected – in unexpected ways – to everyday life, the here and now. An example of this is Elfyn's extraordinary sequence on 'The Theology of Hair' in *Cell Angel* (1996), which manages to be about being female, being Welsh, about sensuality and spirituality, conceived not in terms of the usual Manichaean dualisms, but as part of the same human experience. Lewis, too, as the title of *Parables and Faxes* indicates, is a poet very much of the modern, technological world, an experimental poet, and yet also fascinated by the spiritual. In this regard, contemporary Welsh female poets can be seen to be echoing the impassioned religious concerns of their foremothers a century before, but they are expressing those concerns in a distinctively modern idiom.

Perhaps one of the most influential and reverberant of recent women's writings from Wales is Charlotte Williams's *Sugar and Slate* (2002), which is an appropriately hybrid book. Part memoir, part history, part verse, it tells stories of Wales, of Africa and of Guyana, focusing on the life of one Welsh woman of mixed racial and cultural heritage, and radiating out to trace the unexpected and largely unrecorded connections between black people and Wales over the centuries. Charlotte Williams, the author, is the daughter of the admired Guyanese novelist and artist, Denis Williams, who not unnaturally plays an important role in this narrative. Nevertheless, the author's Welsh mother, Katie Alice, native of Bethesda, Welsh-speaker and lifelong rebel, though she may not be well known to a wide audience, has an even more prominent role to play in her daughter's story. Katie Alice emerges as a real heroine, a matriarch who sprang from a dispossessed past (the orphanage of Bontnewydd) to assert with spirit her own and her daughters' right to be and to belong to Wales.

Divided into three sections, 'Africa', 'Guyana' and 'Wales', the book is not a conventional, linear autobiography. It contains notable gaps and reticences about Charlotte Williams's own life, and at times takes us on fascinating excursions into the lives of others, such as the 'Congo boys'. These two children, aged eight and eleven, arrived at Llandudno pier in 1885, having been brought over from Africa by a Welsh missionary, the Reverend William Hughes. Charlotte Williams clearly empathizes with these isolated, poignant figures, and brings them back to life in her economical, yet often poetically-charged, prose:

> N'Kansa and Kin Kassa were bright boys, eager to learn and to serve the God of the white man. Very soon both the boys had learned to recite Psalms and large passages from the Book of Revelations from memory . . . They were smartly dressed in tailored black serge suits with shiny buttons and wore white handkerchiefs in their top pockets. Little gentlemen; neckties framing their fixed expression . . . They preached the mission in parish after parish throughout North and South Wales, where posters announced that the Reverend William Hughes would speak of his missionary travels and that the *bechgyn duon* (black boys) would sing in Welsh, English, and in their native tongue . . . I've seen the grave of N'kansa at Llanelian, I've seen the grave of Kin Kassa . . . and others. Each of their graves a buried story. I feel that I know something about their voyage across the Atlantic. I think I know what it is like to be stranded at an outpost like Colwyn Bay; dislodged, dislocated . . . I know what it's like to be a curiosity.[21]

The journey is a unifying motif in the book, introduced by a recurring, interrupted scene at Piarco airport in Trinidad, where the narrator is 'in transit' and conversing with a fellow traveller who is taking the same journey, but in the opposite direction. The scene is an apt metaphor for Charlotte Williams's predicament: she feels 'between worlds', in a no man's land, not quite belonging to Wales, Africa or Guyana. Such imagery is found repeatedly in Caribbean writing, from the 'shipwreck' of V. S. Naipaul's characters to the alienation of Jean Rhys's. And yet Charlotte Williams's articulation of it is unique and powerful, and specifically Welsh. Moreover, it also suggests that this contemporary, hybrid text belongs to the tradition of Welsh women's writing which, as we have seen, has always exhibited a fascination with tropes of journeying, displacement and dispossession. Though this might imply a lack of belonging to Wales, paradoxically, perhaps, Welsh women writers, including Charlotte Williams, explore the experience of dispossession ultimately in order to assert their sense of belonging to Wales.

Charlotte Williams is a perceptive writer, adept at drawing connections between people, events and histories that one had previously taken to be quite separate. She begins from the intimate and personal – such as her memories of accompanying her father on an archaeological dig in Africa – and ends with a revelation of the communal history which binds us together:

> The digging took us closer and closer to the answer [to that nagging question 'What could prevail on a man to sell his brother into slavery?'] . . . Iron. The iron bar was the key to the story that bound us all together . . . Iron lust grew beyond the horizon of the village . . . [Iron] from Brymbo, Bersham, and Shotton . . . Iron bars as valuable as gold came from the iron capital of the world: Merthyr . . . It was the ingenious coupling of iron hunger with a sudden increase in the need for labour on the West Indian sugar plantations that sealed a terrible fate . . . In Wales . . . the iron masters grew wealthier and wealthier ploughing back the profits of spices and sugar and slaves to make more and more iron bars and then manacles, fetters, neck collars, chains, branding irons, thumb screws . . . those rusty remnants turning into artefacts on the sites of slave factories and fortresses . . . On the dig with Dad we held the core of this terrible history in our hands. It explained us. All mixed up and intertwined in connections that I never knew.[22]

This highly personal narrative takes the form of a quest: for home, for a wholeness of identity, for acceptance and recognition as a black Welsh woman. Tellingly, it traces not just one journey but a series of journeys and an exploration of particular topographies, from north Wales to Guyana. It reveals unexpected resonances with other women's writing of displacement, in that it is the diasporic experience which helps the individual to construct an adequate imaginative landscape of home. The narrator of *Sugar and Slate* must leave Wales in order to understand her sense of belonging to it; only then can she return.

Two other recent prose volumes which address notions of hybridity and displacement are Trezza Azzopardi's 2001 novel, *The Hiding Place*, and Rachel Trezise's *In and Out of the Goldfish Bowl* (2000), which bear many similarities to each other thematically, if not stylistically. They are representative of the Welsh women's writing of the new millennium, and in many ways contrast starkly with their peers of a century earlier in their focus on conflicting and hybrid identities, family breakdown and domestic abuse. Both have first-person female narrators who tell their own brutalized life-stories and affirm their own unlikely survival.

The Hiding Place is set in what used to be Tiger Bay in the 1960s and focuses on a Maltese-Welsh family. Like Charlotte Williams's *Sugar and Slate*, this novel affirms the place of racially and cultur-ally Other people in the making of modern Wales. Far from the emphasis of some authors of the early decades of the twentieth century on racial and cultural 'purity', Tiger Bay is a place of fluidity and interchange, though Azzopardi certainly does not present it in idealized terms. On the contrary, this is a tough place, where the Gauci family must survive in a poverty partly of their own father's making. In fact, the family is represented in a particularly bleak way; what had been a positive and formative structure in much earlier fiction by Welsh women is exposed by Azzopardi here as a structure which warps and scars, setting siblings against one another, sending the mother to the asylum, the children into 'care' and the father, abandoning them, back to his homeland. Nevertheless, it should be noted that issues such as child abuse and the psychologically and physically scarring potential of the family are addressed in much earlier Welsh fiction, notably in Elena Puw-Morgan's 1943 novel, *Y Graith* (The Scar).

Formally, *The Hiding Place* is a complex novel, which attempts to recreate and interpret a personal history through incomplete and conflicting memories. The novel is set in two distinct times, the 1960s and the present; the nineteen chapters are interspersed with unnumbered passages, mainly in the 'now' of the narrative. The dual chronology adds complexity to the text, suggesting that the past needs to be disinterred and examined in the present in order to knit up the threads of the self into a whole identity (also a primary concern in Charlotte Williams's volume).

The experience of migration, which has figured so strongly in Welsh history and literature, is chronicled both from the father's point of view, in his move from Malta to Wales, and from the mother's – Mary comes down to Cardiff from the Valleys to the north. Both are voluntary exiles, escaping poverty and familial tyranny, and hoping to gain autonomy and freedom in the big city, recently made the capital of Wales. However, both find disappointment and fragmentation, rather than wholeness and fulfilment. They are left with traces or vestiges of what might have once been a whole identity (Maltese and Welsh, respectively), but they are perceived as being hybrid, or 'half-caste', the term used as a racial slur.[23] We are familiar with this 'not-identity' from Williams's *Sugar and Slate*, but in that autobiographical narrative the voice turns the hybrid identity into something positive and celebrated. This is not the case in *The Hiding Place*, partly because the father's sense of failure and alienation is turned upon the mother and children as physical abuse. The struggle becomes not one for national identity and a sense of belonging, but one for sheer physical survival: the children seek a 'hiding place' where they can be safe, their desires shrunk down literally to the size of a rabbit hutch in the backyard, where a child can crouch unnoticed. Images of loss and dispossession – such as houses being burnt and demolished – penetrate the whole text, and in this regard Azzopardi's novel is similar to other late twentieth-century texts by Welsh women writers, such as Glenda Beagan and Clare Morgan.

The occasion for the return of the Gauci sisters to Cardiff is the funeral of their mother, who spent many years in Whitchurch mental hospital. Mary is a complex character, initially an almost archetypal Welsh Mam figure, holding her family together against the odds, but then gradually breaking down herself. Moreover, the narrator Dolores's gradually pieced-together fragments of memory begin to present a picture of a tarnished Mary, not virginal or maternal but weak and abused. Motherhood itself is viewed ambivalently as both nurturing and potentially dangerous, symbolized in a scene of baby rabbits being eaten by their mother. Again, although this picture of breakdown and mental illness is disturbing, it is not entirely new in Welsh women's writing: Kate Roberts's 1962 novella, *Tywyll Heno*, is an earlier example of the exploration of female mental illness in this literary tradition.

The representation of Tiger Bay in Azzopardi's novel contrasts strongly with Leonora Brito's collection of short stories *dat's love* (1995), which presents a much more positive and, frequently, humorous picture of life in the Cardiff docklands. Brito's Caribbean-Welsh mixed-race characters encounter racial prejudice, but they are also clearly part of a cohesive and self-confident community. What is particularly noticeable in many of Brito's stories is the way in which a British identity is emphasized, rather than a Welsh one. The older generation of Caribbean migrants are particularly proud of their home islands' war service and their belonging to the British Empire, as in the humorous story 'Digging for Victory', though the close of the story calls into question that pride.[24] Azzopardi's novel also tends to contradict the picture of a proud black Britishness, though of course the focus of *The Hiding Place* is on the Maltese, rather than the West Indian, community. Yet the view of the modern Cardiff Bay developments provided by Azzopardi is not positive either; the plush new buildings appear false, as if they are hiding something, covering up the past, rather than replacing it with something better. The link between past and present appears broken, existing only in individuals' imperfect memories.

Trezise's novel, *In and Out of the Goldfish Bowl*, is less complex and sophisticated, but it presents a similar vision. The narrator, Rebecca, suffers graphically described sexual abuse from her step-father and subsequent neglect from her mother. The setting is the Rhondda, rather than Cardiff, and the narrator is virulently anti-nationalist, presenting the Penrhys estate and the Rhondda gener-ally as a place of loss, failure and destitution. She mocks notions of national pride; equally, she is contemptuous of notions of British-ness. In this text, the Welsh Mam becomes a drunkard and the heroic Welsh collier is revealed as a rapist. The novel is deliberately iconoclastic, therefore, and clearly therapeutic. Nevertheless, the emphasis finally, as in Azzopardi's novel, is on survival; Rebecca, with a name surely redolent of Welsh history, identifies with her grandmother, who provides an alternative model of Welsh woman-hood and a positive link with what is viewed as an authentic Welsh past which has some moral and cultural value.

Another distinguished recent novel which anatomizes the Welsh family and women's roles within it is Stevie Davies's *Kith and Kin* (2004). Like The *Hiding Place* and *In and Out of the Goldfish Bowl*, *Kith and Kin* has a first-person female narrator, Mara Evans, who tries to disentangle the truth from the web of the past. Again, there is hidden sexual abuse beneath surface respectability, and again it is the grandmother, Nana, who is the figure of respect. The landscape in and around Swansea and the Gower, particularly the grandmother's house, Breuddwyd (Dream), are figured as places of conflict between old and new forms of belonging and kinship.

The tone, form and subject-matter of women's writing published after 1997 are, as we have seen, strikingly varied, much more so than in the writing of Welsh women a century before. Conceptions of Welsh female identity and of the land of Wales itself have changed remarkably from the more essentialist and monolithic ideas espoused by many at the start of the twentieth century. The voices of immigrants to Wales, women of mixed race and mixed cultural background, now stake a claim to Wales and, in turn, alter what it is to be Welsh. Just as the landscape of Wales has metamor-phosed over the century, Welsh women's representations of this Other place has kept pace with that transformation. Despite the differences, stimulating and fascinating for us as readers of their writing, Welsh women over this century are, nevertheless, united by a shared experience of migration, industrialization, war, language loss and a post-colonial reconstruction of identity, all of which they express in their own, distinctive ways.

Conclusion

Yi-Fu Tuan has asserted that 'Place is security, space is freedom'.[1] Twentieth-century Welsh women writers often exemplify this dictum in the ways in which they choose to represent the spaces and places of Wales. They demonstrate how space may be transformed into place, 'as we get to know it better and endow it with value'.[2] Beyond the subjective terms used by Tuan, space also becomes place through physical change, perpetrated by the activities of human beings – mining, quarrying, farming, building, flooding, afforesting. Tuan's emphasis on the human experience of place is valid, though, and this human experience – as opposed to statistical facts and even synthesizing historical narrative – is what creative writers and artists can inimitably convey. Tuan moreover reminds us that attachment to one's native place is a universal phenomenon, in which: 'The . . . land is viewed as mother, and it nourishes; place is an archive of fond memories and splendid achievements that inspire the present.'[3] Time and again, we have seen the Welsh women writers of the twentieth century figuring Wales as a nourishing mother and as a repository of historical memory. In recent works, Welsh women writers have explored how the traditional positive relation of people and place can break down, however, so that place is not an archive of 'fond memories', but a reminder of loss, suffering and dispossession. For, as Jane Aaron and M. Wynn Thomas have pointed out, 'a place is also a people';[4] or, as David Smith would have it, 'a proletariat';[5] rarely do Welsh women writers present us with a flat canvas of picturesque scenes; rather, they give us animated, populated versions of Wales, often invigorated by political consciousness. They frequently express an awareness of the constructed nature of physical space and of the political meanings attached to it. They recognize that, far from being a mere setting or 'backdrop', the places in which their characters live their lives come to be understood as part and parcel of the structure of feeling of a particular location.

In addition to the urban and rural landscapes of Wales, Welsh women's writing demonstrates a continual preoccupation with the concepts of home and homelessness. Gaston Bachelard has argued that the notion of the homeland is the place which unites the individual's public and private experience.[6] The home can be, simultaneously, a private space and a microcosm of the nation. The home, like the wider world, is, moreover, a gendered place, and women writers explore the gendering of Wales more thoroughly and more persistently than most of their male peers. Writing by Welsh women often enacts a principal female character's quest for 'home', a fulfilling gender role and a sense of identity and belonging. Selfhood itself is repeatedly interrogated, often by taking the archetypal image of the woman looking at herself in a mirror. The resultant image is not a simple reflection, however, but a self who, in a sense, is a convergence of disparate influences and meanings, a site of intersection between history, memory and place. Within the domestic environment, women characters are seen over and over again performing apparently mundane household tasks, but in so doing constructing a sense of self, home and belonging. As Gaston Bachelard observes:

> there is ground for taking the house as a *tool for analysis* of the human soul . . . Not only our memories, but the things we have forgotten are 'housed'. Our soul is an abode. And by remembering 'houses' and 'rooms', we learn to 'abide' within ourselves.[7]

In Welsh women's writing, houses and rooms are often imbued with meanings which construct a sense of belonging and identity; the spatial becomes a metaphor for the psychological. The motif of the locked room recurs, reminding us of the gendered spaces of the tale of Bluebeard; philosophically, the motif denotes the creation of an outside and an inside, a 'dialectics of division', as Bachelard would label it, and which, he says, 'philosophers think of in terms of being and non-being'.[8]

The feminist cultural geographer, Dolores Hayden, contends that '[d]wellings, neighbourhoods, and cities designed for homebound women constrain women physically, socially and economically'.[9] Many women in the fictions and poetry studied in this volume have been 'homebound' in one sense or another; the writing itself gives expression to the physical, social and economic restraints experienced by Welsh women in such physical and cultural settings. Whereas most feminist critics, such as Judith Butler, for example, would regard this as evidence of a 'regulatory regime'[10] that legitimizes sexual inequality, reinforcing women's perceived passivity, domesticity and interiority as 'natural', many Welsh women writers ascribe value to the division of gendered space, suggesting that the female domestic space, created and maintained by women, can offer a valid political corrective to the freewheeling male spaces which lie outside. On the other hand, the domestic space can also be the site of abuse and exploitation, a place hidden away from public view, where women suffer silently.

The texts we have examined show clearly that the same spaces can mean conflicting things for people at the same time; women writers often reveal how gender influences and often determines one's relationship with place and one's attitudes towards it. Thus, for example, in Kate Roberts's story 'Y Golled' (The Loss) Annie responds passionately to the untamed mountain landscape, regretting the fact that a small chapel sits there, 'spoiling' the view, whereas her husband Ted is interested only in the chapel and the intense rivalries and intrigues it contains. Spaces and places, then, can be perceived in both positive and negative ways, according to the ideology and gender of the individual. In this regard, Henri Lefebvre makes a useful distinction, already mentioned briefly, between what he terms *dominated* and *appropriated* spaces, often associated with men and women in different ways. He describes *dominated* space as

> a space transformed – and mediated – by technology, by practice. In the modern world, instances of such spaces are legion, and immediately intelligible as such: one only has to think of a slab of concrete or a motorway . . . its origins coincide with those of political power itself.[11]

In contrast, he states that 'natural space modified in order to serve the needs and possibilities of a group . . . has been *appropriated* by that group', going on to add that:

> Peasant houses and villages speak: they recount, though in a mumbled and somewhat confused way, the lives of those who built and inhabited them . . . appropriation cannot be understood apart from the rhythms of time and life . . . Dominated space and appropriated space

may in principle be combined – and, ideally at least, they ought to be combined. But history . . . [is] the history of their separation and mutual antagonism. The winner in this contest, moreover, has been domination.[12]

The Welsh landscape may be understood in these terms, as the appropriated spaces of rural societies – the seaside villages and towns of Allen Raine and Jane Ann Jones, or the farm dwellings of Hilda Vaughan – being superseded and despoiled by the dominated space of the city and industrial ventures. Frequently, the industrial settings, such as quarries, docks and mines, are represented as male worlds, places into which the menfolk disappear and yet from which they return with work to be done by the women – preparing food, washing, even, at times, mourning. Thus, women have an economic and an emotional link with dominated spaces, but they dwell often in an appropriated space. Welsh cities and large towns are clearly dominated spaces, and they are often, perhaps unsurprisingly, represented as alienating places in Welsh women's writing. Citiscapes frequently deny the 'abode' of the individual; as Bachelard observes:

the inhabitants of the big city live in superimposed boxes . . . [which] have no roots . . . from the street to the roof, the rooms pile up one on top of the other, while the tent of a horizonless sky encloses the entire city. But the height of city buildings is a purely *exterior* one . . .'[13]

Similarly, Lefebvre's analysis of such spaces is also negative, with a specifically Marxist inflection:

The arrogant verticality of skyscrapers, and especially of public and state buildings, introduces a . . . phallocratic element into the visual realm; the purpose of this display, of this need to impress, is to convey an impression of authority to each spectator. Verticality and great height have ever been the spatial expression of potentially violent power.[14]

Despite the absence of American-style skyscrapers from most Welsh urban spaces, Lefebvre's observation is borne out by Welsh women's fiction: Dori Llwyd in Elena Puw-Morgan's *Y Graith*, for example, is overawed and dismayed by the large town house in which she is a maid-of-all-work, partly because she perceives its seemingly endless height – the staircases, which she, of course, must clean, appear to go on forever.

In addition to various appropriated and dominated spaces, some writers represent spaces which are not yet mapped or peopled. Eluned Morgan, for example, betrays a curiously modern ecological consciousness in her evocation of the unspoilt wildernesses of the high Andes, although she also extols the specifically Welsh ethnoscape of the Wladfa (the Welsh colony in Patagonia). The wilderness, which occasionally occurs within the geographical boundaries of Wales, especially in Snowdonia, forms a kind of third space, neither appropriated nor dominated, where human identity is swallowed up in the vastness. Jane Aaron has suggested that 'an image which might most characteristically represent the many ways in which Wales has been imagined . . . in pre-1960s women's writing in English . . . would be [an] image of Wales as [a] wild zone'.[15] She goes further to indicate that this wild zone is typically inhabited by the 'social outsider', so that Wales itself is 'figured as a dispossessed, anarchic country, closer to nature than to culture'.[16] Female protagonists in these works have a tendency to embrace this 'wild zone' and the temporary extinction of selfhood which it brings (Allen Raine's 'Welsh witch', Catrin, is a case in point), while male characters, with some exceptions, have a greater tendency to shun it.

Spaces, then, in Welsh women's writing, appear to be emphatically gendered. However, this is not to deny the possibility of change. Certainly, the last century's women's writing in Wales shows how, while spatial organization can be seen as a tool of hegemonic forces which seek to control, contain and organize a population, especially women, it need not necessarily be seen as fixed or static. Women themselves increasingly venture outside their traditionally allocated places and spaces. They often find themselves at sites of contestation, contingent and in flux – shifting sites of resistance as well as complicity. Such sites are termed by cultural geographers *heterotopia*, or shared places which embody the possibility of change. Towards the turn of the century, Wales in women's writing becomes a type of heterotopia in which hybrid identities flourish. Tiger Bay can be seen as an archetypal heterotopia and yet it, too, has now been lost or, at least, transformed into what some writers see as an anonymous dominated space of global capitalism: the Bay.

This transformation of space is obviously connected with historical and social change. Geography and history are interpenetrating systems, rather than easily distinguishable dichotomies. As Doreen

Massey, the feminist cultural geographer, puts it, 'the social is inexorably also spatial . . . [while] the spatial is integral to the production of history, and thus to the possibility of politics'.[17] Massey has argued convincingly that the recuperation of a conception of space as dynamic, social and political, rather than static, passive and inert, is inherently a feminist project, since the hierarchical binary oppositions embodied in space/time, geography/ history have been seen in the past to overlap all too neatly with the negative dichotomy of female/male.

As mentioned in the introduction to this volume, Wales is a heterogeneous entity, and this heterogeneity is represented variously and vividly in the literary works of Welsh women in the twentieth century. Despite the great specificity with which they represent their 'milltir sgwâr' (square mile), be it the Penrhys estate in the Rhondda or a small village near a remote railway station in Flintshire, this volume has revealed that there are unexpected correspondences, interrelationships and continuities between Welsh women's literary works in both languages throughout the century.

One of the ways in which these unexpected correspondences come to light is in the repetition of certain characteristic loci in Welsh women's writing. Looking back over the spatial representations of Wales projected in Welsh women's writing of the twentieth century, we can identify a range of such significant and recurring loci, which may be regarded as '*lieux de memoire*', in Pierre Nora's use of the term.[18] Nora explains that:

> even as traditional memory disappears, we feel obliged assiduously to collect remains, testimonies, documents, images, speeches, any visible signs of what has been, as if this burgeoning dossier were to be called upon to furnish some proof to who knows what tribunal of history.[19]

Many Welsh women writers have regarded themselves as the rememberers, chroniclers and, indeed, sometimes the conscience of Wales. Eluned Morgan is one evident example, and justifies her autobiographical narrative *Dringo'r Andes* (Climbing the Andes) by saying that she was worried lest the land's history would be lost for ever; she shoulders a collective responsibility to speak for a people who think of themselves as 'chosen' and yet have apparently been both punished and forgotten. 'Places of memory' are reverberant repositories of a collective memory which, if read aright, can speak of a people's past and of their cultural identity and allegiances.

Looking back over twentieth-century Welsh women's writing as a whole, it is possible to identify some recurring and reverberant *lieux de memoire*. Although by the end of the century, clearly, the chapel and the coal-mine became dated images of Wales, no longer representative of the economic or cultural life of the majority of the population, yet such images often still remain, lurking in the background even of modern texts, suggesting that they do have a symbolic resonance beyond the literary impulse towards verisimilitude. In early twentieth-century texts, certainly, the chapel is central. The writers evoking the intense excitement of the religious revival of 1904–5, such as Sara Maria Saunders, often provide memorable descriptions of chapels as places, not only of religious worship, but of social interaction and individual quest. Other writers, such as Edith Nepean, present a much more negative view of chapels, as places of oppression and ritual humiliation, as well as being a physical embodiment of an austere and life-denying moral ideology. Whether positive or negative, there is no doubt that the chapel is one of the most potent and enduring of Welsh *lieux de memoire* for women writers. As far as the coal-mine is concerned, it has traditionally been regarded and represented as an emblem of the male experience of south Wales and, as such, more or less out of bounds for women writers. However, Menna Gallie takes us directly into the harsh physical reality of the male, underground world of the coal-mine in the opening pages of her novel, *The Small Mine*. Later in the same novel, the mangled remains of her son are brought back to Flossie's kitchen, dramatizing the interpenetration and interdependence of these male and female gendered places in the Welsh industrial novel. The later history of the mines is suggested in such a poem as Jean Earle's 'Old Tips', which animates the greened-over tip, since it seems to breathe 'warm, greenish smoke' and is a 'mark of home / To my springloaded people.'[20] Some are malevolent, 'secreting runnels / Of dark, treacle death'.[21] The first-person voice of the poem speaks for the Rhondda community, taking possession of the old tips, which speak so eloquently of 'our' past, not an exclusively male or female territory.

In addition to the chapel and the mine, perhaps the white farm is one of the most potent and repeated *lieux de memoire* in women's writing of the last century. Solitary white farmhouses are scattered everywhere in Welsh women's writing, often seen as being like mushrooms 'growing' or nestling in their rural environment. The novels of Hilda Vaughan and Allen Raine offer numerous examples, but they also crop up in much later works, such as the novels of Siân James and Clare Morgan. In Hilda Vaughan's 1942 novel, *Iron and Gold*, for instance, the farm and outbuildings are memorably described as 'like a litter of mice'.[22] Nevertheless, these archetypal 'appropriated' spaces are not invariably idyllic; sometimes the poverty and economic struggle they contain and, to an extent, conceal is the focus of writers' attention, as in many works by Kate Roberts and Elena Puw-Morgan.

Within the farmhouse itself, and in the terraced houses of industrial Wales, the focus of attention is frequently on the kitchen, a space traditionally gendered as female and often figured as such, and as the 'heart' of the household, in many texts throughout the century. Lynette Roberts's much-anthologized 'Poem from Llanybri' offers a vivid evocation of a simple farmhouse kitchen in rural Carmarthenshire.[23] Couched as an invitation (to the poet Alun Lewis), the poem celebrates Welsh traditions and combines a seductive picture of a female space with a sense of a shared literary tradition which transcends gender categories:

> A sit by the hearth with blue flames rising,
> No talk. Just a stare at 'Time' gathering
> Healed thoughts, pool insight, like swan ailing
> Peace and sound around the home, offering
>
> You a night's rest and my day's energy.
> You must come – start this pilgrimage
> Can you come? – send an ode or an elegy
> In the old way and raise our heritage.[24]

Roberts's poem is representative of the positive representations of kitchens as female domains of nurturing and, indeed, rule, which frequently occur in this literary tradition. Nevertheless, the womb-like space can be subverted in some women's writing, which deliberately shows domestic violence and abuse happening here, at the core of women's gendered space. Clare Morgan's short story 'Losing' and Trezza Azzopardi's *The Hiding Place* are recent examples.

Solitary figures on mountain-tops, not unnaturally, given the topography of Wales, crop up frequently in Welsh and Anglo-Welsh writing, especially in men's work. In earlier centuries, Ellis Wynne's sleeping bard gazed at the panorama below him through the fantastically distorted telescope of his satire, while John Dyer's moralizing pedestrian climbed Grongar Hill in order to meditate on human mortality and vanity. Welsh women writers have used the trope rather differently, emphasizing the climb to the mountain-top as a personal journey; the view from the top often becomes an affirmation of belonging to a place and a community. However, Jane Aaron has argued that, typically, fictional protagonists in women's writing gaze 'across the valley', rather than down into the populated areas in the valley below.[25] Marian Parry, in Eigra Lewis Roberts's *Brynhyfryd*, for example, climbs to the top of 'Craig y Gwin' (Wine Crag) to escape from the sterile perfection of her house and to come to a realization about her future direction in life. She gazes nowhere in particular except into her own mind; here, she comes to the epiphanic realization of her own futile stupidity in pining over a lost love for eight years. Another example is Matty Peters, in Eiluned Lewis's *The Captain's Wife*, who climbs to the top of Carn Idris in what is recognizably the Preseli mountains and relishes the panoramic view:

> It was all there, everything that made her universe. She could see the grey city climbing out of the Cathedral hollow, the green treeless country and scattered farmhouses, pink, white and yellow, to each of which [her older brother] Ivor and [cousin] Harry could put a name; the winding road to Silversands . . . the jagged rocks of the Island; and everywhere, round each curve and corner of the land, the curded edges of the sea . . .[26]

Here, the child's perspective is also self-defining; Matty herself is too young yet to be able to identify for herself all the farms below but she certainly recognizes the land as her own; it is where she belongs.

Given that Wales is a stocky peninsula, surrounded on three sides by the sea, it is not surprising to find the sea figuring largely in many texts by Welsh women. As a *lieu de memoire*, the sea obviously has great symbolic potential since it contains so much of human history and has a long tradition of being used as a quasi-allegorical trope for human life – and death. Allen Raine is perhaps the writer who returns most persistently to the sea in her settings and plots. Virtually every one of her novels features a storm at sea and a shipwreck, giving her scope both for some powerful descriptive passages and for inserting complications in her plots. Largely, though, the sea is associated with the menfolk of Raine's fictional world; they are frequently fanatical sailors who become restless when on land for too long. Women, conversely, tend to stay on dry land or, when they venture on to the water, are subject to unfortunate accidents, such as the drowning of Gwenifer's mother in the opening pages of *Queen of the Rushes*. Eiluned Lewis is another author who, in *The Captain's Wife*, evokes vividly both the appeal and danger of the sea. In this novel women, too, such as the main protagonist, Lettice, sail to foreign parts, though not after they have become mothers. The sea and rivers suggest the possibilities and dangers of travel, while the still lakes which abound in Wales and in women's fictional cartography of Wales are, conversely, often associated with the supernatural, as in Hilda Vaughan's *Iron and Gold*.

Also associated with the pleasures and dangers of travel is the recurrent image of the lonely road. Kate Roberts's autobiography *Y Lôn Wen* (The White Lane) offers the archetypal picture of the lonely mountain road, though she imbues it with a symbolic meaning connected with the operation of memory, leading her back into the past. As discussed elsewhere, roads leading away from the isolated farm, over the hill, into the unknown, recur frequently in Welsh women's writing, but often there is a sense of proscription attached to them. Roads lead out for men, but women remain and wait, as in the previously discussed scene from Gillian Clarke's 'Letter from a Far Country'. Later women's writing shakes itself free from that sense of proscription, but the quasi-allegorical weight of the road as an emblem of the individual's journey through life is not lost. In the early twentieth-century writings, perhaps the most frequently alluded-to work of literature (excluding the Bible) is Bunyan's *The Pilgrim's Progress* (or the Welsh version, *Taith y Pererin*). Bunyan's topographical and allegorical imagination leaves its mark on Welsh women's writing for many years.

Another dominant feature of the open countryside which is often used by Welsh women writers in symbolic ways is the heap of ancient stones. In Gwyneth Vaughan's *Plant y Gorthrwm* the three standing stones are christened 'Hope, Patience, and Love', representing the perennial virtues of the *gwerin* who meet beneath them and defy their oppressors. In other works, such as poems by Gillian Clarke and Merryn Williams, the ancient stones simply exist, unmoralised, as emblems of memory and continuity.

Borderlands figure prominently in a number of texts by Welsh women. Some represent actual borderlands, such as those between England and Wales, as in the work of Margiad Evans, but often the notion of the border is explored in more symbolic ways. Since migration is such a common experience both in twentieth-century Welsh history and literature, fictional characters are constantly traversing borders and experiencing the cultural shifts and 'Othering' which that experience imposes upon them. Charlotte Williams's *Sugar and Slate*, for example, is very much a narrative about border experiences and the attempts to construct an identity not riven by borders. But the migrant experience is also chronicled in a number of earlier works in both languages, such as Elena Puw-Morgan's *Y Graith* and Marion Eames's *I Hela Cnau*.

One final *lieu de memoire* which figures in some works by women writers is the cave. As we have seen, Allen Raine's 'Welsh witch' frequents the cave below the village which everyone else shuns in superstitious fear, since they regard it as haunted by the ghosts of the drowned. The 'Otherness' of Catrin, the Welsh witch, is underlined by her frequenting of such a spot. In a later work, Doris in Kate Bosse-Griffiths's novel, *Mae'r Galon wrth y Llyw* (The Heart's at the Tiller) has her first, powerful sexual experiences in a cave on the Gower. The cave, for these two Welsh women writers, appears to stand as the hidden place, associated with taboo – madness or sexuality – and, interestingly, affording shelter to transgressive female characters. In the imaginary topography of Welsh women's writing, the cave is one of the opposites of the chapel, two confined spaces where women find different kinds of solace, one socially sanctioned and the other condemned.

There are many other resonant and recurrent topographical images which are used by Welsh women writers as places of memory and as markers of cultural difference. The places explored here indicate that Welsh women writers do construct a distinctively Welsh topography in their work, largely through the use of symbolic places, which frequently act as types of synecdoche for the land of Wales as a whole. As Ian Baucom has observed, with regard to the ways in which English national identity is continually constructed and reconstructed by reference to place,

> the locale ... serves a disciplinary and nostalgic discourse on ... national identity by making the past visible, by rendering it present, by acting as what Pierre Nora calls a *lieu de memoire* that purports to testify to the nation's essential continuity across time. But because even the hardiest *lieu de memoire* is mutable, because it not only occupies space but is occupied by living subjects who, as they visit, inhabit, or

pass through it, leave their estranging marks upon it, the locale also serves as the site in which the present re-creates the past, as a 'contact zone.'[27]

In a sense, Welsh women's writing as a body of literature is a 'contact zone' in which the present recreates the past, not only in overtly historical novels, such as Marion Eames's *Y Stafell Ddirgel*, but also in texts which use myth, dream and memory to explore the contemporary individual's relation with ancestors and heritage, as we find, for example, in Gillian Clarke's 'The King of Britain's Daughter'.

Juxtaposed with the *lieux de memoire* described above is the constant presence and potential threat or temptation of 'elsewhere', especially colonial lands, such as America, Patagonia, South Africa and Australia, which entice Welsh characters, primarily men, towards them and away from their womenfolk, who often stay behind in Wales. English cities, especially London and Liverpool, loom large as alternative dwelling-places, but often these places are blighted because the Welsh female migrants who do go there are exploited as servants or subjected to racial denigration. Nevertheless, the English city is frequently treated as a place of ambivalence, which offers freedom from a restrictive, traditional chapel culture, but at the same time strips the individual of the moral protection which that very culture provides. Dilys Cadwaladr's Welsh Shakespearean sonnet, 'Llundain' (London), expresses this ambivalence well, both in form and content:

Ddinas y drychiolaethau wedi'r hwyr
  A'th wyll yn noddfa i fleiddiaid chwim y nos,
Dilewyd gwahaniaethau'r ffyrdd yn llwyr
  Ac un â'r butain dlawd yw'r forwyn dlos.
Trwstan yw traed y cibddall ar dy stryd,
  Ni chilia sant rhag baeddu ei fysedd glân
Ar ysgwydd gwalch na ddysgodd ddim o'i grud
  Ond hen dafodiaith lithrig uffern dân.
Crechwen yr hen sy'n awr i'th heol di,
  Ac nid oes gainc ond udo'r crwniwr prudd;
Ni chyfyd plentyn bach ei gân na'i gri
  A llwm yw bron y fam a'i breichiau rhydd:
Ond neithiwr bu i tithau dan y lloer
Ddinas hiraethus, ryw ogoniant oer.[28]

[City of apparitions after dark
Your murk the haven of the swift wolves of night,

The differences of ways are quite rubbed out
And the poor whore and lovely maid are one.
Uncertain are the feet of the half-blind on your street,
The saint deigns to soil his clean fingers
On the shoulder of a tramp who learned nothing in life
But the old fluent dialect of hell's flames.
The raucous laugh of old age is now your sound
And there's no tune but the wailing of the sad crooner;
There's no sign of the song or cry of a small child
And the mother's breast is dry, her arms empty;
And yet last night you bore under the moonlight,
Nostalgic city, a kind of cold majesty.]

Some Welsh women writers construct Wales as a wild landscape of mountains and sea; however, other female writers hardly mention the topography of Wales at all, focusing attention instead on interior, domestic spaces. In many early texts, female characters work out of doors, engaged in agricultural labour which is rooted in the world of Nature. Nature is often uncooperative and indifferent, posing problems and causing discomfort, for example, when Dori in *Y Graith* is forced to walk over the mountain in the dark to get to the nearest railway station, and her boots soon become soaking wet and muddy, further impeding her slow progress. Whereas writers such as Kate Roberts and Siân James are, in this way, unsentimental and realistic about Nature, other Welsh women writers, further removed, perhaps, from actual agricultural labour themselves, tend to endow it with special, even mystical significance: Eiluned Lewis, Margiad Evans and Brenda Chamberlain would be examples of this tendency. There is a shift in the later part of the century to city- and townscapes, not unnaturally reflecting the shifting demographic of the population of Wales. However, the close relationship between the urban and the rural is often retained in Valleys women's writing, where the 'mountain' is as integral and close a part of the community's experience as is the street and the factory or mine.

Places need to be mapped, not only by cartographers, but by creative writers, including women; the latter, as I hope to have shown, produce a distinct literary cartography and a necessary one for our greater understanding of what Wales is and has been. From the beginning of the century, Welsh women writers have been engaged in a process of appropriation and reappropriation of the native place, against a background initially of imperialism and latterly of globalization. Literary topographies are important because they are implicitly political and not static; in turn, they inform people's views of Wales and even change what it means to live here. Literary representations of place can become more power-fully real than 'reality', as the extraordinary appeal, for example, of 'Hardy's Wessex' demonstrates. The poet Tennyson is reputed to have said, when first visiting Lyme Regis, 'Don't talk to me of the Duke of Monmouth. Show me the exact spot where Louisa Musgrove fell!'[29] Once Welsh women's writing becomes as well known as the works of Jane Austen, it may be that literary tourists will eagerly visit Tresaith, for glimpses of the Welsh witch, or Llanybri, to speak to the 'Gods with Stainless Ears'.

According to Amy Dillwyn, in her 1880 novel *The Rebecca Rioter*, landscape forms character: her eponymous hero is harsh, rugged and rebellious, fundamentally because he was born and raised in Upper Killay, known in Dillwyn's time and from her class perspective as a particularly lawless place. Though we might nowa-days be suspicious of the tendency of the late Victorians to create deterministic human categories according to location or race, there is still truth in the notion that there is a mutually formative relation between a place and a people. Contemporary sociological research in Wales repeatedly supports this view; as Graham Day asserts, 'the social features of life in Wales . . . grow . . . out of the landscape it inhabits'.[30] Nowhere is this truth more evident than in the pages of Welsh women's writing in the twentieth century.

Notes

Introduction

1   Susanne Hagemann, 'Women and nation', in Douglas Gifford and Dorothy McMillan (eds), *A History of Scottish Women's Writing* (Edinburgh: Edinburgh University Press, 1997), p. 323.
2   R. S. Thomas, 'Unity', transl. by Katie Gramich of 'Undod', the J. R. Jones Memorial Lecture, 1985, in *R. S. Thomas: Selected Prose*, ed. Sandra Anstey, 3rd edn (Bridgend: Seren, 1995), p. 155.
3   Deirdre Beddoe, *Out of the Shadows: A History of Women in Twentieth-Century Wales* (Cardiff: University of Wales Press, 2000), p. 179.
4   Ibid.
5   Virginia Woolf, *Three Guineas*, in *A Room of One's Own and Three Guineas*, ed. Michèle Barrett ([1928; 1938] Harmondsworth: Penguin, 1993), p. 234.
6   Virginia Woolf, *Orlando*, ed. Rachel Bowlby ([1928] Oxford: Oxford University Press, 1992).
7   Benedict Anderson, *Imagined Communities: Reflections on the Origins and Spread of Nationalism* (London: Verso, 1991); Ernest Gellner, *Nations and Nationalism* (Oxford: Blackwell, 1983); Eric Hobsbawm, *Nations and Nationalism since 1780* (Cambridge: Cambridge University Press, 1990); Eric Hobsbawm and Terence Ranger (eds), *The Invention of Tradition* (Cambridge: Cambridge University Press, 1983).
8   A. D. Smith, *The Antiquity of Nations* (Cambridge: Polity, 2004), p. 247.
9   The terms 'appropriated' and 'dominated' are used by the cultural geographer Henri Lefebvre and are discussed further in the Conclusion pp. 199–200.
10 Moelona, *Alys Morgan*, in *Dwy Ramant o'r De* (Dolgellau: E. W. Evans, Swyddfa'r 'Goleuad', 1911), discussed in chapter 1.
11 John Stuart Mill, *On Liberty; representative government; the subjection of women: three essays* (London: Oxford University Press, 1912).
12 For an admirable analysis of the language of the Blue Books, see Gwyneth Tyson Roberts, *The Language of the Blue Books: The Perfect Instrument of Empire* (Cardiff: University of Wales Press, 1998).
13 Dorian Llywelyn, *Sacred Place, Chosen People* (Cardiff: University of Wales Press, 1999), p. 3.
14 Bill Ashcroft *et al.*, *The Empire Writes Back* (London: Routledge, 1989), p. 9.

[15] Menna Elfyn, 'Siapiau o Gymru', in *Eucalyptus: Detholiad o Gerddi/Selected Poems 1978–1994* (Llandysul: Gomer, 1995), p. 98.

1 Sacred Place: 1900–1920

[1] One example is the invention of the so-called 'long nineteenth century', taken to begin in about 1780, with the result that Romanticism can be embraced as an integral part of the period.

[2] This Report has been the subject of a number of illuminating scholarly studies in recent years, including Gwyneth Roberts's aforementioned *The Language of the Blue Books* and Jane Aaron, *Pur fel y Dur* (Cardiff: University of Wales Press, 1998).

[3] The Welsh phrase means 'The Treason of the Blue Books', a term which clearly suggests that the government report created strong political and national opposition within Wales.

[4] Virginia Woolf, 'Mr Bennett and Mrs Brown' (London: Hogarth, 1924), p. 1.

[5] 'The Angel in the House' was an 1854 poem by Coventry Patmore extolling conjugal love; Virginia Woolf identified the image of the domestic angel as the one who had to be killed, metaphorically, if a women wished to become a writer. See Woolf's 'Professions for Women', first published in *Death of the Moth*, 1942.

[6] 'Buddug' (Catherine Prichard), 'Cranogwen', in *Caniadau Buddug* (Caernarfon: Swyddfa 'Cymru', 1911); repr. and trans. into English in Katie Gramich and Catherine Brennan (eds), *Welsh Women's Poetry 1460–2001* (Dinas Powys: Honno, 2003), pp. 142–3.

[7] The phrase 'T. S. Eliot ends idea of poetry for ladies' is used by James Joyce in a note to *Finnegans Wake*.

[8] 'Ceridwen Peris', 'Cân Gwraig y Gweithiwr/Song of the Worker's Wife', in Gramich and Brennan (eds), *Welsh Women's Poetry 1460–2001* op. cit., pp. 154–5.

[9] 'Cranogwen', 'Fy Ngwlad', in ibid., p. 140.

[10] Winnie Parry, *Sioned: Darluniau o Fywyd Gwledig yng Nghymru* [Sioned: Pictures of Rural Life in Wales] (Caernarfon: Swyddfa 'Cymru', 1906), p. 40.

[11] Ibid., p. 119.

[12] Ibid., p. 123.

[13] Winnie Parry, 'Fy Ffrog Newydd', *Cerrig y Rhyd* (Caernarfon: Cwmni'r Cyhoeddwyr Cymreig, 1907) p. 64.

[14] Saunders Lewis, letter to Kate Roberts, 23 May 1934, in Dafydd Ifans (ed.) *Annwyl Kate, Annwyl Saunders: Gohebiaeth 1923–1983* (Aberystwyth: National Library of Wales, 1992), p. 105.

[15] Kate Roberts, letter to Saunders Lewis, 22 October 1928, ibid., p. 47.

[16] See John Williams, 'Women at work in Nineteenth-Century Wales', in his *Was Wales Industrialised?: Essays in Modern Welsh History* (Llandysul: Gomer, 1995), pp. 58–78, and Deirdre Beddoe, *Out of the Shadows: A History of Women in Twentieth-Century Wales* (Cardiff: University of Wales Press, 2000).

[17] Fanny Edwards, *Cit* (Wrecsam: Swyddfa 'Cymru'r Plant', 1908), pp. 204–5.

[18] This was a common epithet for Wales adopted in the late Victorian period,

probably in response to the allegations made in the Blue Books of 1847. It refers to the practice at the time of judges donning white gloves when there were no criminal cases to be tried in court.

19 '[m]i awn i'r temprans i gael bwyd', Edwards, *Cit*, p. 74.
20 For further details see Marion Löffler, 'A romantic nationalist', *Planet*, 121 (1997), 58–6.
21 Stephen Knight, *A Hundred Years of Fiction* (Cardiff: University of Wales Press, 2004), p. 16.
22 'The Dau Wynne', *A Maid of Cymru* (London and Carmarthen: Simpkin, Marshall & Co. and W. Spurrell & Son, 1901), p. 25.
23 Ibid., p. 17.
24 Ibid., p. 27.
25 Ibid., p. 29.
26 Ibid., p. 31.
27 Ibid., p. 35.
28 Ibid., p. 37.
29 Ibid., p. 52.
30 Ibid., p. 77.
31 Ibid., pp. 96–7.
32 Ibid., p. 103.
33 Ibid., p. 106.
34 Ibid., p. 128.
35 Ibid., p. 154.
36 Ibid., p. 159.
37 Ibid., p. 160.
38 Ibid., p. 214.
39 Ibid., p. 216.
40 Ibid., p. 297.
41 Mallt Williams, 'David', in Jane Aaron (ed.), *A View Across the Valley* (Dinas Powys: Honno, 1999), pp. 14–26.
42 Eluned Morgan, *Gwymon y Môr* [1909], repr. in *Dringo'r Andes a Gwymon y Môr*, ed. Ceridwen Lloyd-Morgan and Kathryn Hughes (Dinas Powys: Honno, 2001), p. 99.
43 Eluned Morgan, *Dringo'r Andes* [1904] repr. in ibid., p. 3.
44 Ibid., p. 8.
45 Ibid., p. 22.
46 Ibid., p. 44.
47 Ibid., p. 51.
48 Ibid.
49 Eluned Morgan, *Gwymon y Môr*, in ibid., p. 137.
50 Ibid., p. 144.
51 Ernst Gellner, *Nationalism* (London: Phoenix, 1998), p. 72.
52 Gwyneth Vaughan, *O Gorlannau y Defaid* (London and Carmarthen: David Nutt and W. Spurrell & Son, 1905), p. 46.
53 Ibid., p. 73.
54 Ibid., p. 74.
55 Ibid., p. 203.
56 Sara Maria Saunders, 'Rhagymadrodd' [Foreword], *Y Diwygiad ym Mhentre Alun* (Wrecsam: Hughes a'i Fab, 1907), p. v.

57 Sara Maria Saunders, 'Gwraig Watkin Jones', *Llithiau o Bentre Alun* (Wrecsam: Hughes a'i Fab, 1908), p. 39.
58 For a gender-inflected analysis of Raine's *Queen of the Rushes*, see my introduction to the Honno Classics edition, 1998.
59 Saunders, *Y Diwygiad ym Mhentre Alun*, p. 6.
60 Ibid., p. 9.
61 Saunders, *Llithiau o Bentre Alun*, p. 32.
62 Saunders, *Y Diwygiad ym Mhentre Alun*, p. 72.
63 Beddoe, *Out of the Shadows*, pp. 11–12.
64 Gwyneth Vaughan, *Plant y Gorthrwm* (Cardiff: Educational Publishing Co., 1908), p. 176.
65 Ibid., p. 86.
66 Ibid., p. 110.
67 Ibid., p. 56.
68 Ibid., p. 154.
69 Ibid., p. 7.
70 Ibid., p. 146.
71 Quoted on frontispiece of Allen Raine, *Torn Sails* (London: Hutchinson, 1898).
72 Quoted on frontispiece of Allen Raine, *By Berwen Banks* (London: Hutchinson, 1899).
73 Gwyn Jones, *The First Forty Years: Some Notes on Anglo-Welsh Literature* (Cardiff: University of Wales Press, 1957), pp. 5–28.
74 Sally Roberts Jones, *Allen Raine* (Cardiff: University of Wales Press, 1979), p. 26.
75 Allen Raine, *A Welsh Witch* (London: Hutchinson, 1902), p. 208.
76 Ibid., p. 14.
77 Allen Raine, *A Welsh Singer* (London: Hutchinson, 1897), p. 8.
78 Ibid., pp. 60–1.
79 Raine, *A Welsh Witch*, p. 286.
80 Ibid., p. 317.
81 Kirsti Bohata has discussed racial othering in Welsh fiction in her chapter 'Stereotypes of alterity: race, sexuality and gender', in *Postcolonialism Revisited* (Cardiff: University of Wales Press, 2004), pp. 29–58, and in her article 'Apes and cannibals in Cambria: images of racial and gendered other in Gothic writing in Wales', in *Welsh Writing in English: A Yearbook of Critical Essays*, 6 (2000), 119–43.
82 Raine, *A Welsh Singer*, p. 358.
83 Raine, *Torn Sails* (London: Hutchinson, 1898), pp. 7–8.
84 Raine, *Garthowen* (London: Hutchinson, 1900), p. 21.
85 Raine, *A Welsh Witch*, p. 153.
86 Raine, *By Berwen Banks*, p. 18.
87 Raine, *Torn Sails*, pp. 196–7.
88 Ibid., p. 173.
89 Ibid., p. 186.
90 Ibid., pp. 100–1.
91 Ibid., p. 105.
92 Raine, *By Berwen Banks*, p. 98.
93 E.g. *By Berwen Banks*, p. 145.

94   *A Welsh Witch*, p. 164.
95   Ibid., p. 170.
96   Ibid., p. 216.
97   Ibid., p. 237.
98   Raine, *On the Wings of the Wind* (London: Hutchinson, 1903), p. 146.
99   Based on the Welsh word *defod* 'rite'; ibid., p. 198.
100 Raine, *Garthowen*, p. 28.
101 Ibid., p. 144.
102 Ibid., p. 143.
103 Raine, *By Berwen Banks*, pp. 284–5.
104 Raine, *Under the Thatch* (London: Hutchinson, 1910), p. 8.
105 Raine, 'Home, Sweet Home: A True Story', in *All in a Month* (London: Hutchinson, 1908), pp. 179–96. The story is reproduced in Aaron (ed.), *A View Across the Valley*.
106 Edith Nepean, Acknowledgement, facing title-page of *Gwyneth of the Welsh Hills* (London: Stanley Paul & Co, 1917).
107 Ibid., p. 47.
108 Ibid., p. 154.
109 Jones, *Allen Raine*, p. 92.
110 Ibid., p. 196.
111 Sally Roberts Jones, *Allen Raine* (Cardiff: University of Wales Press, 1979) p. 80.
112 Derek Walcott, 'Another Life', *Collected Poems* (London: Faber, 1986) p. 294.
113 Bertha Thomas, 'The Madness of Winifred Owen', *Picture Tales from Welsh Hills* (Chicago and London: F. G. Browne & Co. and T. Fisher Unwin, 1913), p. 9. This story is also reprinted in Aaron (ed.), *A View Across the Valley*.
114 Ibid., *Picture Tales from Welsh Hills*, p. 33.
115 Ibid., p. 39.
116 For example, in *Traed mewn Cyffion* (Feet in Chains, 1936) by Kate Roberts, discussed later, and in Emyr Humphreys's 1958 novel, *A Toy Epic*.
117 Thomas, *Picture Tales from Welsh Hills*, p. 68.
118 Ibid., p. 84.
119 Ibid., p. 147.
120 Ibid.
121 Ibid., p. 38.
122 Ibid., p. 168.
123 Ibid., p. 173.
124 Ibid., p. 177.
125 A similar link is suggested in other early works by Welsh women writers; see, for example, the poem 'Red or White?' by Emily Jane Pfeiffer, in *Welsh Women's Poetry 1460–2001*, p. 115, and the story 'A Brave Welshwoman' by Allen Raine, in *All in a Month*, pp. 241–53.
126 Thomas, *Picture Tales from Welsh Hills*, p. 180.
127 Ibid., p. 233.
128 See, for example: Kate Roberts, *O Gors y Bryniau* (1925), Eigra Lewis Roberts's *Brynhyfryd* (1959) and Dorothy Edwards, *Rhapsody* (1927), all discussed later; Gwyn Thomas, *Meadow Prospect Revisited*, ed. Michael Parnell (1992), and D. J. Williams, *Storïau'r Tir Glas* (1936).
129 'Moelona', *Rhamant y Rhos* ([1907] Aberdâr: Pugh a Rowlands, Swyddfa'r

'Leader' a'r 'Darian', 1918); 'Moelona', *Dwy Ramant o'r De* (Dolgellau: E. W. Evans, Swyddfa'r 'Goleuad', 1911).
130 'Moelona', *Rhamant y Rhos*, p. 17.
131 'Moelona', *Alys Morgan*, in *Dwy Ramant o'r De*, p. 8.
132 Ibid., p. 33.
133 Ibid., p. 43.
134 'Moelona', *Rhamant Nyrs Bifan*, in *Dwy Ramant o'r De*, p. 79.
135 'Moelona', *Bugail y Bryn* (Dolgellau: Swyddfa'r 'Cymro', 1917), p. 123.
136 Roger Williams Jones, 'Moelona', in Mairwen and Gwynn Jones (eds), *Dewiniaid Difyr: Llenorion Plant Cymru hyd tua 1950* (Llandysul: Gomer, 1983), pp. 38–42.
137 'Moelona', *Teulu Bach Nantoer* (Wrecsam: Hughes a'i Fab, 1913), available at: http://www.llyfrau.org/gsdl/cgi-bin/library.exe
138 Ibid., p. 7.
139 'Ffug-chwedl' was, however, a commonly used neologism in the period to denote the new genre of the novel.
140 Ibid., p. 25.
141 Ibid., p. 27.
142 Ibid., p. 57.

2 Fallen Place: 1921–1945

1 See Katie Gramich, 'Gorchfygwyr a chwiorydd: storïau byrion Dorothy Edwards a Kate Roberts yn y dauddegau' [Conquerors and sisters: the short stories of Dorothy Edwards and Kate Roberts in the 1920s], in M. Wynn Thomas (ed.), *DiFfinio Dwy Lenyddiaeth Cymru* (Caerdydd: Gwasg Prifysgol Cymru, 1995), pp. 80–96.
2 Gramich, 'Gorchfygwyr a chwiorydd', and Stephen Knight, *A Hundred Years of Fiction* (Cardiff: University of Wales Press, 2004).
3 Arnold Bennett, quoted in Roland Mathias, *Anglo-Welsh Literature: An Illustrated History* (Bridgend: Seren, 1986), p. 79.
4 Dorothy Edwards, 'The Conquered', in *Rhapsody* (London, Wishart & Co., 1927), p. 53.
5 Ibid., p. 54.
6 Ibid., p. 62.
7 Ibid., p. 69.
8 Moelona, *Cwrs y Lli* (Wrecsam: Hughes a'i Fab, 1927), p. 50.
9 Moelona, *Ffynnonloyw* (Llandysul: Gwasg Gomer, 1939), p. 73.
10 Ibid., p. 113. Here, clearly, Nan becomes a member of the moderate NUWSS (National Union of Women's Suffrage Societies), which established its first branch in Wales in 1907. The militant group was the WSPU (Women's Social and Political Union), founded by Emmeline Pankhurst in 1903. See Deirdre Beddoe, *Out of the Shadows: A History of Women in Twentieth-Century Wales* (Cardiff: University of Wales Press, 2000), pp. 40–6.
11 Moelona, *Ffynnonloyw*, p. 91.
12 Ibid., p. 115.
13 Ibid., pp. 115–16.
14 Ibid., p. 123.

¹⁵ Ibid., p. 134.
¹⁶ Ibid., p. 114; Kate Gramich and Catherine Brennan (eds), *Welsh Women's Poetry 1460–2001* (Dinas Powys: Honno, 2003), pp. 162–3.
¹⁷ Hilda Vaughan, quoted on the back cover of *A Thing of Nought* (London: Lovat Dickson & Thompson, 1934).
¹⁸ Ibid., p. 28.
¹⁹ Gillian Clarke, 'Letter from a Far Country' in Gramich and Brennan (eds), *Welsh Women's Poetry 1460–2001*, p. 227.
²⁰ Hilda Vaughan, *The Soldier and the Gentlewoman* (London: Victor Gollancz, 1932), p. 113.
²¹ Ibid., pp. 25–6.
²² For an account of the legend and a reprinting of an early retelling of it see Jane Aaron introduction and the appendix to the 2002 reprint of *Iron and Gold*, published by Honno Press.
²³ See, for instance, Jane Aaron's account of this in 'Y Flodeuwedd gyfoes: llên menywod 1973–1993', in M. Wynn Thomas (ed.), *DiFfinio Dwy Lenyddiaeth Cymru* (Caerdydd: Gwasg Prifysgol Cymru, 1995), pp. 190–208.
²⁴ Kate Bosse-Griffiths, 'Fy Chwaer Efa' [My Sister Eve], *Fy Chwaer Efa* (Dinbych: Llyfrau Pawb, 1944); reprinted in *Cariadau* (Talybont: Y Lolfa, 1995), pp. 21–55.
²⁵ Ibid., p. 46.
²⁶ E. Tegla Davies, 'Cyflwynwn nofel fuddugol cystadleuaeth Llyfrau'r Dryw Llandebie [*sic*]', *Y Faner*, undated cutting (*c*.1941).
²⁷ Kate Bosse-Griffiths, *Anesmwyth Hoen* (Llandybïe: Llyfrau'r Dryw, 1941), p. 51.
²⁸ Ibid., p. 60.
²⁹ Jane Ann Jones, 'Fel angylion', in *Storïau Hen Ferch* (Aberystwyth: Gwasg Aberystwyth, 1937), p. 39.
³⁰ Ibid., p. 44.
³¹ Jane Ann Jones, 'Porthi Nwydau', ibid., p. 71.
³² Ibid.
³³ Jane Ann Jones, 'Taledigaeth y Gwobrwy', ibid., pp. 99–105.
³⁴ Elena Puw-Davies (later, Morgan), *Nansi Lovell: Hunangofiant Hen Sipsi* (Aberystwyth: Gwasg Aberystwyth, 1933), p. 93.
³⁵ Elena Puw Morgan, *Y Wisg Sidan* ([1939] Llandysul: Gwasg Gomer, 1995), p. 237.
³⁶ Ibid., p. 265.
³⁷ Ibid., p. 38.
³⁸ Ibid., p. 124.
³⁹ Elena Puw-Morgan was born in 1900 and lived until 1973 but she published no more novels after *Y Graith* in 1943. Instead, she dedicated herself to caring for ailing relatives and later was herself afflicted by a lingering illness.
⁴⁰ Beddoe, *Out of the Shadows*, p. 31.
⁴¹ Ibid., p. 32.
⁴² Elena Puw-Morgan, *Y Graith* (Dinbych: Gwasg Gee, 1943), p. 113.
⁴³ Ibid., pp. 114, 111.
⁴⁴ Founded in 1925.
⁴⁵ Ibid., p. 201.
⁴⁶ Ibid., p. 246.

47 See 'The madwoman in the hayloft: women and madness in the literatures of Wales', in Katie Gramich and Andrew Hiscock (eds), *Dangerous Diversities: The Changing Faces of Wales* (Cardiff: University of Wales Press, 1998), pp. 18–33.

48 Kate Roberts, 'Y Man Geni', in *O Gors y Bryniau* ([1925] Caerdydd: Hughes a'i Fab, 1992), pp. 3–7.

49 Raymond Williams, *The Welsh Industrial Novel* (Cardiff: University College of Wales Cardiff, 1979), p. 18.

50 Eiluned Lewis, *Dew on the Grass* (London: Macmillan, 1934) p. 15. A version of the following reading of the novel appears as our introduction to the Honno Classics edition (2007).

51 Ibid., p. 17.

52 Ibid., p. 16.

53 Ibid.

54 Proverbs 19: 12, the *Authorized Version*.

55 Lewis, *Dew on the Grass*, p. 45.

56 Ibid., p. 190.

57 Ibid., p. 54. It is interesting to note that the surname 'Lovell' is also used by Elena Puw-Morgan and Allen Raine to indicate characters' Romany origins.

58 Ibid., p. 209.

59 Ibid., p. 26.

60 Ibid., p. 45.

61 Ibid., p. 46.

62 Ibid., p. 61.

63 Ibid., p. 78.

64 Ibid., p. 69.

65 Ibid., p. 84.

66 Ibid., p. 109.

67 Ibid., p. 121.

68 Ibid., p. 122.

69 Ibid., p. 67.

70 Ibid., p. 209.

71 Eiluned Lewis, *The Captain's Wife* (London: Macmillan, 1943), p. 1.

72 Ibid., p. 2.

73 Ibid., p. 88.

74 A parallel explored further in Dorian Llywelyn, *Sacred Place, Chosen People* (Cardiff: University of Wales Press, 1999).

75 Lewis, *The Captain's Wife*, p. 84.

76 Ibid., p. 103.

77 Eiluned Lewis, 'The Birthright', *Morning Songs and Other Poems* (London: Macmillan, 1944), p. 23; also in Lewis, *Dew on the Grass*, facing title-page; also reproduced in Gramich and Brennan (eds), *Welsh Women's Poetry 1460–2001*, pp. 164–5.

78 Margiad Evans, *Country Dance* ([1932] London: John Calder, 1978), pp. 60–1.

79 Ibid., p. 55.

80 Quoted in Moira Dearnley, *Margiad Evans* (Cardiff: University of Wales Press, 1982), p. 13.

81 Evans, *Country Dance*, p. 3.

82 Ibid., p. 17.

83 Evans, *The Wooden Doctor* ([1933] Dinas Powys: Honno, 2005), p. 72.

84 Ibid., p. 109.

85 Ibid., p. 147.

86 Ibid., 154.

87 P. J. Kavanagh, Introduction to *Autobiography*, Margiad Evans (London: Calder & Boyars, 1943), p. iii.

88 R. Merfyn Jones, *The North Wales Quarrymen 1874–1922* (Cardiff: University of Wales Press, 1981), p. 38.

89 Kate Roberts, 'Newid Byd', *O Gors y Brynian* ([1925] Caerdydd: Hughes a'i Fab, 1992), p. 48.

90 Vaughan, *A Thing of Nought*, p. 51.

91 Kate Roberts, 'Y Golled', *Rhigolau Bywyd* (Aberystwyth: Gwasg Aberystwyth, 1929), p. 12.

92 Kate Roberts, *Traed mewn Cyffion* (Abertawe: C.E. Watkins, 1971) ch. 4; English trans. by John Idris Jones, *Feet in Chains* (Ruthin: John Jones Publishing, 1996). All English translations that follow are taken from the latter work.

93 See Beddoe, *Out of the Shadows*, ch. 2 ff. For a more extensive account of Welsh women's writing and war, see my chapter in *Wales at War: Critical Essays on Literature and Art*, ed. Tony Curtis (Bridgend: Seren, 2007).

94 Roberts, *Traed mewn Cyffion*, p. 158.

95 Ibid.

96 Ibid., p. 163.

97 Ibid., p. 164.

98 Ibid., pp. 172–4.

99 Ibid., p. 176.

100 Ibid., p. 178.

101 Kate Roberts, letter to Saunders Lewis, 8 March 1961, in *Annwyl Kate, Annwyl Saunders: Gohebiaeth 1923–1983* (Aberystwyth: National Library of Wales, 1992), p. 191.

102 Roberts, *Traed mewn Cyffion*, pp. 186–7.

103 Ibid., p. 191.

104 For a discussion of Kate Roberts and feminism, see Delyth George, 'Kate Roberts – ffeminist?', *Y Traethodydd*, 140 (1985), 185–201.

105 Judith Butler, *Gender Trouble: Feminism and the Subversion of Identity* (London: Routledge, 1990), p. 24.

106 For instance, Matty, in *The Captain's Wife*, reflects sorrowfully, 'sometimes the longing to be a boy and go to sea was unendurable. She was the only girl in the family. Was it possible that God had made a mistake?' (p. 173).

107 Kate Roberts, 'Y Taliad Olaf', *Ffair Gaeaf* (Dinbych: Gwasg Gee, 1937), p. 46.

108 Kate Roberts, interview with Gwyn Erfyl, in Rhydwen Williams (ed.), *Kate Roberts: Ei Meddwl a'i Gwaith* (Llandybïe: Christopher Davies, 1983), p. 32.

109 Hilda Vaughan, *Pardon and Peace* (London: Macmillan, 1945), p. 4.

110 Ibid., p. 195.

111 Ibid., p. 20.

112 Ibid., p. 37.

113 Kate Roberts, review in *Y Llenor*, 1937, quoted in Eigra Lewis Roberts (ed.), *Merch yr Oriau Mawr* (Caernarfon: Tŷ ar y Graig, 1981), p. 27.

114 Rhiannon Davies Jones, quoted in ibid., p. 65.

115 Dilys Cadwaladr, 'Braslun o ysgrif Hon a hon', in ibid., p. 65.

116 Dilys Cadwaladr, 'Bara', in Gramich and Brennan, *Welsh Women's Poetry 1460–2001*, p. 166.

117 Dilys Cadwaladr, 'Yr Hen Oruchwyliaeth', *Storïau* (Wrecsam: Hughes a'i Fab, 1936), pp. 119–30.

118 Ibid., pp. 41–8.

119 Ibid., pp. 71–6.

120 See Dilys Cadwaladr, 'Atgofion 2', quoted in Roberts (ed.), *Merch yr Oriau Mawr*, p. 16.

121 Dilys Cadwaladr, 'Dyn Call', *Storïau*, p. 96.

122 Ibid., pp. 109–15.

123 Ibid., pp. 99–105.

124 Ibid., p. 105.

125 Caradoc Evans, 'Be This Her Memorial', *My People* ([1915] Bridgend: Seren, 1987).

126 Lynette Roberts, 'Gods with Stainless Ears', in her *Collected Poems*, ed. Patrick McGuinness (Manchester: Carcanet, 2005), pp. 43–78.

127 Patrick McGuinness, lecture on Lynette Roberts delivered at the Association for Welsh Writing annual conference, Gregynog Hall, Powys, April 2005.

128 Tony Conran, 'Lynette Roberts: war poet', *The Cost of Strangeness* (Llandysul: Gomer, 1983), p. 191.

129 Roberts, 'Gods with Stainless Ears', Part III, *Collected Poems*, p. 59.

130 Ibid., Part I, p. 47.

131 Ibid., Part IV, p. 61.

132 Ibid., Part V, pp. 68–9. 'Catoptric': relating to mirrors or reflections.

133 See Lily Tobias, *The Nationalists and Other Goluth Studies* (London: C. W. Daniel, 1921), and Jasmine Donahaye, '"A dislocation called a blessing": three Welsh-Jewish perspectives', in *Welsh Writing in English: A Yearbook of Critical Essays*, 7 (2001–2), 154–73. The rediscovery of Tobias is largely due to the research and scholarship of Donahaye.

134 Jasmine Donahaye, Introduction to *Eunice Fleet* ([1933] Dinas Powys: Honno, 2004), p. xvii.

135 Ibid., p. xix.

3 Awakening Place: 1946–1977

1 Deirdre Beddoe, *Out of the Shadows: A History of Women in Twentieth-Century Wales* (Cardiff: University of Wales Press, 2000), p. 134. For further details of this 'sortie', see Mari A. Williams, '*Where is Mrs Jones Going?*': *Women and the Second World War in South Wales* (Aberystwyth: Board of Celtic Studies, 1995), and her *A Forgotten Army: Female Munitions Workers of South Wales 1939–1945* (Cardiff: University of Wales Press, 2002).

2 Christopher W. Newman, *Hilda Vaughan* (Cardiff: University of Wales Press, 1981), p. 3.

³   Judith Maro's wartime experiences are recounted in the anthology *Iancs, Conshis a Spam: Atgofion Menywod o'r Ail Ryfel Byd*, ed. Leigh Verrill-Rhys (Dinas Powys: Honno, 2002), pp. 125–36 and 146–61.

⁴   See Myfanwy Haycock, *Hill of Dreams* (Cwmbran: Cwmbran Community Press, n.d.), p. 5. Her verse was first published in newpapers, such as the *Western Mail*.

⁵   Jane Ann Jones, *Y Bryniau Pell* (Dinbych: Gwasg Gee, 1949), p. 20.

⁶   Ibid., p. 37.

⁷   Ibid., p. 50.

⁸   Ibid., p. 89.

⁹   Kate Roberts, *Stryd y Glep* (Dinbych: Gwasg Gee, 1949), p. 7.

¹⁰ Ibid., p. 21.

¹¹ Ibid., p. 92.

¹² Kate Roberts, *Y Byw Sy'n Cysgu* (Dinbych: Gwasg Gee, 1956), p. 82.

¹³ Ibid., p. 96.

¹⁴ This goes some way to explaining the unexpected translation of the novel's title in the most recent version in English: *The Awakening*, trans. Siân James (Bridgend: Seren, 2006).

¹⁵ John Osborne, *Look Back in Anger* (London: Faber, 1957), p. 15.

¹⁶ Kate Bosse-Griffiths, *Mae'r Galon wrth y Llyw* (Aberystwyth: Gwasg Aberystwyth, 1957), p. 32.

¹⁷ Ibid., p. 113.

¹⁸ Ibid., p. 149.

¹⁹ Margiad Evans, 'To My Sister Sian', *A Candle Ahead* (London: Chatto & Windus, 1956), pp. 25–6; also repr. in Katie Gramich and Catherine Brennan (eds), *Welsh Women's Poetry 1460–2001* (Dinas Powys: Honno, 2003), pp. 182–3.

²⁰ Evans, 'To My Sister Siân', p. 26; Gramich and Brennan (eds), *Welsh Women's Poetry 1460-2001*, p. 183.

²¹ Eigra Lewis Roberts, *Brynhyfryd* (Aberystwyth: Gwasg Aberystwyth, 1959), p. 9.

²² Ibid., p. 12.

²³ Ibid.

²⁴ Ibid., p. 98.

²⁵ Ibid., p. 33.

²⁶ Ibid., p. 92.

²⁷ Ibid., p. 182.

²⁸ Eigra Lewis Roberts, *Tŷ ar y Graig* (Llandysul: Gomer, 1966), p. 45.

²⁹ Ibid., p. 53.

³⁰ Ibid., pp. 38–9.

³¹ Kate Roberts, *Y Lôn Wen* (Dinbych: Gwasg Gee, 1960), pp. 10–11.

³² Ibid., p. 20.

³³ Ibid., p. 30.

³⁴ Ibid., pp. 56–7.

³⁵ Ibid., pp. 152–3.

³⁶ Kate Roberts, 'Te yn y Grug', *Te yn y Grug* ([1959] Dinbych: Gwasg Gee, 1987), p. 41; 'Tea in the Heather', trans. by Joseph Clancy, in his volume *The World of Kate Roberts: Selected Stories 1925–1981* (Philadelphia: Temple

University Press, 1991), p. 193. This volume contains good English translations of several of the Kate Roberts texts discussed in this book.

37   Ibid., Roberts, p. 41; Clancy, p. 194.

38   Ibid., Roberts, p. 42; Clancy, p. 194.

39   Ibid., Roberts, p. 43; Clancy, p. 195.

40   Ibid., Roberts, p. 44; Clancy, p. 196.

41   Kate Roberts, 'Dieithrio', *Te yn y Grug*, p. 77; 'Becoming Strangers', *Tea in the Heather*, ed. Clancy, p. 219.

42   Tony Conran, 'The writings of Brenda Chamberlain', *The Cost of Strangeness* (Llandysul: Gomer, 1982), p. 205.

43   Brenda Chamberlain, *Poems with Drawings* (London: Enitharimon Press, 1969).

44   Tony Brown, 'The problems of belonging' in M. Wynn Thomas (ed.), *Welsh Writing in English* (Cardiff: University of Wales Press, 2003), p. 188.

45   Ibid., p. 189.

46   Brenda Chamberlain, *Tide-race* ([1962] Bridgend: Seren, 1987), pp. 31, 36.

47   Brenda Chamberlain, 'Seal cave', in Gramich and Brennan (eds), *Welsh Women's Poetry 1460–2001*, p. 186.

48   Chamberlain, *Tide-Race*, p. 26.

49   See Dot Jones, 'Counting the cost of coal: women's lives in the Rhondda, 1881–1911', in Angela V. John (ed.), *Our Mother's Land: Chapters in Welsh Women's History 1830–1939* (Cardiff: University of Wales Press, 1991), pp. 109–34.

50   Menna Gallie, *The Small Mine* ([1962] Dinas Powys: Honno, 2000), p. 42.

51   Menna Gallie, *Strike for a Kingdom* ([1959] Dinas Powys: Honno, 2003), p. 56.

52   Ibid., p. 87.

53   Ibid., p. 138.

54   Ibid., p. 5.

55   Ibid.

56   Ibid., p. 154.

57   Gallie, *The Small Mine*, p. 80. The relevant lines from R. Williams Parry's sonnet are: 'Ganllath o gopa'r mynydd, pan oedd clych / Eglwysi'r llethrau'n gwahodd tua'r llan, / Ac anhreuliedig haul Gorffennaf gwych / Yn gwahodd tua'r mynydd ... Llithrodd ei flewyn cringoch dros y grib; / Digwyddodd, darfu, megis seren wib'; in Tony Conran's translation: 'A furlong from the crest, when the bells' cry / Of hillbreast churches called us villageward, / And the sun, bright and unsetting in July / Invited to the summits ... His dry red pelt slipped over the rock scar, / And was, and was not – like some shooting star.' The original can be found in *Blodengerdd o Farddoniaeth Gymraeg yr Ugeinfed Ganrif*, eds Gwynn ap Gwilym and Alan Llwyd (Llandysul: Gorner, 1987) p. 45. The translation is in *Welsh Verse*, Tony Conran (Bridgend: Poetry Wales Press, 1986) p. 269.

58   Ibid., p. 54. 'Angel ar y ffordd a diawl ar ben pentan.'

59   Ibid., p. 3.

60   Ibid., p. 28.

61   'Menna Gallie was wary of the label "feminist": Angela V. John, in her Introduction to *Strike for a Kingdom*, p. viii.

62   Beddoe, *Out of the Shadows*, p. 24.

63   Kate Roberts, *Tywyll Heno* (Dinbych: Gwasg Gee, 1962), p. 23.

64   Ibid., pp. 26 ff.

65   Ibid., pp. 95–6.

66   Marion Eames, *Y Stafell Ddirgel* ([1969] Llandysul: Gomer, 1994), p. 178.

67   Marion Eames, *Y Rhandir Mwyn* (Llandybie: Christopher Davies, 1972), p. 244.

68   Jane Edwards, *Dechrau Gofidiau* (Llandysul: Gomer, 1962), p. 16.

69   Ibid., pp. 73–5.

70   Ibid., p. 152.

71   Gwyn Alf Williams, *When Was Wales?* (Harmondsworth: Penguin, 1985), p. 237.

72   Edwards, *Dechrau Gofidiau*, p. 140.

73   Edna O'Brien, *The Country Girls*; *Girl with Green Eyes*; and *Girls in their Married Bliss* (London: Jonathan Cape, 1960; 1962; 1964).

74   See Stephen Knight, *A Hundred Years of Fiction* (Cardiff: University of Wales Press, 2004), p. 173.

75   Moira Dearnley, *That Watery Glass* (Llandybïe: Christopher Davies, 1973), p. 36.

76   See Jane Aaron, 'Y Flodeuwedd gyfoes: llên menywod 1973–1993', in M. Wynn Thomas (ed.), *DiFfinio Dwy Lenyddiaeth Cymru* (Caerdydd: Gwasg Prifysgol Cymru, 1995), pp. 190–208.

77   Ibid., p. 195.

78   Kate Roberts, 'Cathod mewn Ocsiwn', *Hyn o Fyd* (Dinbych: Gwasg Gee, 1964), p. 72.

79   Kate Roberts, 'Dychwelyd', *Gobaith a Storïau Eraill* (Dinbych: Gwasg Gee, 1972), p. 88.

80   Ibid., p. 89.

81   Ibid., p. 91.

82   Ibid., p. 93.

83   Saunders Lewis, 'Queen of Welsh writers' (review of *Hyn o Fyd*), undated cutting.

84   Kate Roberts, 'Y Daith', *Prynu Dol* (Dinbych: Gwasg Gee, 1969), pp. 77–8.

85   Although this version of the story appeared in the volume of the same name in 1969, it had its origins in a radio script by Roberts which was broadcast in December 1957. See Bobi Jones's structural comparison of the differences in the four extant versions of this story in his *Llenyddiaeth Gymraeg 1936–1972* (Llandybïe: Christopher Davies, 1975), pp. 195–202.

86   Kate Roberts, 'Prynu Dol', *Prynu Dol*, p. 28. The English translation here is of course incomplete and inadequate: 'words like *flibbertigibbet (?) shreds, ashes, struggling, brand spanking new.*'

87   *Tynged yr Iaith* (The Fate of the Language) is the title of the crucially influential radio speech given by Saunders Lewis in 1962, which led directly to the founding of Cymdeithas yr Iaith and a campaign of civil disobedience carried out over the next three decades to try to force the authorities to recognize and use the Welsh language.

88   Ned Thomas's *The Welsh Extremist* (Talybont: Y Lolfa, 1971) is an influential text of the period which explicitly analysed the experience of the Welsh as one of colonization; tellingly, Thomas couches the political polemic in terms of a critical analysis of Welsh literature, including the writings of Kate Roberts.

89   Bobi Jones, quoted in Introduction, Clancy (ed.), *The World of Kate Roberts*, p. xiv.
90   Nesta Wyn Jones, 'Cysgodion', *Cannwyll Yn Olau* (Llandysul: Gomer, 1969), p. 22.
91   Ibid., p. 23.
92   Ibid., p. 24.
93   Ibid., p. 33.
94   Ibid., p. 37.
95   Ibid., pp. 41–3.
96   Ibid., p. 43.
97   Nesta Wyn Jones, 'Estroniaid', *Ffenest Ddu* (Llandysul: Gomer, 1973), pp. 14–15.
98   Ibid., p. 20.
99   Ibid., pp. 40–1.
100 Ibid., pp. 57–64.
101 Ibid., p. 62.
102 Nesta Wyn Jones, 'Capel Celyn', in Gramich and Brennan (eds), *Welsh Women's Poetry 1460–2001*, pp. 256–7.
103 Gillian Clarke, 'Clywedog' in ibid., p. 233.
104 Sally Roberts Jones, Author's note in *The Forgotten Country* (Llandysul: Gomer, 1977).
105 Aaron, 'Y Flodeuwedd gyfoes', p. 202. In the original Welsh: 'gall rhannu hunaniaeth ethnig brofi'n gryfach na gwahaniaeth iaith'. Aaron's examples here are the novelists Moira Dearnley, Beti Hughes and Jane Edwards.
106 Sally Roberts Jones, 'Ann Griffiths', *The Forgotten Country*, p. 57.
107 See 'Buddug', 'Yr "Hen" Ann Griffiths' ('Old' Ann Griffiths), in Gramich and Brennan (eds), *Welsh Women's Poetry 1460–2001*, pp. 148–9; Rhiannon Davies Jones, *Fy Hen Lyfr Cownt* (My Old Account Book) ([1961] Llandysul: Gomer, 1996); Eigra Lewis Roberts, *Byd o Amser* (Llandysul: Gwasg Gomer, 1976).
108 Sally Roberts Jones, 'Community', *The Forgotten Country*, pp. 12–13.
109 Roberts Jones, 'New World', ibid., p. 25.
110 Roberts Jones, 'Caretaker, Blarney Castle', ibid., p. 33.

4 Feminist Place: 1978–1996

1   Gillian Clarke, 'Birth', *The Sundial* (Llandysul: Gomer, 1978), p. 29. The same poem is retitled 'Calf' in the *Collected Poems* (Manchester: Carcanet, 1997), p. 15.
2   Gillian Clarke, 'Hearthstone', ibid., p. 114.
3   Gillian Clarke, 'Letter from a Far Country', ibid., p. 45.
4   Ibid., p. 46.
5   Ibid., p. 50.
6   Ibid., p. 54.
7   Ibid., p. 56.
8   Gillian Clarke, Section 6 of 'The King of Britain's Daughter', ibid., p. 173.
9   Gillian Clarke, 'Beudy', ibid., p. 164.

10   Gillian Clarke, 'Llŷr', ibid., p. 68. The river Avon in Stratford is *afon* (river) in Welsh, and King Lear's name is a version of the Welsh name, Llŷr.

11   Gillian Clarke, 'Border', ibid., p. 95.

12   Menna Elfyn, 'Tro'r haul arno', in *Aderyn Bach mewn Llaw: Detholiad o gerddi 1976–1990* (Llandysul: Gomer, 1990), p. 60.

13   Menna Elfyn, 'Anhysbys – An sy'n hysbys', ibid., p. 58.

14   Gillian Clarke, 'Letter from a Far Country', *Collected Poems*, p. 55.

15   Menna Elfyn, 'Wnaiff y gwragedd aros ar ôl?', *Aderyn Bach mewn Llaw*, p. 93.

16   Menna Elfyn (ed.), Rhagymadrodd (Introduction), *Hel Dail Gwyrdd* (Llandysul: Gomer, 1985), p. xvi.

17   Gillian Clarke, 'Ffiw: Referendum Reactions', *New Welsh Review*, 38 (Autumn 1997), 11

18   Ibid., p. 45.

19   Christine Evans, 'Thunder above Llanberis', *Cometary Phases* (Bridgend: Seren, 1989), p. 8.

20   Christine Evans, 'Cometary Phases', ibid., p. 96.

21   Christine Evans, 'Second Language', ibid., pp. 60–1.

22   Christine Evans, 'Llŷn', *Island of Dark Horses* (Bridgend: Seren, 1995), pp. 71–2.

23   Hilary Llewellyn-Williams, 'Capel Mair', *animaculture* (Bridgend: Seren, 1997), pp. 38–9.

24   Catherine Fisher, 'Great-grandmother', *Immrama* (Bridgend: Seren, 1988), p. 23.

25   Ibid.

26   Fisher's resurrection of the forgotten female ancestor is directly comparable with the work of several contemporary Irish women poets, notably Eavan Boland. See her *Outside History* (1990) and *Object Lessons* (1995).

27   Ruth Bidgood, 'Kindred', *Selected Poems* (Bridgend: Seren, 1992), p. 116.

28   Angharad Tomos, *Yma o Hyd* (Talybont: Y Lolfa, 1985), pp. 107–8.

29   Angharad Tomos, *Titrwm* (Talybont: Y Lolfa, 1994), page facing p. 146.

30   Menna Elfyn, 'Cân y di-lais i British Telecom/Song of a voiceless person to British Telecom', *Eucalyptus: Detholiad o Gerddi 1978–1994* (Llandysul: Gomer, 1995), pp. 6–9.

31   Ibid., p. 8. The English given here is R. S. Thomas's translation.

32   Glenda Beagan, 'Scream, Scream', *The Medlar Tree* (Bridgend: Seren, 1992), p. 32.

33   Ibid., p. 31.

34   Glenda Beagan, 'Shaman', *Vixen* (Dinas Powys: Honno, 1996), p. 67.

35   Glenda Beagan, 'Triskel', ibid., p. 66.

36   Gillian Clarke, Hilary Llewellyn-Williams and Angharad Jones are other poets who wrote on Blodeuwedd at this time. Critical analysis of this phenomenon can be found in Jane Aaron, 'Y Flodeuwedd gyfoes: llên menywod 1973–1993', in M. Wynn Thomas (ed.), *DiFfinio Dwy Lenyddiaeth Cymru* (Caerddydd: Gwasg Prifysgo/Cymru, 1995), pp. 190–208.

37   Glenda Beagan, 'Blodeuwedd', *Vixen*, p. 9.

38   Jean Earle, 'Grandma's House', *Visiting Light* (Bridgend: Seren, 1987), p. 20.

39   Ibid.

40   Ibid., p. 21.

41 Jean Earle, 'Quaker's Yard Junction, 1950', ibid., pp. 44–5.
42 Gweneth Lilly, *Orpheus* (Llandysul: Gomer, 1984), p. 23.
43 Ibid., p. 24.
44 Ibid., p. 170.
45 Ibid., p. 170.
46 Siân James, *A Small Country* ([1979] Bridgend: Seren, 1989), pp. 131–2.
47 Ibid., p. 160.
48 Ibid., p. 161.
49 Ibid., p. 133.
50 Ibid., p. 180.
51 Ibid., p. 189.
52 Siân James, *Love and War* ([1997] Bridgend: Seren, 2004), p. 22.
53 Ibid., p. 217.
54 Ibid., p. 85.
55 Siân James, *Storm at Arberth* (Bridgend: Seren, 1994), p. 128.
56 Ibid., p. 63.
57 Catherine Merriman, *State of Desire* (London: Pan, 1996), p. 198.
58 Ibid., p. 13.
59 Ibid., p. 14.
60 Siân James, 'Happy as Saturday Night', *Not Singing Exactly* (Dinas Powys: Honno, 1996), p. 201.
61 Ibid., p. 202.
62 Ibid., p. 207.
63 Clare Morgan, 'Losing', in Alun Richards (ed.), *The New Penguin Book of Welsh Short Stories* (Harmondsworth: Penguin, 1993), pp. 358–67.
64 Ibid., p. 365.
65 Ibid., pp. 366–7.
66 Ibid., p. 359.
67 'Is there a women's poetry?', Symposium, *Poetry Wales*, 23 (1987), 52.
68 Ibid.
69 Manon Rhys, *Cysgodion* (Llandysul: Gomer, 1993), p. 11.
70 Siân Evans, *Little Sister* in Jeff Teare (ed.), *New Welsh Drama II* (Cardiff: Parthian, 2001), p. 96.
71 Marian Eames, *I Hela Cnau* (Llandysul: Gomer, 1978), pp. 104, 101. An English translation of the novel by Eames herself is also available: *The Golden Road* (Llandysul: Gomer, 1990).
72 See Ruth McElroy, 'Cymraes oddi cartref?: Welsh women writing home and migration', *Welsh Writing in English: A Yearbook of Critical Essays*, 3 (1997), 134–56.
73 Eames, *I Hela Cnau*, p. 206.
74 Ibid., pp. 208–9.
75 Ibid., p. 209.
76 McElroy, 'Cymraes oddi cartref?, p. 137.
77 Lucinda Coxon, *Waiting at the Water's Edge* (Bridgend: Seren, 1995), p. 45.
78 Ibid., p. 16.
79 Ibid., p. 75.
80 Ibid., p. 97.
81 Ibid., p. 97.
82 Ibid., p. 112.

83 Gillian Clarke, 'Letter from a Far Country', *Collected Poems*, p. 46.
84 Eluned Phillips, 'Clymau', *Cerddi Glyn-y-Mêl* (Llandysul: Gomer, 1985), p. 72.
85 Ibid., p. 80.
86 Ibid., p. 76.
87 Eluned Phillips, 'Y Perthi Coll', in Gramich and Brennan (eds), *Welsh Women's Poetry* p. 190.
88 Ibid.
89 Menna Elfyn, 'Eucalyptus', in Kate Gramich and Catherine Brennan (eds), *Welsh Women's Poetry 1460–2001* (Dinas Powys: Honno, 2003), pp. 290–1. Translation by Tony Conran.
90 Ibid.
91 Gillian Clarke, *Collected Poems*, pp. 152–3; Joyce Herberts, 'When I Stood There Among Bullets' in Gramich and Brennan (eds), *Welsh Women's Poetry* p. 196.
92 Merryn Williams, 'Black Mountain Cairns', in Gramich and Brennan (eds), *Welsh Women's Poetry* p. 335.
93 Menna Elfyn, '*Cwfaint/Nunnery*', *Cell Angel* (Newcastle upon Tyne: Bloodaxe, 1996), pp. 30–1. Translation by Gillian Clarke.
94 Menna Elfyn, 'Blwyddyn Y Pla/The Year of the Plague', ibid., pp. 104–5. Translation by Tony Conran.
95 Elaine Showalter, *Sister's Choice: Tradition and Change in American Women's Writing* (Oxford: Oxford University Press, 1994), p. 7.
96 Tony Conran, 'Introduction', *Welsh Verse* (Bridgend: Poetry Wales Press, 1986).

5 Hybrid Place: 1997–2005

1 Such as Stephen Knight, *A Hundred Years of Fiction* (Cardiff: University of Wales Press, 2004); Kirsti Bohata, *Postcolonialism Revisited* (Cardiff: University of Wales Press, 2004); Jane Aaron and Chris Williams (eds), *Postcolonial Wales* (Cardiff: University of Wales Press, 2005)
2 Sharon Morgan, *Magic Threads*, in Hazel Walford Davies (ed.), *One Woman, One Voice* (Cardiff: Parthian, 2000), p. 17.
3 Ibid., p. 20.
4 Ibid., p. 23.
5 Ibid., p. 36.
6 Ibid.
7 Hazel Walford Davies, 'Modulations of monologue', in ibid., p. 8.
8 Angharad Price, *O! Tyn y Gorchudd* (Llandysul: Gomer, 2002), p. 11.
9 Ibid., p. 147.
10 Gwyneth Lewis, Preface to *Keeping Mum* (Newcastle upon Tyne: Bloodaxe, 2003), p. 9.
11 Gwyneth Lewis, 'Mother Tongue', ibid., p. 15.
12 Menna Elfyn, 'Rhagair', *Perffaith Nam* (Landysul: Gomer, 2005), p. 9.
13 Menna Elfyn, 'Molawd i'r Lleuad (ardrothwy rhyfel)', ibid., p. 66.
14 Menna Elfyn, 'Botwm i'r Botwm Bol', ibid., p. 33.
15 Menna Elfyn, 'Y Forwyn Goch', ibid., p. 141.

16 Ibid., p. 139.
17 Menna Elfyn, 'Bronnau Ffug', ibid., pp. 123–5.
18 Menna Elfyn, 'Ymwelydd', ibid., p. 119.
19 Menna Elfyn, 'Ia Cymru', ibid., p. 30.
20 Menna Elfyn, 'Melltith y Maman', ibid., p. 105.
21 Charlotte Williams, *Sugar and Slate* (Aberystwyth: Planet, 2002), p. 37.
22 Ibid., p. 49.
23 Trezza Azzopardi, *The Hiding Place* (London: Picador, 2001), p. 153.
24 Leonora Brito, *dat's love* (Bridgend: Seren, 1995), pp. 67–74.

Conclusion

1   Yi-Fu Tuan, *Space and Place: The Perspective of Experience* (London: Edward Arnold, 1977), p. 3.
2   Ibid., p. 6.
3   Ibid., p. 154.
4   Jane Aaron and M. Wynn Thomas, 'Pulling you through changes: Welsh writing in English before, between and after two referenda', in M. Wynn Thomas (ed.), *A Guide to Welsh Literature, Volume VII: Welsh Writing in English* (Cardiff: University of Wales Press, 2003), p. 280.
5   David Smith (ed.), *A People and a Proletariat: Essays in the History of Wales* (London: Pluto Press, 1980).
6   Gaston Bachelard, *Poetics of Space* ([1958] Boston: Beacon Press, 1994).
7   Ibid., p. xxxvii.
8   Ibid., pp. 211–12.
9   Dolores Hayden, 'What would a non-sexist city be like? Speculations on housing, urban design, and human work', in Stimpson *et al.* (eds), *Women and the American City* (Chicago and London: University of Chicago Press, 1981), p. 168.
10 Judith Butler, *Gender Trouble: Feminism and the Subversion of Identity* (London: Routledge, 1990), p. 6.
11 Henri Lefebvre, *The Production of Space*, trans. Donald Nicholson-Smith (Oxford: Blackwell, 1991), p. 164.
12 Ibid., pp. 165–6.
13 Bachelard, *Poetics of Space*, pp. 26–7.
14 Lefebvre, *The Production of Space*, p. 98.
15 Jane Aaron (ed.), Introduction to *A View Across the Valley* (Dinas Powys: Honno, 1999), p. x.
16 Ibid., p. xii.
17 Doreen Massey, *Space, Place and Gender* (London: Polity, 1994), pp. 265, 269.
18 Pierre Nora, 'Between memory and history: *les lieux de memoire*,' trans. Marc Roudebush, *Representations*, 26 (Spring 1989), 7–25.
19 Ibid., 13–14.
20 Jean Earle, 'Old Tips', in Gramich and Brennan, *Welsh Women's Poetry 1460–2001*, p. 170.
21 Ibid.
22 Hilda Vaughan, *Iron and Gold* ([1948] Dinas Powys: Honno, 2002), p. 40.

23 Lynette Roberts, 'Poem from Llanybri', in Gramich and Brennan, *Welsh Women's Poetry 1460–2001*, pp. 175–6.

24 Ibid., p. 176.

25 Aaron (ed.), Introduction to *A View Across the Valley*, p. xii.

26 Eiluned Lewis, *The Captain's Wife* (London: Macmillan, 1943), pp. 99–100.

27 Ian Baucom, *Out of Place: Englishness, Empire and the Locations of Identity* (Princeton University Press, 1999), pp. 5–6. The theory of the 'contact zone' is elaborated by Mary Louise Pratt in her *Imperial Eyes: Travel Writing and Transculturation* (New York: Routledge, 1992).

28 Dilys Cadwaladr, 'Llundain', in Eigra Lewis Roberts (ed.), *Merch yr Oriau Mawr* (Caernarfon: Tŷar y Graig, 1981), p. 22.

29 Quoted in Simon Trezise, *The West Country as a Literary Invention: Putting Fiction in its Place* (Exeter: University of Exeter Press, 2000). Louisa Musgrove is a character in Jane Austen's novel, *Persuasion*.

30 Graham Day, *Making Sense of Wales: A Sociological Perspective* (Cardiff: University of Wales Press, 2002), p. 14.

Bibliography

Primary sources

Aaron, Jane (ed.), *A View Across the Valley: Short Stories by Women from Wales c.1850–1950* (Dinas Powys: Honno, 1999).

Azzopardi, Trezza, *The Hiding Place* (London: Picador, 2001).

Beagan, Glenda, *The Medlar Tree* (Bridgend: Seren, 1992).

——, *Vixen* (Dinas Powys: Honno, 1996).

——, *Changes and Dreams* (Bridgend: Seren, 1997).

Bidgood, Ruth, *The Given Time* (Bridgend: Seren, 1972).

——, *Selected Poems* (Bridgend: Seren, 1992).

Bielski, Alison, *Across the Burning Sand* (Llandysul: Gwasg Gomer, 1970).

——, *Discovering Islands* (Bristol: Xenia Press, 1979).

——, *That Crimson Flame: Selected Poems* (Salzburg and Oxford: University of Salzburg, 1996).

Bosse-Griffiths, Kate, *Anesmwyth Hoen* (Llandybïe: Llyfrau'r Dryw, 1941).

——, *Fy Chwaer Efa* (Dinbych: Llyfrau Pawb, 1944).

——, *Mae'r Galon wrth y Llyw* (Aberystwyth: Gwasg Aberystwyth, 1957).

——, *Cariadau* (Talybont: Y Lolfa, 1995).

Brito, Leonora, *dat's love* (Bridgend: Seren, 1995).

'Buddug', *Caniadau Buddug* (Caernarfon: Swyddfa 'Cymru', 1911).

Cadwaladr, Dilys, *Storïau* (Wrecsam: Hughes a'i Fab, 1936).

——, 'Partners', in *GK's: A Miscellany of the First 500 Issues of GK's Weekly*, intro. G. K. Chesterton (London: Rich and Cowan, 1936), pp. 266–71.

——, *Bara: Pryddest* (Llandysul: Gwasg Gomer, 1945).

Chamberlain, Brenda, *The Green Heart* (Oxford: Oxford University Press, 1958).

——, *Tide-Race* ([1962] Bridgend: Seren, 1987).

——, *The Water Castle* (London: Hodder & Stoughton, 1964).

——, *A Rope of Vines* (London: Hodder & Stoughton, 1965).
——, *Poems with Drawings* (London: Enitharmion, 1969).
Clancy, Joseph (ed.), *The World of Kate Roberts: Selected Stories 1925–1981* (Philadelphia: Temple University Press, 1991).
Clarke, Gillian, *The Sundial* (Llandysul: Gomer, 1978).
——, *Letter from a Far Country* (1982) .
——, *Selected Poems* (Manchester: Carcanet, 1985).
——, *Letting in the Rumour* (Manchester: Fyfield, 1989).
——, *The King of Britain's Daughter* (Manchester: Carcanet, 1993).
——, *Collected Poems* (Manchester: Carcanet, 1997).
——, *Five Fields* (Manchester: Carcanet, 1998).
——, *Making the Beds for the Dead* (Manchester: Carcanet, 2004).
Coxon, Lucinda, *Waiting at the Water's Edge* (Bridgend: Seren, 1995).
'Cranogwen' (Sarah Jane Rees, *Caniadau* (Dolgellau: Robert Oliver Rees, 1870).
Davies, Hazel Walford (ed.), *One Woman, One Voice: Plays* (Cardiff: Parthian, 2000).
Davies, Rhiannon, *Cerddi Afreolaidd* (Dinbych: Gwas Gee, n.d.).
Davies, Stevie, *Kith and Kin* (London: Phoenix, 2004).
Dearnley, Moira, *That Watery Glass* (Llandybïe: Christopher Davies, 1973).
Eames, Marion, *Y Stafell Ddirgel* ([1969] Llandysul: Gomer, 1994).
——, *Y Rhandir Mwyn* ([1972] Llandybïe: Christopher Davies, 1990).
——, *I Hela Cnau* (Llandysul: Gomer, 1978).
——, *Seren Gaeth* (Llandysul: Gomer, 1985).
——, *The Golden Road* (Llandysul: Gomer, 1990).
——, *Y Ferch Dawel* (Llandysul: Gomer, 1992).
Earle, Jean, *Visiting Light* (Bridgend: Seren, 1987).
——, *Selected Poems* (Bridgend: Seren, 1990).
——, *The Sun in the West* (Bridgend: Seren, 1995).
——, *The Bed of Memory* (Bridgend: Seren, 2001).
Edwards, Dorothy, *Rhapsody* (London: Wishart & Co., 1927).
——, *Winter Sonata* (London: Wishart & Co., 1928).
Edwards, Fanny, *Cit* (Wrecsam: Swyddfa 'Cymru'r Plant', 1907).
Edwards, Jane, *Dechrau Gofidiau* (Llandysul: Gomer, 1962).
——, *Byd o Gysgodion* (Llandysul: Gomer, 1964) .
——, *Bara Seguryd* (Llandysul: Gomer, 1969).
——, *Dros Fryniau Bro Afallon* (Llandysul: Gomer, 1976).
Elfyn, Menna, *Eucalyptus: Detholiad o Gerddi/Selected Poems 1978–1994* (Llandysul: Gwasg Gomer, 1995).
——, *Mwyara* (Llandysul: Gomer, 1976).
——, *Stafelloedd Aros* (Llandysul: Gomer, 1978).
——, *Tro'r Haul Arno* (Llandysul: Gomer, 1982).

——, *Mynd Lawr i'r Nefoedd* (Llandysul: Gomer, 1986).
——, *Aderyn Bach Mewn Llaw* (Llandysul: Gomer, 1990).
——, *Cell Angel* (Newcastle on Tyne: Bloodaxe, 1996).
——, *Cusan Dyn Dall/Blind Man's Kiss* (Manchester: Carcanet, 2001).
——, *Perffaith Nam* (Landysul: Gomer, 2005).
——, (ed.), *Hel Dail Gwyrdd* (Llandysul: Gomer, 1985).
——, (ed.), *O'r Iawn Ryw* (Dinas Powys: Honno, 1991).
Elis, Meg, *I'r Gad* (Taalybont: Y Lolfa, 1975).
——, *Carchar* (Talybont: Y Lolfa, 1978).
Evans, Christine, *Looking Inland* (Bridgend: Poetry Wales Press, 1983).
——, *Falling Back* (Bridgend: Poetry Wales Press, 1986).
——, *Cometary Phases* (Bridgend: Seren, 1989).
——, *Island of Dark Horses* (Bridgend: Seren, 1995).
Evans, Margiad, *Country Dance* ([1932] London: John Calder, 1978).
——, *The Wooden Doctor*, ed. Sue Asbee ([1933] Dinas Powys: Honno, 2005).
——, *Autobiography* (London: Calder & Boyars, 1943).
——, *The Old and the Young*, ed. Ceridwen Lloyd-Morgan ([1948] Bridgend: Seren, 1998).
——, *A Ray of Darkness* ([1952] London: John Calder, 1978).
——, *A Candle Ahead: Poems* (London: Chatto & Windus, 1956).
Evans, Siân, 'Little Sister', in Jeff Teare (ed.) *New Welsh Drama II* (Cardiff: Parthian, 2001).
Fisher, Catherine, *Immrama* (Bridgend: Seren, 1988).
——, *The Unexplored Ocean* (Bridgend: Seren, 1994).
——, *Altered States* (Bridgend: Seren, 1999).
Furnival, Christine, *Prince of Sapphires* (Breakish: Aquila, 1976).
——, *Towards Praising* (Swansea: Christopher Davies, *c*.1978).
Gallie, Menna, *Strike for a Kingdom* ([1959] Dinas Powys: Honno, 2003).
——, *The Small Mine* ([1962] Dinas Powys: Honno, 2003).
Gramich, Katie and Catherine Brennan (eds), *Welsh Women's Poetry 1460–2001* (Dinas Powys: Honno, 2003).
Gwylim, Gwynn ap and Alan Llwyd (eds), *Blodengerdd o Farddoniaetn Gymraeg yr Ugeinfed Garinf* (Llandysul: Gomer, 1987).
Haycock, Myfanwy, *Hill of Dreams* (Cwmbran: Cwmbran Community Press, n.d.).
Herbert, Joyce, *Approaching Snow* (Bridgend: Poetry Wales Press, 1983).
Howell, Florence, *Jane Wogan* (Aberystwyth: Gwasg Aberystwyth, 1935).
Hughes, Ellen, *Sibrwd yr Awel* (Pwllheli: Robert Owen, *c*.1885).

——, *Murmur y Gragen* (Dolgellau: E. W. Evans, 1907).

Hywel, Elin ap, *Pethau Brau* (Talybont: Y Lolfa, 1982).

James, Siân, *A Small Country* ([1979] Bridgend: Seren, 1999).

——, *Storm at Arberth* (Bridgend: Seren, 1994).

——, *Not Singing Exactly*, ed. Katie Gramich (Dinas Powys: Honno, 1996).

——, *Love and War* ([1997] Bridgend: Seren, 2004).

Jones, Angharad, *Y Dylluan Wen* (Llandysul: Gomer, 1995).

Jones, Einir, *Daeth Awst, Daeth Nos* (Abertawe: Barddas, 1991).

Jones, Jane Ann, *Storïau Hen Ferch* (Aberystwyth: Gwasg Aberystwyth, 1937).

——, *Y Bryniau Pell* (Dinbych: Gwasg Gee, 1949).

Jones, Nesta Wyn, *Cannwyll yn Olau* (Llandysul: Gomer, 1969) .

——, *Ffenest Ddu* (Llandysul: Gomer, 1973).

Jones, Rhiannon Davies, *Fy Hen Lyfr Cownt* (Llandysul: Gomer, 1961).

——, *Lleian Llan-Llŷr* ([1965] Caernarfon: Gwasg Gwynedd, 1990).

Jones, Sally Roberts, *Strangers and Brothers* (Port Talbot: Alun Books, 1976).

——, *The Forgotten Country* (Llandysul: Gomer, 1977).

——, *Relative Values* (Bridgend: Poetry Wales Press, 1985).

Lewis, Eiluned, *Dew on the Grass* (London: Macmillan, 1934).

——, *Dew on the Grass* ed. Katie Grammich (Dinas Powys: Honno, 2007).

——, *December Apples: Poems* (London: Lovat Dickson and Thompson, 1935).

——, and Peter Lewis, *The Land of Wales* (London: B. T. Batsford Ltd., 1937).

——, *The Captain's Wife* (London: Macmillan, 1943).

——, *Morning Songs, and Other Poems* (London: Macmillan & Co. Ltd., 1944).

——, *In Country Places* (London: Macmillan, 1951).

——, *The Leaves of the Tree* (London: Peter Davies, 1953).

Lewis, Gwyneth, *Parables and Faxes* (Newcastle upon Tyne: Bloodaxe, 1995).

——, *Zero Gravity* (Newcastle upon Tyne: Bloodaxe, 1998).

——, *Keeping Mum* (Newcastle upon Tyne: Bloodaxe, 2003).

Lilly, Gweneth, *Orpheus* (Llandysul: Gomer, 1984).

Llewellyn-Williams, Hilary, *The Tree Calendar* (Bridgend: Poetry Wales Press, 1987).

——, *animaculture* (Bridgend: Seren, 1997).

Maro, Judith, *Hen Wlad Newydd* (Talybont: Y Lolfa, 1974).

Merriman, Catherine, *Silly Mothers* (Dinas Powys: Honno, 1991).

——, *State of Desire* (London: Pan, 1996).

'Moelona', (Elizabeth Mary Jones) *Dwy Ramant o'r De* (Dolgellau: E. W. Evans, Swyddfa'r 'Goleuad', 1911).

——, *Teulu Bach Nantoer, Ffug-Chwedl i Blant* (Wrecsam: Hughes a'i Fab, 1913).

——, *Bugail y Bryn* (Dolgellau: Swyddfa'r 'Cymro', 1917).

——, *Rhamant y Rhos* (Aberdar: Pugh a Rowlands, Swyddfa'r 'Leader' a'r 'Darian', 1918).

——, *Cwrs y Lli* (Wrecsam: Hughes a'i Fab, 1927).

——, *Breuddwydion Myfanwy* (London: Foyle, 1928).

——, *Ffynnonloyw* (Llandysul: Gwasg Gomer, 1939).

Morgan, Clare, *An Affair of the Heart* (Bridgend: Seren, 1996).

Morgan, Elin Llwyd, *Duwieslebog* (Talybont: Y Lolfa, 1993).

——, *Rhwng y Nefoedd a Las Vegas* (Talybont: Y Lolfa, 2004).

Morgan, Eluned, *Dringo'r Andes* [1904] *a Gwymon y Mor* [1909], ed. Ceridwen Lloyd-Morgan and Kathryn Hughes (Dinas Powys: Honno, 2001).

Morgan, Sharon, *Magic Threads* in *One Woman, One Voice: Plays* ed. Hazel Walford Davies (Cardiff: Parthian, 2000).

Nepean, Edith, *Gwyneth of the Welsh Hills* (London: Stanley Paul & Co. Ltd., 1917).

——, *Cambria's Fair Daughter* (London: Stanley Paul & Co. Ltd., 1923).

O'Brien, Edna, *The Country Girls; Girl with Green Eyes;* and *Girls in their Married Bliss* (London: Jonathan Cape, 1960; 1962; 1964).

Parry, Winnie, *Sioned: Darluniau o Fywyd Gwledig yn Nghymru*, (Caernarfon: Swyddfa 'Cymru' 1906); repr. with a new intro. by Margaret Lloyd Jones (Dinas Powys: Honno, 1988).

——, *Cerrig y Rhyd* (Caernarfon: Cwmni'r Cyhoeddwyr Cymreig, 1907).

'Peris, Ceridwen,' (Alice Gray Jones), *Caniadau Ceridwen Peris* (Caernarfon: Llyfrfa'r Methodistiaid Calfinaidd, 1934).

Phillips, Eluned, *Cerddi Glyn-y-Mel* (Llandysul: Gomer, 1985).

Price, Angharad, *Tania'r Tacsi* (Llandysul: Gomer, 1999).

——, *O! Tyn y Gorchudd* (Llandysul: Gomer, 2002).

Pugh, Sheenagh, *Beware Falling Tortoises* (Bridgend: Poetry Wales Press, 1987).

——, *Selected Poems* (Bridgend: Seren, 1990).

——, *Sing for the Taxman* (Bridgend: Seren, 1993).

——, *Id's Hospit* (Bridgend: Seren, 1997).

——, *The Beautiful Lie* (Bridgend: Seren, 2002).

Puw-Davies, Elena (later Puw-Morgan), *Nansi Lovell: Hunangofiant Hen Sipsi* (Aberystwyth: Gwasg Aberystwyth, 1933).

Puw-Morgan, Elena, *Y Wisg Sidan* ([1939] Llandysul: Gwasg Gomer, 1995).

——, *Y Graith* (Dinbych: Gwasg Gee, 1943).

'Raine, Allen', (Anne Adaliza Beynon Puddicombe) *A Welsh Singer* (London: Hutchinson, 1897).
——, *Torn Sails* (London: Hutchinson, 1898).
——, *By Berwen Banks* (London: Hutchinson, 1899).
——, *Garthowen* (London: Hutchinson, 1900).
——, *A Welsh Witch* (London: Hutchinson, 1902).
——, *On the Wings of the Wind* (London: Hutchinson, 1903).
——, *Hearts of Wales* (London: Hutchinson, 1905).
——, *Queen of the Rushes* [1906], ed. Katie Gramich (Dinas Powys: Honno, 1998).
——, *All in a Month and Other Stories* (London: Hutchinson, 1908).
——, *Neither Storehouse nor Barn* (London: Hutchinson, 1908).
——, *Where Billows Roll* (London: Hutchinson, 1909).
——, *Under the Thatch* (London: Hutchinson, 1910).
Rhys, Manon, *Cwtsho* (Llandysul: Gomer, 1988).
——, *Cysgodion* (Llandysul: Gomer, 1993).
Richards, Alun (ed) *The New Penguin Book of Welsh Short Stories* (Harmondsworth: Penguin, 1993).
Roberts, Eigra Lewis, *Brynhyfryd* (Aberystwyth: Gwasg Aberystwyth, 1959).
——, *Tŷ ar y Graig* (Llandysul: Gomer, 1966).
——, *Fe Ddaw Eto* (Llandysul: Gomer, 1976).
——, *Byd o Amser* (Llandysul: Gomer, 1976).
——, (ed.), *Merch yr Oriau Mawr: Dilys Cadwaladr* (Caernarfon: Ty ar y Graig, 1981).
Roberts, Kate, *O Gors y Bryniau* ([1925] Caerdydd: Hughes a'i Fab, 1992).
——, *Rhigolau Bywyd* (Aberystwyth: Gwasg Aberystwyth, 1929).
——, *Traed mewn Cyffion* ([1936] Abertawe: C. E. Watkins, 1971).
——, *Feet in Chains* trans. John Idris Jones (Ruthin: John Jones, 1996).
——, *Ffair Gaeaf a Storïau Eraill* (Dinbych: Gwasg Gee, 1937).
——, *Stryd y Glep* (Dinbych: Gwasg Gee, 1949).
——, *Y Byw Sy'n Cysgu* (Dinbych: Gwasg Gee, 1956).
——, *Te yn y Grug* (Dinbych: Gwasg Gee, 1959).
——, *Y Lôn Wen* (Dinbych: Gwasg Gee, 1960).
——, *Tywyll Heno* (Dinbych: Gwasg Gee, 1962).
——, *Hyn o Fyd* (Dinbych: Gwasg Gee, 1964).
——, *Tegwch y Bore* (Llandybïe: Christopher Davies, 1967).
——, *Prynu Dol* (Dinbych: Gwasg Gee, 1969).
——, *Gobaith a Storïau Eraill* (Dinbych: Gwasg Gee, 1972).
——, *Yr Wylan Deg* (Dinbych: Gwasg Gee, 1976).
——, *The Awakening* trans. Siân James (Bridgend: Seren, 2006).
Roberts, Lynette, *Collected Poems*, ed. Patrick McGuinness (Manchester: Carcanet, 2005).

Rubens, Bernice, *I Sent a Letter to my Love* (London: W. H. Allen, 1975).

——, *Yesterday in the Back Lane* (London: Abacus, 1996).

Ruck, Berta, *Intruder Marriage* (London: Hutchinson, 1945).

Saunders, Sara Maria, *Y Diwygiad ym Mhentre Alun* (Wrecsam: Hughes a'i Fab, 1907).

——, *Llithiau o Bentre Alun* (Wrexham: Hughes a'i Fab, 1908).

Thomas, Bertha, *Picture Tales from Welsh Hills* (Chicago and London: F. G. Browne & Co. and T. Fisher Unwin, 1913).

Tobias, Lily, *The Nationalists and Other Goluth Studies* (London: C. W. Daniel, 1921).

——, *My Mother's House* (London: Allen & Unwin, 1931).

——, *Eunice Fleet* [1933], ed. Jasmine Donahaye (Dinas Powys: Honno, 2004).

Tomos, Angharad, *Yma o Hyd* (Talybont: Y Lolfa, 1985).

——, *Si Hei Lwli* (Talybont: Y Lolfa, 1991).

——, *Titrwm* (Talybont: Y Lolfa, 1994).

——, *Wele'n Gwawrio* (Talybont: Y Lolfa, 1997).

Trezise, Rachel, *In and Out of the Goldfish Bowl* (Cardigan: Parthian, 2000).

Vaughan, Gwyneth, *O Gorlannau y Defaid* (London and Carmarthen: David Nutt and W. Spurrell & Son, 1905).

——, *Plant y Gorthrwm* (Cardiff: Educational Publishing Co., 1908).

Vaughan, Hilda, *The Battle to the Weak* (London: Queensway, 1925).

——, *Her Father's House* (London: Heinemann, 1930).

——, *The Soldier and the Gentlewoman* (London: Victor Gollancz, 1932).

——, *A Thing of Nought* (London: Lovat Dickson & Thompson, 1934).

——, *Pardon and Peace* (London: Macmillan, 1945).

——, *Iron and Gold* [1948], ed. Jane Aaron (Dinas Powys: Honno, 2002).

Verrill-Rhys, Leigh (ed.), *Iancs, Conshis a Spam: Atgofion Menywod o'r Ail Ryfel Byd* (Dinas Powys: Honno, 2002).

Williams, Charlotte, *Sugar and Slate* (Aberystwyth: Planet, 2002) .

Williams, R. Bryn (ed.), *Eluned Morgan: Bywgraffiad a Detholiad* (Llandysul: Gomer, 1948).

Wooff, Erica, *Mud Puppy* (London: The Women's Press, 2002).

'Wynne, The Dau', (Mallt and Gwenffreda Williams), *A Maid of Cymru: A Patriotic Romance* (London and Carmarthen: Simpkin, Marshall & Co. and W. Spurrell & Son, 1901).

Secondary sources

Aaron, Jane, 'A national seduction: Wales in nineteenth-century women's writing', *New Welsh Review*, 7/3, 27 (1994), 31–8.

——, 'Finding a voice in two tongues: gender and colonization' in Jane Aaron, Teresa Rees, Sandra Betts and Moira Vincentelli (eds), *Our Sisters' Land: The Changing Identities of Women in Wales* (Cardiff: University of Wales Press, 1994), pp. 183–98.

——, 'The hoydens of Wild Wales: representations of Welsh women in Victorian and Edwardian fiction', *Welsh Writing in English: A Yearbook of Critical Essays*, 1 (1995), 23–39.

——, 'Y Flodeuwedd gyfoes: llên menywod 1973–1993', in M. Wynn Thomas (ed.), *DiFfinio Dwy Lenyddiaeth Cymru* (Caerdydd: Gwasg Prifysgol Cymru, 1995), pp. 190–208.

——, *Pur fel y Dur: Y Gymraes yn Llen Menywod y Bedwaredd Ganrif ar Bymtheg* (Cardiff: University of Wales Press, 1998).

——, and Chris Williams (eds), *Postcolonial Wales* (Cardiff: University of Wales Press, 2005).

Anderson, Benedict, *Imagined Communities: Reflections on the Origins and Spread of Nationalism* (London: Verso, 1991).

Asbee, Sue, 'Margiad Evans's *The Wooden Doctor*: illness and sexuality', in *Welsh Writing in English: A Yearbook of Critical Essays*, 9 (2004), 33–49.

Ashcroft, Bill, Helen Tiffin and Gareth Griffiths, *The Empire Writes Back* (London: Routledge, 1989).

Bachelard, Gaston, *The Poetics of Space*, trans. Maria Jolas (Boston: Beacon, 1994; original French edn 1958).

Baucom, Ian, *Out of Place: Englishness, Empire and the Locations of Identity* (Princeton University Press, 1999).

Beddoe, Deirdre, 'Images of Welsh women', in Tony Curtis (ed.), *Wales: The Imagined Nation* (Bridgend: Poetry Wales Press, 1986), pp. 225–38.

——, *Out of the Shadows: A History of Women in Twentieth-Century Wales* (Cardiff: University of Wales Press, 2000).

Bohata, Kirsti, *Postcolonialism Revisited* (Cardiff: University of Wales Press, 2004).

——, 'Apes and Cannibals in Cumbria, images of racial and gendered other in Gothic writing in Wales', in *Welsh Writing in English: A Yearbook of Critical Essays*, 6 (2000), 119–43.

Boland, Eavan, *Outside History* (Manchester: Carcanet, 1990).

——, *Object Lessons: The Life of the Woman and the Poet in Our Time* (Manchester: Carcanet, 1995) .

Brown, Tony, 'The problems of belonging', in M. Wynn Thomas (ed.), *Welsh Writing in English* (Cardiff: University of Wales Press, 2003).

Butler, Judith, *Gender Trouble: Feminism and the Subversion of Identity* (London: Routledge, 1990).

Butler, Susan (ed.), *Common Ground: Poets in a Welsh Landscape* (Bridgend: Poetry Wales Press, 1985).

Carter, Harold, *Culture, Language and Territory: Diwylliant, Iaith a Thiriogaeth* (London: British Broadcasting Corporation, 1988).

Cavaliero, Glen, Introduction to Eiluned Lewis, *Dew on the Grass* (Woodbridge: Boydell and Brewer, 1984).

Clarke, Gillian, 'Beginning with Bendigeidfran', in Jane Aaron, Teresa Rees, Sandra Betts and Moira Vincentelli (eds), *Our Sisters' Land: The Changing Identities of Women in Wales* (Cardiff: University of Wales Press, 1994), pp. 287–93.

——, 'Ffiw: Referendum Reactions' *New Welsh Review*, 38 (Autumn 1977).

Colley, Linda, *Britons: Forging the Nation, 1707–1837* (New Haven: Yale University Press, 1992).

Conran, Tony, 'The writings of Brenda Chamberlain', *Anglo-Welsh Review*, 46 (Spring 1972), 19–23, and in *The Cost of Strangeness* (Llandysul: Gomer, 1982).

——, 'Lynette Roberts – War Poet' in *The Cost of Strangeness*.

——, (ed.), *Welsh Verse* (Bridgend: Poetry Wales Press, 1986).

Curtis, Tony (ed.), *Wales: The Imagined Nation* (Bridgend: Seren, 1986).

——, (ed.), *Wales at War: Critical Essays in Literature and Art* (Bridgend: Seren, 2007).

Davies, Diane, 'The voice and vision of Jean Earle', *Poetry Wales*, 242 (1988), 35–9.

Davies, E. Tegla, 'Cyflwynwn nofel fuddugol cystadleuaeth Llyfrau'r Dryw Llandebie [sic]' *Y Faner*, undated cutting (c. 1941).

Day, Graham, *Making Sense of Wales: A Sociological Perspective* (Cardiff: University of Wales Press, 2002).

Dearnley, Moira, *Margiad Evans* (Cardiff: University of Wales Press, 1982).

Donahaye, Jasmine, '"A dislocation called a blessing": three Welsh-Jewish perspectives', *Welsh Writing in English: A Yearbook of Critical Essays*, 7 (2001–2), 154–73.

Elfyn, Menna (ed.), *Trying the Line: Tribute to Gillian Clarke at 60* (Llandysul: Gomer, 1997).

Evans, Caradoc, *My People* ([1915] Bridgend: Seren, 1987).

Fish, Angela, 'Flight-deck of experience', *New Welsh Review*, 52 (1992), 60–4.

Gellner, Ernest, *Nations and Nationalism* (Oxford: Blackwell, 1983).

——, *Nationalism* (London: Phoenix, 1998).

George, Delyth, 'Kate Roberts – ffeminist?', *Y Traethodydd*, 140 (1985), 185–201.

Gifford, Douglas and Dorothy Macmillan (eds), *A History of Scottish Women's Writing* (Edinburgh: Edinburgh University Press, 1997).

Gramich, Katie and Andrew Hiscock (eds), *Dangerous Diversities: The Changing Faces of Wales* (Cardiff: University of Wales Press, 1998).

Harris, John, 'Queen of the Rushes: Allen Raine and her public', *Planet*, 97 (1993), 64–72.

Hayden, Dolores, 'What would a non-sexist city be like? Speculations on housing, urban design, and human work', in Stimpson *et al.* (eds), *Women and the American City* (Chicago and London: University of Chicago Press, 1981).

Hobsbawm, Eric, *Nations and Nationalism since 1780* (Cambridge: Cambridge University Press, 1990).

——, and Terence Ranger (eds), *The Invention of Tradition* (Cambridge: Cambridge University Press, 1983).

Holman, Kate, *Brenda Chamberlain* (Cardiff: University of Wales Press, 1997).

Holt, Constance Wall, *Welsh Women: An Annotated Bibliography of Women in Wales and Women of Welsh Descent in America* (Metchuen, NJ: Scarecrow Press, 1993).

Hooker, Jeremy, *The Presence of the Past* (Bridgend: Poetry Wales Press, 1987).

——, 'Ceridwen's daughters: Welsh women poets and the uses of tradition', *Welsh Writing in English*, 1 (1995), 128–44.

Hopwood, Mererid, *Singing in Chains: Listening to Welsh Verse* (Landysul: Gomer, 2004).

Humphreys, Emyr, *A Toy Epic* (Bridgend: Seren, 1989).

Ifans, Dafydd (ed.), *Annwyl Kate, Annwyl Saunders: Gohebiaeth 1923–1983* (Aberystwyth: National Library of Wales, 1992).

John, Angela V. (ed.), *Our Mother's Land: Chapters in Welsh Women's History 1830-1939* (Cardiff: University of Wales Press, 1991).

Jones, Bobi, *Llenyddiaeth Gymraeg 1936–1972* (Llandybïe: Christopher Davies, 1975).

Jones, Gareth Elwyn and Dai Smith (eds), *The People of Wales* (Llandysul: Gomer, 1999).

Jones, Gwyn, *The First Forty Years: Some Notes on Anglo-Welsh Literature* (Cardiff: University of Wales Press, 1957).

Jones, Iorwen Myfanwy, 'Merched Llên Cymru o 1850 i 1914' (unpub. M.A. thesis, University of Wales, Bangor, 1935).

Jones, Mairwen and Gwynn Jones, *Dewiniaid Difyr* (Llandysul: Gwasg Gomer, 1983).

Jones, R. Merfyn, *The North Wales Quarrymen 1874–1922* (Cardiff: University of Wales Press, 1981).

Jones, S. Beryl, 'Dorothy Edwards as a writer of short stories', *Welsh Review*, 7 (1948), 184–93.

Jones, Sally Roberts, *Allen Raine* (Cardiff: University of Wales Press, 1979).

Knight, Stephen, '"The hesitations and uncertainties that were the truth": three women writers of Welsh industrial fiction', in H. Gustav Klaus and Stephen Knight (eds), *British Industrial Fictions* (Cardiff: University of Wales Press, 2000).

——, *A Hundred Years of Fiction* (Cardiff: University of Wales Press, 2004).

Lefebvre, Henri, *The Production of Space*, trans. Donald Nicholson-Smith (Oxford: Blackwell, 1991; original French edn, 1974).

Lewis, Gwyneth, 'On writing poetry in two languages', *Modern Poetry in Translation*, 7 (Spring 1995), 80–3.

Lloyd-Morgan, Ceridwen, 'From temperance to suffrage?', in Angela V. John (ed.), *Our mother's land: Chapters in Welsh Women's History, 1830–1939* (Cardiff: University of Wales Press, 1991), pp. 135–58.

——, 'Portrait of a border writer: the life and work of Margiad Evans', *Planet*, 107 (Oct./Nov., 1994), 45–54.

——, *Margiad Evans* (Bridgend: Seren, 1998).

Llywelyn, Dorian, *Sacred Place, Chosen People: Land and National Identity in Welsh Spirituality* (Cardiff; University of Wales Press, 1999).

Löffler, Marion, 'A romantic nationalist', *Planet*, 121 (1997), 58–6.

Mathias, Roland, *Anglo-Welsh Literature: An Illustrated History* (Bridgend: Seren, 1986).

McElroy, Ruth, 'Cymraes oddi cartref?: Welsh women writing home and migration', *Welsh Writing in English: A Yearbook of Critical Essays*, 3 (1997), 134–56.

Massey, Doreen, *Space, Place and Gender* (London: Polity Press, 1994).

Mill, John Stuart, *On Liberty; representative government; the subjection of women: three essays* (London: Oxford University Press, 1912).

Morgan, Clare, 'Exile and the kingdom: Margiad Evans and the mythic landscape of Wales', *Welsh Writing in English: A Yearbook of Critical Essays*, 6 (2000), 89–118.

Morgan, Derec Llwyd, *Bro a Bywyd Kate Roberts* (Caerdydd: Cyngor Celfyddydau Cymru, 1981).

Newman, Christopher W., *Hilda Vaughan* (Cardiff: University of Wales Press, 1981).

Nora, Pierre, 'Between memory and history: *les lieux de memoire*', trans. Marc Roudebush, *Representations*, 26 (Spring 1989), 7–25.

Osborne, John, *Look Back in Anger*, (London: Faber, 1957).

Parnell, Michael, 'The novels of Bernice Rubens: an introduction', *New Welsh Review*, 31 (1990), 43–5.

Parry, Idris, 'Margiad Evans and tendencies in European literature', *Transactions of the Honourable Society of Cymmrodorion* (1971), 224–36.

Parry, R. Palmer, 'Winnie Parry a'i Gwaith', *Taliesin*, 46 (1983), 10–41.

Peach, Linden, 'Incoming tides: the poetry of Gillian Clarke', *New Welsh Review*, 1 (Summer, 1988), 75–81.

——, *Ancestral Lines: Culture and Identity in the Work of Six Contemporary Poets* (Bridgend: Seren Books, 1993).

Poetry Wales, Symposium: 'Is there a women's poetry?', 23 (1987)

Pratt, Mary Louise, *Imperial Eyes: Travel Writing and Transculturation* (New York: Routledge, 1992).

Prys-Williams, Barbara, *Twentieth-Century Autobiography* (Cardiff: University of Wales Press, 2004).

Roberts, Gwyneth Tyson, *The Language of the Blue Books: The Perfect Instrument of Empire* (Cardiff: University of Wales Press, 1998).

Rowlands, John (ed.) *Sglefrio ar Eiriau* (Llandysul: Gomer, 1992).

Showalter, Elaine, *A Literature of their Own: British Women Writers from Brontë to Lessing* (Princeton: Princeton University Press, 1977).

——, *Sister's Choice: Tradition and Change in American Women's Writing* (Oxford: Oxford University Press, 1994).

Smith, A. D., *The Antiquity of Nations* (Cambridge: Polity, 2004).

Smith, Dai, *Wales: A Question for History* (Bridgend: Seren, 1999).

Smith, David (ed.), *A People and a Proletariat: Essays in the History of Wales* (London: Pluto Press, 1980).

Smith, Kenneth R., 'The portrait poem: reproduction of mothering', *Poetry Wales*, 24/1, (1988) 48–54.

——, 'Poetry of place: the haunted interiors', *Poetry Wales*, 24/2, (1988) 59–65.

——, 'A vision of the future', *Poetry Wales*, 24/3, (1988) 46–52.

——, 'Praise of the past: the myth of eternal return in women writers' *Poetry Wales*, 24/4, (1988) 50–8.

Stephens, Meic (ed.), *The New Companion to the Literature of Wales* (Cardiff: University of Wales Press, 1998).

Stevenson, Anne, 'The compassionate sensibility of Christine Evans', *Poetry Wales*, 25/2 (September 1989), 13–15.

Stevenson, Lucy, 'Two drafts of an unpublished story by Dorothy Edwards', *Welsh Writing in English: A Yearbook of Critical Essays*, vol. 10 (2005), 160–89.

Thomas Gwyn, *Meadow Prospect Revisited* ed. Michael Parnell (Bridgend: Seren, 1992).

Thomas, Lucy, 'In search of the sandcastle dynasty: colonialism and the novels of Allen Raine' (unpub. MA thesis, Cardiff University, 2004).

Thomas, M. Wynn, *Internal Difference: Twentieth-Century Writing in Wales* (Cardiff: University of Wales Press, 1992).

——, *Corresponding Cultures: The Two Literatures of Wales* (Cardiff: University of Wales Press, 1999).

——, (ed.), *DiFfinio Dwy Lenyddiaeth Cymru* (Caerdydd: Gwasg Prifysgol Cymru, 1995).

——, (ed.), *A Guide to Welsh Literature, Volume VII: Welsh Writing in English* (Cardiff: University of Wales Press, 2003).

Thomas, Ned, *The Welsh Extremist* (Talybont: Y Lolfa, 1971).

Thomas, R. S., 'Unity' trans. by K. Gramich, in *R. S. Thomas: Selected Prose* ed. Sandra Anstey (Bridgend: Seren, 1995).

Trezise, Simon, *The West Country as a Literary Invention: Putting Fiction in its Place* (Exeter: University of Exeter Press, 2000).

Tuan, Yi-Fu, *Space and Place: The Perspective of Experience* (London: Edward Arnold, 1977).

Walters, Irene, 'Facing annihilation: genre, gender and social issues in the works of Eiluned Lewis' (unpub. MA thesis, Trinity College, Carmarthen, 1998).

Williams, D. J., *Stonäu'r Tir Glas* (Llandysul: Gomer, 1936).

Williams, Gwyn Alf, *When Was Wales?* (Harmondsworth: Penguin, 1985).

Williams, John, 'Women at Work in Nineteenth-Century Wales' in his *Was Wales Industrialized?: Essays in Modern Welsh History* (Llandysul: Gomer, 1995) pp. 58–78.

Williams, Mari A., *'Where is Mrs Jones Going?': Women and the Second World War in South Wales* (Aberystwyth: Board of Celtic Studies, 1995).

——, *A Forgotten Army: Female Munitions Workers of South Wales, 1939–1945* (Cardiff: University of Wales Press, 2002).

Williams, Raymond, *The Welsh Industrial Novel* (Cardiff: University College of Wales Cardiff, 1979).

Williams, Rhydwen (ed.) *Kate Roberts: Ei Meddwl a'i Gwaith* (Llandybïe: Christopher Davies, 1983).

Williams, Siân Rhiannon, 'Y Frythones: portread cyfnodolion merched y bedwaredd ganrif ar bymtheg o Gymraes yr oes', *Llafur*, 4: 1 (1984), 43–56.

Woolf, Virginia, *A Room of One's Own and Three Guineas*, ed. Michèle Barrett ([1928; 1938] Harmondsworth: Penguin, 1993).

——, *Orlando*, ed. Rachel Bowlby (Oxford: Oxford University Press, 1972).

——, 'Professions for Women', in *Collected Essays*, vol. 2, (London: Chatto and Windus, 1972).

——, 'Mr Bennett and Mrs Brown', in *A Woman's Essays* ed. Rachel Bowlby (London: Penguin, 1992).

Index